'The secret of the Gospel of J[...]nd attentively, you can not only n[...]to deeper and deeper friendship wi[...]his secret in a vivid, accessible, and surprising way.'

David F. Ford, *Regius Professor of Divinity Emeritus,*
University of Cambridge

'Immediately engaging, Ian Galloway's fascinating book provides a refreshingly new approach to John's Gospel. Both those who are familiar with the gospel text and those new to the faith will find themselves captivated and stimulated by the journey. Above all they will be attracted to the figure of Christ himself who emerges clear and inspirational throughout the narrative as someone we can know, follow and thoroughly trust.'

Terry Virgo, *founder of the Newfrontiers international family of churches*

'In entering any spectacular building, you see so much more if you have a passionate, knowledgeable and engaging guide. Ian Galloway is that guide as we enter John's Gospel in this encouraging and challenging book. But most of all he introduces us to the person at the centre of it all, Jesus.'

David Wilkinson, *Principal of St John's College, Durham University*

'A unique blend of spirituality and theology, this warm and engaging book invites you into an encounter with Jesus through the rich narrative of John's Gospel. The ease and creativity of Ian's style draws the reader into discovering wonderful hidden depths and theological insight in the text. I believe that this book will prove to be a treasure trove for those wanting to understand and communicate the Gospel in fresh and compelling ways.'

Lynn Green, *General Secretary of the Baptist Union*

'This book is beautiful. It is somehow pastoral, personal, lyrical and devotional. It will move you. It will make you think. It will teach you. It is deep and will make you deeper. It is rich and will enrich you. Rarely have I found myself inhabiting a book as much as I did while reading Called to be Friends.'

Andy McCullough, *author of Global Humility and The Bethlehem Story*

'Ian's book beautifully takes us on a journey through John's Gospel, convincing us of not only the possibility of a living friendship with Jesus, but the biblical imperative to do so. He enables us to chew on scripture and wrestle with truths in a way that is imminently practical and deeply personal to our understanding of the kind of friendship God truly offers us.'

Rachel Turner, *presenter of the Parenting for Faith course by the Bible Reading Fellowship*

'The book invites us to look with fresh eyes at who Jesus is and what believing in him entails. It does what it says on the tin; it issues both the challenge and opportunity to not only learn more about Jesus but ultimately that we might come to know and become friends of Christ. For seekers, enquirers, those who are new or who have been believers for many years, this helpful and easily accessible book encourages us to journey in the company of John's Gospel with a writer who communicates with both a knowledge of the text and a knowing of its subject, Christ, the life giver who invites us all into the company of his transforming friendship.'

Roy Searle, *a founder and Companion of the Northumbria Community*

'For both academic theologian and ordinary person, Ian takes you on a journey with a grasp of John's Gospel and a fresh insight into it which can't but fail to both stretch your mind and nourish your soul.'

Mark Elder, *leader of the theology track within Freshstreams network of churches*

'Ian Galloway really grasps the essence of the Johannine message, he sees the power and value of each story and by observing the literary style that is unique to John, he understands the heartbeat of the fourth Gospel. The story is told with a relational passion that is true to the character and nature of John's Gospel.'

Stephen McQuoid, *General Director of Gospel Literature Outreach*

First published in Great Britain in 2021 by Hodder & Stoughton
An Hachette UK company

This paperback first published in 2022

1

A CIP catalogue record for this title is available from the British Library

Paperback ISBN 978 1 529 35683 0
eBook ISBN 978 1 529 35684 7

Typeset in Monotype Bembo by Manipal Technologies Limited

Printed and bound in Great Britain by Clays Ltd, Elcograf S.p.A.

Hodder & Stoughton policy is to use papers that are natural, renewable and recyclable
products and made from wood grown in sustainable forests. The logging and
manufacturing processes are expected to conform to the environmental regulations of
the country of origin.

Hodder & Stoughton Ltd
Carmelite House
50 Victoria Embankment
London EC4Y 0DZ

www.hodderfaith.com

Called to Be Friends

Unlocking the heart of John's Gospel

IAN GALLOWAY

HODDER

For Heather, whose wealth of wisdom, depth of insight and devotion to Jesus are a constant inspiration and continuous joy, and without whom none of this would have happened.

Contents

Introduction: That You May Know Him

God wants you to know him. Just that single sentence fills me with excitement. 'I have called you friends,' says Jesus, 'for everything that I learned from my Father I have made known to you.' (15:15)

You have been called to be friends with Jesus. And friendship with Jesus means that you can know God. Because everything that Jesus knows of his Father he makes known to you.

But what does it mean to be friends? How does one person connect deeply with another?

First, friendship forms when I see you in action. Some of my best friends have come about by us doing stuff together. When I see what you do, I see something of you. It is the same with God. Serving in any capacity helps us to see God at work and thus get to know him. Running a food bank. Campaigning against human slavery. Leading worship. Teaching children. Praying for the sick. All these and more are opportunities to get to know God because we see him at work first-hand. Knowing God is not separate from serving God. Each invigorates the other. This book is practical. I want you to see Jesus in action. And I invite you to get involved. To help you be great friends with God.

Second, friendship forms when I understand you. To get to know me there are some important things you should probably know about me. You need to hear my story. It is the same with God. You need to know God's story. There are vital truths about God to explore and understand. If you don't study the Scriptures, you will be in danger of creating God in your own image. The Bible takes a rather stern view of this. It is called idolatry. The study of God is essential for friendship with God. Good theology leads to great friendship. This book is full of truth. To help you be deep friends with God.

Third, friendship forms when I experience you. Love is the shared experience of one another. My wife loves me. We've done stuff together. We've renovated houses. We have raised five children. We planted and led a thriving church in northern England. We've learnt to scuba dive and visited some beautiful places. And she understands me – more than I like, sometimes. But her love for me is more than something I see from what she does or understand from what she says. Her love is something I experience within myself. In the touch of her hand. In the beating of my heart. In the welling-up of her love within my soul. So it is with God. God wants you to know him. And that means receiving his love for you, his joy over you and his delight in you. To be friends with God is to experience deep within yourself that you are loved by God. As you read you may need to pause. To let God near. To help you be close friends with God.

I have been praying for you. Praying that as you read this book, you will be deeply refreshed in your friendship with Jesus. You may have been following him for decades. You may be just exploring spiritual things and are asking lots of questions. You are so welcome. You may have recently discovered Jesus and decided to follow him. Wherever you are in your journey of faith, I am praying for you. The most refreshing, energising, life-giving thing you can do is to nurture your friendship with God and to enjoy the experience of being loved by him. The Apostle Paul, one of the great church leaders and teachers of the first century, repeatedly prays for this in a letter he wrote to the churches he was serving. He prays that God's people would know God better (Eph. 1:17). He prays that those following Jesus would have the power to grasp how deep the love of Christ is, and 'to know this love that surpasses knowledge' (Eph. 3:16–19).

That is my prayer for you.

Because right at the heart of being a follower of Jesus is an experience of being drawn into friendship with God. To follow Jesus is to know God as a Father and a Friend. Normally, when we make a friend, the other person is present to us through being there in the flesh. People make themselves known in and through their bodies. We speak, we touch, we laugh and we cry. So how does friendship with God work, given the challenges there are to pursuing deep friendship with a divine, eternal being who has no bodily existence that we can see?

John's Gospel answers that question.

The Gospel Is a Temple Space

In Old Testament times the temple was the space where God dwelt. He was actually there. Like I am here, in my study, writing this. The Jewish Temple in Jerusalem and the Tabernacle or Tent in the desert before it were like a room in God's heavenly house, but located on earth. The idea of the Gospel as temple space draws on this. It means that by jumping into the Gospel and either hearing it or reading it, you will not just see what Jesus did or understand what Jesus said.

You will meet Jesus himself.

And that experience will transform you. You will find yourself friends with God. The whole Bible is like this, of course. But John, through a very careful process of selection, has taken this profound idea to a whole new level. The Gospel is constructed as a beautiful house. As you go inside you will find Jesus.

The Gospel Is Written with an Elegant Structure

It has proved very difficult to explain why John has organised his Gospel in the way that he has. Both the stories he has chosen and the way he has written it are very different from the other three Gospels. But John is also deeply connected to the other Gospels, and the whole New Testament, in multiple ways, large and small. Explaining this in a way that takes account of all the evidence has proved difficult. Some proposals stress the differences. Other proposals emphasise the connections. What is more, determining a coherent organising structure to the Gospel that makes sense of the whole has proved elusive. Those proposed have either been so general as to be of little value, or they have been so disputed that none have found widespread acceptance.

Rather than using historical–critical approaches to John, useful though those are, this book uses narrative analysis, which is taking the text as it is. I am going to take you on a journey into the text so that you can see how John has written his Gospel and understand why he has written it this way. My purpose in this is profoundly personal. You will be greatly helped by seeing how the Gospel has been so elegantly written. Grasping the structure of the Gospel will help you to meet with Jesus and deepen your friendship with God. This might seem a bold claim, but it will make more sense after you have read the book.

The whole point of grasping the structure of the Gospel is to better understand the meaning of each story. When we see the whole tree, a leaf makes so much more sense. However, we all tend to extract the bits of the Bible that we like. In doing this we can easily distort their meaning. This book aims to help you grasp the whole Gospel of John so that you can understand each part of it much more deeply and truly. And the purpose of understanding the meaning of Scripture deeply and truly is to come closer to God and become good friends. Understanding the narrative structure of John is not a pointless pursuit for a few sad people. It is a very helpful ingredient in deepening your friendship with God.

The Gospel Has the Entire Old Testament Underneath

One thing that you are going to discover as you read this book is that when you read John you are also reading the entire Old Testament. This isn't obvious at first because John only very occasionally quotes directly from the Old Testament. What is more, he has written his Gospel in one continuous flowing style, which makes it very difficult to identify any of his possible sources, including the Old Testament.

His method is not to mention the odd verse. He draws in whole chapters at a time. Sometimes several chapters at once. Theologians have a word for this. They call it intertextuality. What is happening is that other stories are being included into the story that you are reading. Mary Shelley's novel *Frankenstein* does this. John does it so much that it slightly does your head in. But what happens is that the stories become rich, deep and full of meaning. This is one of the reasons why John's Gospel is so popular. You don't have to understand all the intertextuality to read John. But it makes it a much better experience if you do. There isn't enough space in this book to cover all the intertextuality that John has deployed. But we will make a good start.

Intertextuality also helps to keep us safe. One danger we face is creating a Jesus of our own imagination from the bits of the Bible that we like. By drawing into his Gospel the whole Hebrew Bible, the author helps us to see the fullness of Jesus and to appreciate the depth of the one who is calling us to be friends.

When We Read the Gospel, Word and Spirit Work Together

The Word of God is the means God has chosen to make himself known. Without the Scriptures we would not have the faintest idea what God is like. However, I know from personal experience that it is possible to study the Scriptures without any personal relationship with God. We need the work of the Spirit of God to enable us to know God. John's Gospel tells us that the Spirit comes to make God known (14:16–21). The presence of the Spirit brings the living reality of Jesus out from the page as we read his Word. To be friends with God, both Word and Spirit are needed. Unfortunately, the Christian world has become somewhat polarised in the last century over these two aspects. There are those who rightly emphasise the sufficiency of the Scriptures. There are those who rightly point to the necessity of the work of God by the Spirit. John's Gospel shows that they have always worked together.

Jesus came to reveal his Father by being himself. As you immerse yourself in the Gospel you will see that Jesus knew who he was from the stories of his Bible. His identity and his self-awareness are drawn completely from the Scriptures. When the Spirit comes, he reveals Jesus to us in the same way that the incarnate Jesus made himself known to his friends. From the Scriptures. The Gospel was written to be a space where that can happen for us.

Finding Friendship

These amazing features of the Gospel all work together to create an immersive and exciting experience for the reader. There are very rich details in the stories that reveal who Jesus is. The elegant structure creates a temple space for you to meet with Jesus; to see, understand and experience him. The Old Testament stories sitting underneath add huge depth to this wonderful process of encountering Jesus and finding friendship.

This why there is such a huge synergy in the Gospel. Each story is deliberately connected to and works powerfully with all the other stories. This creates energy. John's Gospel is strangely gripping and can move you deeply as you read.

How This Book Is Organised

The book is in four parts.

In Part One, we will look at the big idea of us being called to be friends with God, the challenges to knowing God and the Gospel as a temple space. I will tell you a bit more of my story and give you an overview of the structure that creates the space and answers the challenges we all have to knowing God.

In Part Two your journey into the Gospel begins. The temple structure of the Gospel will be revealed. We will look in detail at each part of the elegant literary structure of John and what it means for you, all designed to help you grasp the Gospel, meet with Jesus and deepen your friendship.

In Part Three, we go inside. The structure of John is not just a flat system. It is multidimensional. As each part comes together the temple space is created, and we are invited to go inside and meet with God. In chapters 15–17 there is what I have called the 'timeless time'. The clock stops in the narrative at the end of chapter 14 and doesn't start again until the beginning of chapter 18. We hear Jesus speaking to us from the timeless time, where it is always now. We discover that our friendship with him has become so close that he is in us and we are in him, as branches on a vine. The author wants us to read the Crucifixion story and the Resurrection story from this perspective of being in Christ, which is what the Apostle Paul does in his writings. He invites us to look back at the death and resurrection of Jesus as those who are in him. Both authors want us to see that Jesus' story is our story, his death is our death and his life is our life.

Finally, in Part Four, we will reflect on our journey and sum up what it means to be friends of God.

Enjoy the book!

PART ONE

Friends of God

I

Called to Be Friends

Invitation and Challenge

Jesus loves people. He is irrepressible. You can't turn a page in the Gospel without meeting someone experiencing a life-changing encounter with Jesus. Scholars have shown that one of John's principles in selecting his material was to tell the stories of representative people – people like you and me.

Maybe you are like Nathanael. Nathanael is a faithful man. He is longing for people to live God's way. He sees all the corruption and deception in the world around him and he wants nothing to do with it. But he feels overlooked. Jesus comes into Nathanael's life with huge affirmation. Jesus sees the good in Nathanael and speaks it out loud. The effect on Nathanael is galvanising (1:45–51).

Turn over a page. Maybe you are like Nicodemus. Nicodemus is a highly educated and respectable man. He is very influential and well thought of in his community. But Jesus can see that what Nicodemus needs is not more learning, but new life from God. Jesus isn't afraid to tell him so. Nicodemus blusters a bit. But then he goes quiet. Because new life is what he needs (3:1–9).

Turn over the page. Maybe you are feeling broken, rejected and all alone. You look back over your life and see so much pain and wreckage. You avoid people. You wonder what people are saying about you. You feel a failure. You are certainly not good enough for friendship with God. Jesus offers life-giving friendship to a person in that place. The transformation that happens in her life is nothing short of astonishing (4:7–42).

Turn over another page. Maybe you feel trapped and forgotten. You are just part of the crowd. You are going nowhere. Jesus goes

3

to meet someone like that. He finds a man who hasn't walked for thirty-eight years (5:1–6). Thirty-eight years. That is a lot of lying around on your mat. Jesus checks with him that he wants to be well. Then, with just a word, Jesus sends him off into town, carrying the mat that reminded him every day of his difficult life (5:8). Ironically, the mat-carrying thing causes trouble, because it is a Saturday, a Sabbath. Mat-carrying on a Saturday is against the local regulations (5:9–10). But we are jumping ahead.

Turn over another page. Jesus offers life to a whole bunch of rather sceptical people who don't want to hear who Jesus truly is (6:26–59). They aren't convinced. They find what Jesus says quite difficult. Which it is. Very difficult. So they walk away (6:66). Jesus turns to his friends and followers, who are still getting to know him. They are reading the story of his life as it happens before their very eyes. Jesus asks them, 'Do you want to stick around with me? Or is this all a bit too challenging for you?' One of his friends says this: 'Lord, to whom shall we go? You have the words of eternal life.' (6:68).

If you want the transforming life that comes from getting deeply connected to Jesus, then you are reading the right book. But I may as well warn you now: it's going to be challenging. There may be a few times when you feel like walking away.

To start with, Jesus makes people think. I want this book to be an exciting journey of discovery for you. Things are so much more compelling when you find them out for yourself. I don't want to tell you what to think. But I do want to make you think, sometimes quite deeply.

Second, Jesus offers life, but he also makes demands. I can't pretend that it is otherwise. He is not alone in this, of course.

Third, all good things require a bit of application. Losing weight, running 10km, learning to scuba dive, making a great friend. None of these happens without some follow through. You will need a bit of grit to get the most from this book. Growing into a deep friendship with God is going to require something from you. Loving another is not a passive experience; it requires investment and active engagement.

Ask my wife.

Eternal Life

As we jump into the Gospel of John, we will see something very striking about Jesus: the extraordinary depth of his own relationship with God. Jesus lives in close communion with God. There is constant two-way communication and deep trust. It's a living relationship: 'Jesus gave them this answer: "Very truly I tell you, the Son can do nothing by himself; he can do only what he sees his Father doing, because whatever the Father does the Son also does. For the Father loves the Son and shows him all he does"' (5:19–20).

Uniquely in John's Gospel, Jesus draws back the veil on his own relationship with God as Son to Father. What he reveals of his Son–Father relationship is very attractive. However, it also gets him into serious trouble. His relationship with God threatens the authorities. Someone who talks in depth with God is a big problem if you happen to be one of the people in charge. More than that, it is theologically difficult for them. The religious authorities are fiercely protective of the doctrine of monotheism. Monotheism is the truth that there is One Holy Eternal Creator God who is Judge of all. But in trying to protect God's uniqueness and oneness they have so confined God as a Single Separate Other that there is no space for them to understand Jesus. So they reject him. In their minds he is claiming something impossible: equality with God through a Father–Son relationship. Huge rows develop, and John's Gospel is full of them. Both Jesus and the authorities use the Bible to support their positions. They aren't arguing about whether the Bible is the Word of God. They are arguing about what it means. So it is painful for Jesus to live in intimate friendship with God. It means that many people rule him out before he even begins.

However, that does not deflect him. He is intent on bringing others into the same place of enjoying close friendship with God (1:12). Jesus repeatedly invites people to come to him and to receive life (5:21; 6:29–35; 7:37–8). Our understanding of what Jesus means by life grows as we go through the Gospel. But peeking ahead a little, Jesus sums up what life is all about when he is just hours away from his own death: 'Now this is eternal life, *that they know you, the only true God*, and Jesus Christ, whom you have sent' (17:3, italics added).

What is eternal life? What is this gift of life that is so alive not even death can put an end to it? To have eternal life is to know God. Eternal life is a gift that enables me to relate to God in the same way as Jesus did. To know the Father as a friend.

This means, of course, that eternal life has already begun. Eternal life is not some future state of bliss that has no connection to current reality. Eternal life is not something that starts after my death. Eternal life begins when I step into friendship with God. Theologians call this 'realised eschatology'. It means that the way things are going to be in eternity have already started in current reality, at least in part. Friendship with God is a rich gift that only Jesus can give. He can give it, because of who he is: 'Jesus answered, "I am the way and the truth and the life. No one comes to the Father except through me"' (14:6).

Is it possible to have a relationship with God? To know God? God the all knowing, all wise, all everything you can think of. How can the smallness of I have a genuine relationship with the greatness that is God? Is personal friendship with God truly available? We will see that John addresses the challenges to knowing God from the beginning of the Gospel. Because deep and abiding friendship with God is where the author wants to take you.

Drawing Close

Jesus connects very deeply and very quickly with people. He has extraordinary relational strength. Once people get through their initial uncertainties, they feel very drawn to him. In the Gospel, a couple of people who are feeling really unsure about Jesus have extraordinary experiences. They suddenly realise that Jesus knows them. Either Jesus has deep intuitive insight or he has a God-given gift. Or both. One of the people he meets is so changed and healed by the experience that she immediately invites others to meet Jesus (4:39–41). Jesus goes viral in the village. It starts with her encountering Jesus. Then, because of what happens to her, everyone wants to meet him.

Discovering that Jesus knows you is a very exciting moment. Suddenly, nothing is hidden. He can see around the corners of your heart. He can see the good that sits inside you. He can see the potential that is in you, which others have not yet seen. He can also see where things have gone horribly wrong. No one enjoys that sort of stuff coming out into the light, but Jesus has a gentle way of insisting that it does. He is able to create the safe spaces where our past failures can get not just painfully re-examined but also resolved and healed.

What we will discover in the Gospel is that Jesus is genuinely interested in you. Jesus is going to lead you into the place where you know that you are known, and you are loved. We all want to do good stuff like serving the poor, bringing justice to the nations, stopping climate change, caring for our kids, earning a living and loving our neighbours. There is so much to be done. But to flourish in life we must be loved. Otherwise what we do becomes who we are, and that is not healthy.

In the Gospel of John, we meet a somewhat mysterious, unnamed disciple who eventually acquires something of an identity: 'the disciple whom Jesus loved' (13:23). The Gospel teases us as to who he is, where he is from and whether he might be the author of the Gospel or not. We'll get to that later. It is the description of the disciple that the author wants us to notice. He leans back on Jesus during a meal. He is held. He is comforted. He is close. Jesus speaks softly into his ear. He is the disciple whom Jesus loved. That kind of relationship is something we all deeply desire, especially, perhaps, with Jesus.

We are made to have close friends. We are made to be known. We are made to be loved. This is where Jesus wants us to live. He knows that to receive love is to receive life.

Drifting Apart

More than forty years ago, and completely to my surprise, I discovered that the resurrection was true, Jesus was alive, and that he was inviting me to be his friend.

But what I started to notice is that my friendship with Jesus easily got pushed to the edge of my life. I had the first heady days of discovering that I was a friend of God. My poor flatmates got to hear all about it. But I needed that to become more enduring. I needed to put friendship with Jesus deep down in the very heart of who I am.

7

Even more alarmingly, I began to see that it was possible for friendship with God to become peripheral to the life of the Church. That sounds ironic, and believe me, it eventually becomes tragic. But it is a story that I have heard too many times. One of the great promises God makes to his people is that we will all know him (Jer. 31:34). When relationship with God ceases to be at the centre of Christian community, the results can be catastrophic. The author of John's Gospel knows all too painfully that it is possible to do religious things without knowing God. The outcome is disastrous, and John wants us to avoid it (8:31–43).

What happens when relationship with God is not foundational to life, either personally or in the church community?

Living God's Way Becomes Difficult

The obedience that comes from knowing Jesus is very different from trying harder. Without a living relationship with God, Christianity descends into moralism. And moralism has failed. One sure way of getting people to do things is to tell them not to. We need more than just instruction. It is friendship with God that empowers us to become like God.

Church Stops Being Family

When church is family, those who are part of the church know that they are children of a loving Father who forgives them and receives them gladly. So they forgive and receive each other gladly. Well, most of the time. There is only one ethical instruction in the entire Gospel of John: 'love one another'. Jesus tells his friends that what they have received from him they are to give to each other: 'As I have loved you, so you must love one another' (13:34).

Without love for Jesus, church stops being family. In my experience, church then descends into something else. It can look like a salesforce – peddling forgiveness of sins, life after death and possibly miracles as well. It's sad when a church feels like it is offering a product for sale, rather than introducing people to a person they know. Or church can become an organisation that exists for the ego of its leaders. The church becomes a monument to them, the bigger the better. Or church can become a social action task force doing good works.

It is good that good things happen, but the church is so much more than a charity. Without the energy that comes from knowing God, it eventually runs out of steam. Or church simply becomes a religious group going through rituals that have been hollowed out of their true meaning and power, which is the kind of church I grew up in.

Worship and Prayer Become Rituals

Worship and prayer are foundational to enjoying God. In prayer and worship our hearts connect deeply with God. However, it is sadly possible for our friendship with God to grow cold and distant. When this happens, the practices of prayer and participation in worship become human centred rather than life giving and God focused. Prayer descends into religious practice. This can be shouting to God, or earnest seriousness, or even silent sitting. But without relationship with God, prayer becomes religious duty. Worship too becomes focused on the process. Did I like the music? Or the lyrics? Or those leading and singing? Did it give me a good feeling?

I Remain at the Centre of My Life

Without friendship with God, I am tempted to believe that God is there to answer my prayers and bring me blessings. This view of life is built on the delusion that I can control God. Now, of course, God does answer my prayers and he does bless me. But only because he is a patient, kind, gracious Father. It is not because I am in charge of God or because I am the centre of everything.

But without relationship with God, the world revolves around me: my interests, my financial needs, my relationship needs, my ambitions, my political persuasions, my fulfilment. There is only one problem with this. It doesn't. The world doesn't revolve around me and God doesn't revolve around me. When I get to know God, I suddenly realise that I am not the centre of everything. God is. This is a healthy place to live. Because it is a true and authentic place.

All of this points to something you already know: that it is essential to actively invest in your friendship with God – which is what this book is all about.

2

Knowing God

The Challenges

We want to know God and desire friendship with him. But we all face significant challenges to knowing God.

The Otherness of God

God is not like me. How can I know the eternal God? How can I know a God who stands outside time and sees all things? How can I know the creator God, the maker of the heavens and the earth with their vast expanse through time and space? How can I know a God whose wisdom and knowledge are evidently so far beyond me? I struggled just trying to learn French. How can I know a holy God whose being is one of utter purity? The Prophet Isaiah had an encounter with God. You can read about it in his book. All Isaiah could say was, 'I am ruined' (Isa. 6:1–5).

The Absence of God

Another struggle that we have is the absence of God. Where is God? This is a real problem for many people, particularly those who are interested in the possibility of God. It isn't just tragedy or suffering that makes people question the reality of God. It is the challenge of connecting with a God who cannot be seen or touched. When it comes to forging a friendship with one another there is a lot we can give to that. We can have meals together. We can sit in each other's homes. We can go for walks. We can go to parties. We can go on holiday to special places. We can talk to each other. We can watch each other and see what matters to each other. How can I get to know God when he dwells in heavenly reality? As Isaiah says, God doesn't live in my world (Isa. 34:5).

What can I do in the face of the absence of God? Where can I turn? Where can I go to meet with God?

Our Weakness Within

Even when building human relationships, we struggle with each other. For me to get to know you I have to stop talking and start listening. I have to make room for you in my mind. It's not just about opening my home to you. It's making space in my heart for you. And it's not just hearing the words you say. We can often struggle to truly understand what other people mean. Friendship comes when I connect to your heart behind your words.

We also have difficulty being open about ourselves. We all find it hard to be open, honest, vulnerable and real. Vulnerability with other people is something every human being craves. We love to be known. But we struggle to reveal ourselves so that we can be known.

What is the answer?

This is where the Gospel of John begins.

The Word

John begins at the beginning. 'In the beginning was the Word, and the Word was with God, and the Word was God' (1:1).

This first sentence of John's Gospel is very deliberately built on the first sentence of the Hebrew Bible, John's own Bible, which we now call the Old Testament: 'In the beginning God' (Gen. 1:1). What an extraordinary thing to do.

John has taken this phrase and edited it. It is a very bold, confident move. John is not just skilled in biblical studies. He also feels completely able to make such a change. Editing Scripture in this way is not for the faint-hearted or the unqualified. What he does is write into the Scripture a short explanation of what it means. He does not take anything away from the original meaning. Neither does he distort the text into a different meaning. What he does is open up the meaning. He deepens and extends what is already there. Bible teachers do this all the time. They say more words, or write more words, in order to draw out the true meaning of the Bible. Theologians call this process 'exegesis'. John's objective in this piece of exegesis is to place Jesus in the middle of his own Scriptures. Later on, his writing was itself recognised as Scripture, which is why it is in our Bible.

John can see that there is more to be said between the word 'beginning' and the word 'God'. Becoming friends with Jesus has revealed to him that there is more to be said about God. 'In the beginning God' becomes '*In the beginning* was the Word, and the Word was with God, and the Word was *God*' (1:1, italics added).

What does he mean?

He writes the word 'Word' three times. 'In the beginning was the *Word*. The *Word* was with God. The *Word* was God.'

Words are very important. Words are what separate us from the rest of creation. Words are what we use to make ourselves known. Can you imagine not being able to use words at all, not being able to explain anything? I am a speaking man, a self-revealing man, made in God's image. For you to get to know me, I have to open up and speak of who I am. John the author is saying that from the very beginning God is a God who explains himself; he is a speaking God. From the very beginning God is self-revealing.

In this highly creative and theologically imaginative move, John uses what God does in Genesis 1 and applies it back to God himself. In Genesis 1 God creates by speaking his Word (Gen. 1:3). God speaks and things come into being. John takes that idea and moves it back into eternity, back into the nature of God. Before there was any speaking and creating *by* God, there was speaking and revealing *of* God. God spoke and made himself known. Before any creation *by* the Word there is self-revelation *of* the Word.

This Word that God speaks is not a sound that represents something else. When I say 'dog' you know what I mean. 'Dog' is a word that represents the animal. This Word isn't like that. This Word is a person, the very person of God, with God in the beginning. 'In the beginning was the Word, and the Word was with God, and the Word was God. He was with God in the beginning' (1:1–2).

God doesn't speak sounds; he speaks himself. God speaks himself to reveal himself through himself. In his very nature from all eternity, God is a being who makes himself known. Just to make clear that this happens before any creation starts, just to make sure that we get it, John goes on to say, 'Through him all things were made; without him nothing was made that has been made' (1:3).

And that is about as good a summary as you can get of Genesis 1. God speaks. Through his Word things are made. Many other New Testament scriptures refer to the story of creation in Genesis 1 and include Jesus in the middle in the same way (such as Col. 1:15–16; Heb. 1:2–3; 1 Cor. 8:6). Just not quite so elegantly.

God is a self-revealing God. This addresses the challenge we identified earlier of the otherness of God. How can I know the eternal God who dwells beyond time and space? How can I know the creator God with immeasurable knowledge and wisdom? Because that God is also a self-revealing God. In his very nature God makes himself known. He speaks himself to reveal himself through himself. This is still good Jewish monotheism. But with Jesus in the middle.

What about the next challenge? The absence of God? What has God done about that?

Made Flesh

As is normal in the Gospel of John, one profound thought is quickly followed by another: 'The Word became flesh and made his dwelling among us' (1:14).

The Word that is God became God in human flesh. Everything that is God was brought into human existence in the person of Jesus. God didn't stop being God when he came as Jesus Christ. Jesus is not lite, fat-free God. Nothing was subtracted when God became flesh. It does not say that a bit of God became flesh. The Word became flesh. God wasn't subtracted; humanity was added. Not for nothing is Jesus called Immanuel, which means God with us.

And to underline this point, John writes, 'and made his dwelling among us'. The phrase 'made his dwelling' is the Greek word *skenoo*. It means to pitch your tent. To tabernacle. We are now in the book of Exodus, the second book of the Bible. In the story of the Exodus, God sets his people free from slavery in Egypt, calls them to himself in the desert and dwells among them. He instructs Moses to build a very special tent, called the Tabernacle. And in the tent is found the very presence of God. As Greg Beale describes in his book, *The Temple and the Church's Mission*, the Tabernacle in the desert and then the Temple in Jerusalem were both built to a profound specification.[1] The Temple was a space within a space within a space. Each space in the Temple represented a much larger space in reality, and the spaces they represented became larger the further in you went. Theologians call this a 'microcosm'. It is the cosmos in micro-form. The outer court stood for the earth. It was decorated with trees and animals. The next space, called the 'holy place', stood for the visible heaven and its light sources. It was shrouded in deep-blue curtains and lit by seven lights on a golden lampstand. The inmost place, called the Most Holy Place, stood for the invisible, heavenly dimension of the cosmos, where God and his heavenly hosts dwelt. The people of Israel knew that God wasn't somehow just beyond Venus or hidden behind the moon. They knew that God was above and beyond all things. But they also knew that he had chosen to dwell with them. He had built an extension to heaven on earth. When Israel went to the tent, they went to meet with God. They were a people called to live close to God.

When both Moses and Solomon 'finished the work' of building the Tabernacle (Exod. 40:33–5) and Temple (2 Chr. 5:1–14), the *shekinah* glory of God came and filled the space: 'Then the cloud covered the tent of meeting, and the glory of the Lord filled the Tabernacle. Moses could not enter the tent of meeting because the cloud had settled on it, and the glory of the Lord filled the Tabernacle.'

This is how John's Gospel describes Jesus: 'We have seen his glory, the glory of the one and only Son, who came from the Father, full of grace and truth' (1:14).

Jesus is the presence of God on earth. He is the pitching of God's tent. He is the revealing of God's glory. But Jesus is also completely and fully human. In the Gospel of John, Jesus' friends have meals with him. They sit and talk with him. They go for walks. They go to parties. They go on holiday to Jerusalem to celebrate the Festivals. They talk to him. They watch him. They see how he lives. They see what matters to him. They see how he relates to different people. They are walking with God, talking to God, getting to know God.

The author of the Gospel of John was brought up as a Jew and is now a follower of Jesus. He is not about to throw away his monotheism. God being one God is one of the deepest, most significant truths in Judaism and therefore in Christianity. So John has a problem. How on earth can he explain this? How can he describe the relationship between Jesus and God? John turns to the relationship that Jesus himself uses to describe this mystery: Father and Son (1:14).

As soon as you say Father, there is Son. Father is not Father without Son. Without a child, a father is not a father; he is an adult. Father cannot be said without saying Son. Saying Father and Son without Mother means that Son is not formed from union. Son is not descendant. Son is not nurtured or raised. The Son is, just as the Father is. If Father exists by his own divine will then Son exists by the same will. Son is not created. Uncreated Son is as much a participant in the divine will of being Father and Son as Father. Otherwise, Son has a beginning, which means that before that beginning God was not Father.

Now before mothers feel excluded and women generally feel marginalised, please let me point out that God as Father and Son is nothing at all to do with human gender, apart from the very obvious and specific application to the incarnate Jesus himself. The use of the words Father and Son have nothing to do with maleness and femaleness. Father and Son exist before there are fathers and mothers, sons and daughters. When God creates humanity in his image, he makes them male and female (Gen. 1:27). The male is not more in the image of God than the female. The female is not a lesser image-bearer of God than the male. God, as we now understand him to be Father and Son and Spirit, images himself into humanity, male and female. The fathers bear the image of the Father and the Son and the Spirit. The mothers bear the image of the Father and the Son and the Spirit. The sons and daughters are made in the likeness of the Father and the Son and the Spirit. To describe God as Father and

Son is not in any way to imply that maleness is more like God than femaleness, although obviously some men want you to believe this. The assumed superiority of the male is something we are all trying to be freed from.

As Alister McGrath points out in his book, *Christian Theology*, it was Karl Rahner who argued that the way God reveals himself to us is the way that God is.[2] Father and Son is not a back projection of family life onto God. It is the way God exists. We shall see more of what that means as we look further into the Gospel of John.

To say Father and Son is to speak of relationship and separation. There cannot be relationship without separation. But the strength of relationship transforms the separation. The separation is sufficient to be able to say, 'I am Father, you are Son.' But this leads to the possibility of God existing as a divine duality, which is an impossibility. There cannot be two Gods. But separation sufficient to say Father and Son is needed. How can the oneness of God be preserved while talking about the separateness that is the Father and the Son? It is because the separation is accompanied by a relationship that is so comprehensive and complete that Father and Son are one. All that is Father is found in Son and all that is Son is found in Father. Father and Son are a unity not a duality. The theologians call this relationship 'perichoresis', which means the mutual indwelling of the persons. The Father is so in the Son and the Son so in the Father that they are one. One God.

It is important to recognise that the author of the Gospel of John does not call himself a Trinitarian Christian. He lived at a time when that term was not used. The first recorded use of the word 'Trinity' is by Theophilus of Antioch in the late second century. But it was Tertullian, writing in the early third century, who explicitly defined the Trinity as Father, Son and Holy Spirit. He had to invent several new words to explain what he meant by one God in three persons. There was lots of discussion and debate about this, but it was finally put into an agreed form of words in the Nicene Creed in AD 325, and amended in Constantinople in AD 381:

We believe in one God, the Father Almighty, Maker of heaven and earth, and of all things visible and invisible. And in one Lord Jesus Christ, the Son of God, begotten of the Father, Light of Light, very God of very God, begotten, not made, consubstantial with the Father; by whom all things were made both in heaven and on earth; who for us men, and for our salvation, came down from heaven, and was incarnate by the Holy Ghost and of the Virgin Mary, and was made man.

Although the Gospel writer cannot be described as Trinitarian, it is immediately obvious that the formulation of the doctrine of the Trinity has drawn significantly on the Gospel of John. From the time of Jesus, there was a journey to go on to arrive at the Christian doctrine of the Trinity. But John's Gospel puts up lots of signposts that all point in that direction.

John's Gospel tells us that the Son and the Father know each other very closely, very intimately: 'No one has ever seen God, but the one and only Son, who is himself God and is in the closest relationship with the Father, has made him known' (1:18).

I love that translation in the New International Version (NIV): 'in the closest relationship with'. The Greek word there is *kolpos*. It means the front of the body between the arms. That is why the older translations say 'the only begotten Son, which is in the bosom of the Father' (KJV). The newer translations avoid this language because they don't want the teenage boys giggling at the back. The Father and Son live in an eternal embrace. Their knowledge, their wisdom, their insight, their likes, their dislikes, everything about them flows back and forth between them. They are so close that they are one.

The word 'made known' is the Greek word *exegemai*. It means to unfold, to declare, to draw out in a narrative. It is where we get the word 'exegesis', which means to explain and unfold the meaning of the Bible. Jesus unfolds and explains all that God is. He is in the embrace of God. He is the explanation of God. He is enfolded in God. He unfolds God.

In the person of Jesus the fullness of God is found in human form. The absence of God is no more.

Now I know what you are thinking. Jesus the physical man, the Word made flesh is no longer with us. Aren't we back to the heavenliness of God? Aren't we back to the absence of God? Jesus being God in the flesh was all very well for the disciples at the time of Jesus. But what about us?

The Gospel of John addresses this head on.

By the Spirit

The conclusion that John's Gospel comes to is that it is better for us now than it was for the disciples of the incarnate Jesus. There is more opportunity for us to know God now than there was to know God then. We can be closer to God than they could. There is something even better than Jesus in the body. We have Jesus in the Spirit.

In the Gospel of John, there is a whole section of Jesus' teaching about this. It is one of the many unique features of the Gospel. Jesus tries to prepare his disciples for the huge change that is going to come so suddenly upon them. He says that the experiences of the first disciples who walked with Jesus in the flesh are not going to be lost. Theirs was not a special experience that we can't have. We too live with Jesus. We too walk with Jesus. We too eat with Jesus. We too go on holiday with Jesus. Not Jesus in the flesh. It's better than that: Jesus by the Spirit:

> If you love me, keep my commands. And I will ask the Father, and he will give you another advocate to help you and be with you forever – the Spirit of truth. The world cannot accept him, because it neither sees him nor knows him. But you know him, for he lives with you and will be in you. I will not leave you as orphans; I will come to you. (14:15–18).

It would be good to pause at this point and read 14:15–27. In that section, Jesus says the same thing many times. You would think he was trying to make a point. And you would be right.

First, Jesus teaches that we are God's covenant people who live a life of love and obedience. 'If you love me, keep my commands' (14:15).

This is Jesus quoting straight from the Prophet Jeremiah (Jer. 31:33–4). Jeremiah looks forward to a time when God is going to build a new covenant relationship with his people. One of the key features of this new relationship is that we will all know God. Another incredible aspect is that God will write his law on our hearts. In the Exodus story the law was written by God on two stone tablets to be taught to the people by Moses. In the new covenant relationship that we have with God, the law isn't something outside us. God writes the way he wants us to live within us. Obedience isn't something we try to live up to. Obedience is something we live out because God writes obedience to his Word into us. It's out of love for Jesus that we obey him.

Jesus says this, three more times (14:21, 23, 24). That's emphatic. We are new covenant people. We are friends of God. We know God, love God and obey God.

Second, Jesus says God will come; the Spirit will be sent: 'And I will ask the Father, and he will give you another advocate to help you and be with you for ever – the Spirit of truth' (14:16).

Jesus asks the Father who sends the Spirit of truth. God asks God to send God. The Spirit of truth is called an advocate. The word there in Greek is *paracletos*, which means 'one who is called alongside'. Jesus walked alongside Simon. The disciple whom Jesus loved leant back on Jesus. You walk with Jesus by the Spirit. You lean back on Jesus in the Spirit.

This truth is repeated multiple times:

- 'But you know him, for he lives with you and will be in you' (14:17)
- 'I will not leave you as orphans; I will come to you' (14:18)
- 'Before long, the world will not see me any more, but you will see me. Because I live, you also will live' (14:19)
- 'On that day you will realise that I am in my Father, and you are in me, and I am in you' (14:20)
- The one who loves me will be loved by my Father, and I too will love them and show myself to them' (14:21)
- 'My Father will love them, and we will come to them and make our home with them' (14:23)
- 'But the Advocate, the Holy Spirit, whom the Father will send in my name, will teach you all things and will remind you of everything I have said to you' (14:26)

The challenge of the absence of God was overcome by God coming in the flesh in the person of Jesus. The challenge of the absence of

God is overcome even more by the Father and the Son coming in the person of the Spirit. He comes and makes his home with you. He lives with you. He is in you. Jesus reveals himself to you.

The presence of the incarnate Jesus in the flesh is not better than the presence of Jesus by the Spirit. The presence of the Spirit *is* the presence of Jesus. In fact, the body is not necessarily the best vehicle for revealing the person. There are limitations. To start with, the closer you get to someone the less you can see of them. When you give someone a hug what you are really looking at is half an ear. The body is a means. But it is also a hindrance. The body can deceive us. God looks at the heart. People look at the appearance. Both these statements are true. And appearances can be deceptive.

Jesus by the Spirit is a closer, more intimate friendship for everyone.

So that just leaves the challenge of the weakness we have within, the challenge we have in making space for Jesus in our hearts.

The Weakness Within

For me to know you, I need to make space for you in my heart and in my mind. We tend to fill our minds with ourselves. We are very self-preoccupied. We are mostly self-absorbed. We are usually self-interested. It's time to repent. It is time to say, 'Lord I want to know you. Help me to stop thinking of myself all the time.'

In this book, I am going to help you to turn your eyes upon Jesus. I want you to look fully at him. I want you to stop thinking about yourself and start thinking about him. We are going on a journey, a journey of discovery of Jesus. I am going to repeatedly invite you to read the Scriptures. When you do this, try not to think about yourself and your life. Try to turn your gaze upon Jesus to know him.

All friendship takes application. No friendship happens by accident. There is that initial spark. Something happens that connects you. But then choices are made. It is the same with Jesus. You have to go and sit near him, sit next to him. You have to make space in your heart and in your diary for him. As you go on your journey of discovery of who Jesus is, there is no need to rush. Take as long as you like. It has taken me twenty years to write this book.

3

Temple Space

Life in His Name

John the author tells us why he has written the Gospel: 'Jesus performed many other signs in the presence of his disciples, which are
not recorded in this book. But these are written that you may believe
that Jesus is the Messiah, the Son of God, and that by believing you
may have life in his name (20:30–1).

John the author is completely up front. He has selected his stories.
He has chosen his material very carefully and has organised it very
deliberately. But why?

'But these are written *that you . . .*' (20:31, italics added). John the
author wrote for you. He wrote with you in mind. When people
write their story, most people write about themselves. I like the music
of Bruce Springsteen. I bought his book, *Born to Run*, as a birthday
present for my wife. It's all about Bruce. He is not thinking about
you. He is writing about himself. John is completely different. He is
writing *for* you. John has hidden himself so cleverly in his Gospel that
to start with you don't even notice he is there. He is not writing to be
well known. He is writing for you.

John the author isn't writing to his church or to the churches he
serves. We aren't eavesdropping on another's conversation. Have you
ever read the letter in the New Testament called 2 Corinthians? It is
from the Apostle Paul to the church in Corinth, a church he helped
to start. There's obviously been lots of correspondence between Paul
and the people in the church. You can tell that there have been major
disagreements. When you read 2 Corinthians, you feel like you are
listening in to one half of a phone call. Not with John. This book has
been written for you.

'But these are written that you may *believe*' (20:31, italics added). That word 'believe' is a verb. Verbs are things that we do. Run. Cook. Drink. Believe. In John, believe is never a noun. The problem with thinking about belief as a noun is that it can become something that I possess. In John's Gospel, believing is always an active response to the person of Jesus. Believing occurs when people meet with Jesus. Believing is deeply connected to discovering who Jesus is and receiving him as he is: 'that you may believe that *Jesus is the Messiah, the Son of God*' (20:31).

This is why, as Tom Wright points out in his book, *Simply Christian*, believing is inextricably linked to loyalty and obedience.[1] If I believe that Jesus is King and Son of God, I will live for him (loyalty) and live to please him (obedience). This is the same language used by the Apostle Paul, who described himself as sent to call people who didn't know God to 'the obedience that comes from faith' (Rom. 1:5; 16:26). This is not a return to works-based religion where I try by my efforts to earn God's favour and forgiveness. This is the reality that believing, like loving, shows itself to be truly present by the life lived, not only by the words spoken. If I believe in Jesus who by his death forgives all my sins, I will live free of all guilt. If I believe that my true worth is measured by his love for me, then I will live free of all shame and pretence. If I believe that Jesus as Son calls me as his friend to know his Father, I will live a life of deep devotion. Believing is active response, not merely mental assent.

That verb 'believe' is in the tense that means it is something that has happened. I have embarked on a life of living for Jesus, which for me happened more than forty years ago. But John doesn't stop there: 'that you may believe that Jesus is the Messiah, the Son of God, *and that by believing . . .*' (20:31, italics added). Believing is something that is happening now. I am actively trusting Jesus right now. Believe is something that I started doing in the past. Believing is something I am doing now. Is John's Gospel written so that people will start on their journey of friendship with God? Yes. 'These are written that you may believe.' Is John's Gospel written for people who do believe to help them to deepen their friendship with God? Yes. 'These are written that you may believe, and that by believing . . .'

This is where John brings it altogether and states his purpose for writing in the way he has: 'by believing you may *have life* in his name'

(20:31, italics added). The action of believing leads to life. As we have seen, life, eternal life, is knowing God and becoming friends with God. This is why John has written his Gospel. It is the reason he has written it in the way that he has: that you may become friends with God.

What is more, he has written it. This might sound obvious. But it is in the *writing* that John has accomplished his purpose of helping you to become friends with God and to deepen your friendship with God. 'But these are *written* that you may believe' (20:31, italics added).

As Sandra Schneiders says in her book *Jesus Risen in Our Midst*, 'the locus of revelation . . . is the text itself and "the event of revelation takes place in the interaction between text and reader"'.[2] It is one thing to write a book that describes the past or looks back at the life of a well-known person. It is quite another thing to write a book and say, 'Read my book. When you read my book, you will meet someone and form a deep friendship.' But that is what John has done.

To deliver on this extraordinary purpose of enabling you to meet with Jesus and become friends with God, John has taken the ideas of Temple theology and has applied them to his Gospel. John's Gospel has been written carefully and prayerfully as a Temple in Words, a literary temple. The Gospel is where you hear the story of God. But more than that, it has been written to be a place to go and meet with God.

This is not a new idea.

The Psalms are a literary temple. When Solomon's Temple was destroyed by the Babylonians and the Jewish people were taken into exile, they had to develop new ways of meeting with God. The Psalms were compiled as a literary temple. They provided a place where God's people in exile, without a physical space to go and meet with God, could still encounter him. Of all the poems in Israel, the ones that we have in our Bibles were deliberately organised to retell the whole story of Israel in poetic song and provide a space where God's people could celebrate and meet with God. John has done the same thing. But without all the singing, and with Jesus in the middle of the story.

I have a book called *Norwegian Wood* by Lars Mytting. It's about how to chop and dry and stack wood. When I read it, I learn lots. But when I am reading it, I am not chopping any wood. I have another book called *The Gardener's Year* by Alan Titchmarsh. It is great stuff about gardening. But when I read the book, I am not out in the garden. My hands are not in the soil. I have another book called *100 Diving Sites: Underwater Paradises Around the Globe* by Paul Munzinger. It's a beautiful book with lovely pictures. But when I read the book I'm not diving. I'm not underwater.

John is different. John has written his Gospel so that *as you read it*, by the work of the Holy Spirit through the Word, you meet with Jesus. John retells the stories of Jesus in such a way that you can know him. The theologians call this 'reader response'. It describes what happens to people when they read the Bible. John wrote his Gospel for you so that your reader response is meeting with Jesus and finding yourself to be a friend of God.

This raises a massive question. How has he done it?

Narrative Panels

Twenty years ago, I was asked to teach the Gospel of John for a whole week to church leaders at a senior level. I was a little surprised to be asked. I thought to myself, 'Better study it properly then.' It was the beginning of an epic journey that became something of an obsession for me. If you have obsessive tendencies you may as well put them to good use.

I began to repeatedly read, study and teach John. The first commentary that I read in preparation for that teaching week was by Don Carson, called *The Gospel According to John*, written in 1988. Carson gives a thorough overview of the sweep of studies on John through the ages. In his introduction he ventures a small opinion. Current cutting-edge studies on John are those that take a literary approach, making sense of the text as it stands.[3] Although Carson raises some reservations about these methods, I had a strong sense from God that this is what I should do. All very well, I thought, but what exactly is that?

I had a close look at Carson's analysis of the Gospel and was a bit taken aback. By his own admission, what he had done was list the stories in order and arranged them under vague headings. I studied other narrative analyses from other authors. It was all a little underwhelming. Dividing the Gospel into the Prologue (1:1–18), the Book of Signs (1:19–12:50), the Book of Glory (13:1–20:31), and an Epilogue (21:1–25) seemed to be as good as it got.

As I read and reread the Gospel, one strange detail caught my attention. The Wedding at Cana is described as the 'first of the signs' (2:11). The Healing of the Royal Official's Son is described as the 'second sign' (4:54). First and second. Then nothing. No third or fourth or seventh. Scholars who tried to count subsequent signs seemed to be making the numbers fit their conclusions.

It occurred to me that this might be a literary device. By then I had come to see how many literary devices there were in the Gospel. Perhaps the author was showing that these stories belong together. I studied them side by side and was totally shocked. They have an identical narrative shape. The stories have the same storyboard. They do belong together. You can read all about this in Chapter Four. The next question came to me. Are there any more stories like this in the Gospel? Limiting my initial search to chapters 1–14, for reasons that will become apparent later, I found two more stories that had the same storyboard: The Feeding of the Five Thousand and The Raising of Lazarus. There were developments and interesting differences. Jesus is not a machine but a real person. But they are a set of stories where Jesus is working from the same storyboard and in doing so revealing the consistency of his person.

When we are becoming friends with someone, we discover who they are by listening to what they say and hearing stories of the things that they do. I wondered whether this set of stories was acting in the same way. All of us are hardwired in pattern recognition. We seem to delight in connecting things together in our minds. You can make a face appear to people by assembling a pattern of different coloured sticky notes on a large board. We are doing pattern recognition all the time, especially on each other. Perhaps the stories I had seen in the Gospel were deliberately in a repeating pattern. Without thinking about it, we might be bringing those stories together in our minds, just as we bring together the pattern of coloured sticky notes to reveal a face. I wondered if by bringing together the pattern of the stories in our minds we are discovering that Jesus is real. This is what we do with any friend when we hear their stories. We get to know them as a person, not just listen to their past. We don't deliberately or even consciously do this. We just do it. Maybe this is why people feel so drawn to the person of Jesus when they read the Gospel of John.

I looked at the four stories side by side for a very long time. They are such an odd set. In The Wedding at Cana, reality is changed by pouring in and pouring out of jars. In The Healing of the Royal Official's Son, a healing happens by people walking away from Jesus. In The Feeding of the Five Thousand, bread is multiplied and there is a lot left over. In The Raising of Lazarus, the dead son of a family loved by Jesus is raised back to life.

Another inspired question came to me: 'Where have you seen these stories before, Ian?' It took a while. But I found them all in one place. They are one after the other in 2 Kings 4–5. Every time I teach this, mostly to senior church leaders, I ask the same question. Where have you seen these stories before? No one ever knows. But Jesus is being Elisha. You can read about this in Chapter Six.

I wondered, had I found John's methodology? Are there other sets of stories in the Gospel with the same narrative shape that when put side by side come together and connect with each other? And underneath these sets of stories do we find some Old Testament stories?

I believe I have found John's methodology.

For lack of a better idea, I decided to look at the stories immediately *before* the first sign and immediately *before* the second sign. The same thing stood out: these two stories have the same narrative shape. They belong together. I looked for others like them in chapters 1–14 of the Gospel and found two more with the same storyboard. Flushed with this success, I looked at the stories immediately *after* the first sign and immediately *after* the second sign. The same thing happened: they have the same narrative shape. They too belong together. I looked for others like them in chapters 1–14 of the Gospel and found two more.

From then on, I was hooked. Not only were the stories of the first sign and the second in a repeating pattern, but the other stories around them were in the same repeating pattern. As you read the book, you will discover that the whole Gospel is elegantly formed from these sets of stories that belong together. They work together to reveal Jesus with startling clarity and depth of personality.

Underneath each set of stories, I discovered a different part of the Old Testament.

I started to call these sets of stories narrative panels. I took the idea from art. Sometimes artists don't just paint one picture. They paint several that all work together. Medieval Christian painters often did paintings made up of three panels called a triptych. These paintings show the same scene but from different angles. They are designed to work together and help you to build up a three-dimensional picture in your mind – the sort of picture you would get if you were actually there. This is how these stories in the Gospel work. They enable us to look at Jesus from several perspectives. In doing so, we get to see him and find that we can know him. All great stories, films and documentaries use this technique to draw us in. In the Gospel, the stories are deliberately not adjacent but are placed in repeating sequences. They are arranged like a great symphony where the same melodies repeat at different moments in developing forms. They are like scenes in a play where the full depth and complexity of characters comes gradually to light as we combine insights from different scenes to build a full multidimensional picture of the characters.

I gave the narrative panels names. The four that I found by looking at the first sign and the second sign I called Demonstration stories. In response to a request for help from a significant person, Jesus gets other people to do something that demonstrates who he is. These turn out to be Jesus reliving the Elisha/Elijah signs.

The stories immediately before the Demonstration stories I called Invitation stories. Jesus invites people to know him. He has meals with them, shows that he knows them and ultimately transforms them. These turn out to be based on the stories of the family at the beginning of the Bible, particularly Jacob.

The stories immediately after the Demonstration stories I called Provocation stories. Jesus takes the initiative. He performs a sign that speaks of God's judgment coming against the corruption of Israel's leaders. In these stories Jesus announces that he is coming as God's new King who will put everything right. As God's King he will build a new Temple where God will dwell with his people. Understandably, this provokes the authorities and reveals what is really in their hearts.

They struggle with Jesus and eventually many reject him. Underneath these stories we find the prophetic songs of Isaiah.

The Gospel opens with two witnesses who both speak: John the author and John who baptises. I have, partly for the sake of producing a book of readable length, taken the view that the Narrator figure in the Gospel is the author and I refer to John the author throughout. I realise that this might seem an unwarranted oversimplification, but I do have reasons. Be that as it may, John the author and John who baptises both appear again in chapter 3. So there are just two stories in this panel, which I called Declaration stories. In the two stories the two witnesses point to who Jesus is. Nothing less than the whole story and theology of Israel lies underneath these stories, which is why, if you have ever heard any preaching from them, it can go on for a very long time.

As you may know from trying to read it, John's Gospel is filled with long, unresolved arguments. As Jesus argues with the authorities he speaks of his identity, his authority and his authenticity. Those arguing with him mostly do not believe him and some end up being very opposed to him because of what he says. These stories contain some of our favourite sayings and we often extract these sayings to teach or quote them. There is an irony here because Jesus says them to people who don't believe him. But it is often when we are being opposed that we speak clearly and strongly, and Jesus is no exception. This is why we like what Jesus says but are often slightly confused by the way he says it. What you will discover is that we get a much fuller understanding of Jesus when we put our favourite sayings back into their proper context. I called these arguments Contention stories. There are seven of these. Sitting underneath them are Ezekiel, who is a prophet to the people in Exile, and the story of the Exodus.

Finally, there is one story that sits alone. Interestingly, from a historical–critical point of view it also sits alone. No Condemnation, the story of the woman caught in adultery, may well be in italics in your Bible. That is because the translators are a little uncertain about its origin. We won't go into why they think that, because we are doing narrative analysis, taking the text as we have it. But it is helpful that both historical–critical and narrative analysis agree on this point. I have ended up calling this story Admission. You will see why a bit later.

It would appear that John the author has taken the whole of his Bible and shown us how Jesus is revealed from within all the Hebrew Scriptures. To write the first part of the Gospel he selects twenty-two stories about Jesus which, taken together, locate him within the entire story of Israel.

The big question then was: do these sets of stories occur in the rest of the Gospel, which we now know as chapters 15–21? The short answer is yes, they do.

The Crucifixion story has been written with one of each of the five narrative panels forming part of the story. The incarnate Jesus that we have met in the Gospel is summed up in his death. You can read about this in Chapters Twenty-Five to Twenty-Nine.

In the Resurrection account there are also five stories. They start and finish with an Invitation story and there is no Declaration story. The other interesting feature is that the Provocation and Contention stories have been woven together, with each having two parts. The point is being made very strongly that the risen Jesus is the same Jesus as the incarnate Jesus.

In chapters 15–17 the clock stops, and it is always now – the timeless time. It is constructed in an almost identical way to the Resurrection story. It begins and ends with an Invitation. And the Provocation, Contention and Demonstration panels have been woven together, with each having two parts. The Jesus who is speaking to you now and inviting you to know him is the same Jesus who stood on the shores of Lake Galilee and invited people to know him. John wants us to know that the Jesus we are following is the Jesus whom he saw, touched, knew and loved. Or was it loved by? If you want to have a quick look at this all set out, there is a diagram on page 228 for the first set of ten stories of the Gospel, a diagram on page 229 for the second set of ten stories. The timeless time is shown on page 235, Crucifixion on page 296 and Resurrection on page 327.

How to Read This Book

There is a lot to get through.

To help matters, I have written the book so that you can read it one chapter at a time. You can read the book all the way through if that works for you. But I reckon you will get more from it if you pace yourself.

I have also written a workbook as a companion to this one. You might find that helpful as well. It has handy hints, things to do, space for you to write your thoughts, further reading and deeper questions. I suggest you get to work on it before reading each chapter in this book. Even better, you could meet up with some friends as a book club. You can talk about each chapter and share your thoughts and your journey together.

For our silver wedding anniversary, Heather and I went on two incredible safaris in Tanzania and we learnt to scuba dive in Zanzibar. In both experiences we learnt the same thing: to see living things properly in their natural environment you have to slow down. One of our guides on the safari was from the Masai people. He was tall, incredibly dark skinned and had a very dignified bearing. He also had an extraordinary ability to see living things. We learnt so much from him. After he had helped us to see what he could already see, the animals and birds and snakes were obvious to us. But we couldn't see them until he helped us to see them. After a few days, we started to get the hang of it ourselves. But there were many things that we would never have seen without his help. What I began to realise was that I was in such a hurry inside. Seeing living things can't be rushed. In Zanzibar, the diving was exactly the same. The more we relaxed into the water and the slower we moved (which is harder than it sounds when you are learning to dive), the more we saw.

I want to help you see what is in the Gospel, to take in the view and absorb it all and let the living Jesus rise before your eyes.

PART TWO

Creating the Space

Demonstration

4

Seeing the Signs

First Sign: The Wedding at Cana

Our journey into the depths of John's Gospel now begins. We will start where I did with the first sign, The Wedding at Cana. You can read the story in 2:1–12. You might want to pause now and read the story two or three times before we begin.

When we read the Bible, we often take the approach of dissection. We chop it into pieces and separate all the parts. We can learn a lot that way. But dissection is what we do to dead things. To observe something living is much more like a safari. We have to get up close. We have to stay really quiet. We need to be patient and watch carefully. And there are those exciting moments when a wonderful living creature starts walking towards us.

One of the most effective ways to look into a living story is to ask questions. By doing that, we can see it more completely. We are not trying to extract information and take a bit of it away. We are trying to absorb the whole story. We are taking the text as it is and enjoying the story as it happens. We are simply trying to see what is there.

You can read the questions below and then go straight on and read my answer. But better still, stop after every question. Go back and read the story again. Immerse yourself in it. Then answer the question yourself before moving on to read my answer. One of my deep desires is that you get to read and love the Bible.

Where Does the Story Happen? (2:1)

Cana in Galilee. Each word conveys meaning. If I write Taj Mahal or Eiffel Tower, you are likely to be able to sense something of it and picture it in your mind. Cana is a modest-sized vibrant Jewish village interconnected with other Jewish villages in lower Galilee. It is situated on a limestone outcrop that rises 330 feet above the floor of the Beit Netofa Valley. The village is on an important junction of Roman roads connecting Tarichaea on the Sea of Galilee with Ptolemais (Akko) on the Mediterranean coast. You are about nine miles north of Nazareth and twenty miles west of Capernaum. The sun is hot. The roads are dusty.

There's a large building about fifty or sixty feet long with two rows of interior columns, benches along the sides and finely plastered floors and walls. It's the synagogue, where all community life happens, including worship and teaching. Around the village there are several stepped pools used for Jewish ritual baths. You can see lots of stone vessels because they are not subject to impurity according to Jewish law and are therefore common among Jewish communities at this time.

Family life is going on. Farming. Trading. Cooking. And today, and maybe for a few days, there is a wedding. A wedding in the village. It's a big event with many guests.

Who Is There? (2:1–2)

Jesus, of course. And his mother. We find out at the end of the story that Jesus' brothers are there as well. Maybe a relative is getting married, or possibly a close friend of the family. Jesus' disciples, a small group of people who are starting to gather around him, are invited to the wedding as well. One of them, Nathanael, became a disciple only a few days ago (1:43–51). He had an encounter with Jesus where he felt so connected to him. Nathanael is from Cana (21:2). They are probably all staying at his house.

How Does the Story Start? Who Starts It? (2:3)

Jesus' mum. She is probably the most significant person in Jesus' life. She has held him. She has bathed him. She has nurtured him. She has taught him. She has wondered about him. Now something has started to happen. He has given up his job. He has been baptised, like so many people have, by John who baptises. A few disciples have started to gather around him.

What Does She Say to Him? (2:3)

'They have no more wine.' What does she mean? Is she just making an observation? 'It's sunny today.' No – this is the Middle East. In Middle Eastern culture everyone steps carefully around the thing that really matters. You never go directly to the main issue, especially if you are a woman talking to a man. If we were to translate that into my English culture, what is she asking? 'Help them. Help them, my son. For God's sake, do something. This is a total and complete disaster.'

Running out of wine at a wedding is a massive shame. It is hard for us to understand the significance. But this is a shame culture where these things matter. This couple would forever be known in their village as the family who ran out of wine at their wedding. No one is going to die. But they will be shamed for ever. Shame is in some ways worse than death. Because you have to live with it.

How Does Jesus Respond? (2:4)

It's all very odd. He is very reluctant. Almost rude. It's a rebuff, a strong push-back. 'Woman.' Can you hear him say it? I don't know if you have ever said that to your mum. 'Tea's ready,' says your mum. 'Woman,' says you. I can't see that going down very well in my house. To say 'Woman' isn't disrespectful, but neither is it responsive nor engaging – especially because of what Jesus says next. 'Why do you involve me?' This is an Aramaic expression that is hard to translate but it means, 'Stop bothering me; this is nothing to do with me. And it is nothing to do with you either.' And then, even more mystifying, 'My hour has not yet come.' This is a literary device called a prolepsis. We only find out what his 'hour' is by reading further on in the Gospel, where we discover that his 'hour' is his death. This raises the question – what possible relevance does the crucifixion of Jesus have with a catering problem at a village wedding? We will have to come back to that.

How Does His Mum Respond to That? (2:5)

Does she go all sulky or, as we say in the North East of England, all ragey? No, she doesn't step back; she steps forward. She doesn't give up; she goes on. She tells the servants, 'Do whatever he tells you.' She responds to Jesus' reluctance with faith. Strong faith. What does she think he is going to do? We don't know. But maybe she knows from her experience that Jesus is good at sorting things out when they are going wrong. She seems certain he will do something. Is it a mother's intuition or her experience of Jesus in a previous event we know nothing of? How does she know that Jesus will move so readily from reluctance to resourcefulness? We are left with a large gap in the story. But strangely, gaps in stories make the people in them come closer to us, because we have to step into the story to somehow make sense of it. The mystery draws us in, which is what we do all the time when we make friends with people. What others don't tell us is often the most interesting.

What Happens Next? (2:6–8)

Jesus gives instructions. He completely changes tack. He moves from, 'Nothing to do with me, woman,' to solving the entire problem and then some. What are the instructions? Fill the jars. How many jars? Six jars. How big are they? Between 80 and 120 litres in each jar. They are not a matching set. They have all been borrowed from the neighbours. Every family has a large jar for ritual washing, but each household only needs one. There they are, lined up in the corner under a nice covering to keep the sun off them. There they are, all of them now full. Some water has been spilt on the ground where the servants sloshed it in to get it up to the brim. Now, says Jesus to them, draw some out and take it to the master of the banquet. OK. Who is going to do that? Which servant is going to do that? We don't know. But they do it.

How Does the Miracle Happen? How Does It Actually Work?

The miracle happens in the hands of the servants. It is Jesus who is doing it, but he is also not doing it. What he doesn't do is stop the wedding, stand beside the jars, get everyone to watch and wave his hands over the water while praying loudly. The servants enact the miracle. No one would be paying the blindest bit of attention to them. Servants are there to pour stuff in and out of jars. But reality is changed in them pouring in and drawing out. Water changes into wine in the willing obedience of the servants. In the story, Jesus is off-stage. Nobody else knows that he has anything to do with it. The master of the banquet gives the credit to the bridegroom (2:9–10). 'This is amazing. I've done hundreds of these weddings. Everyone, but everyone, serves the best wine at the start of the wedding. When people have drunk a fair bit and they don't care any more, then they bring out the cheap, nasty stuff. This wine is fantastic. You are bringing it out now. This is the best wedding I have ever been to.'

What Is the Outcome? (2:9–10)

How much wine is there? If we average the jars at 100 litres each, that is 600 litres. Nearly a thousand bottles. It's an abundance. It's a lot more than they need. At the end of the party, some people are going to be happily asking the family: do you mind if I take some of that home with me? A life of shame has been turned into a life-long memory of honour and praise. Their wedding will forever be one of the best wedding parties that ever happened in the village.

Who Knows What Has Really Happened? (2:11)

We are lucky. We are not actually at the party. We have the best view of everybody. The bridegroom knows nothing. The servants know something. But it is Jesus' mum who knows the whole story. She tells the disciples; they see the glory and they come to faith.

How Does the Story Finish? (2:12)

Jesus goes on a journey. They all travel down to Capernaum, which is possibly where his mother is now living, and maybe also Jesus himself. It is twenty miles, pretty much all downhill. There would be lots to talk about.

*

This story has a storyboard:

- A significant person comes to Jesus – *Mum*
- She asks Jesus to help someone else – *They have no more wine*
- Jesus is reluctant – *What is this to me or to you?*
- She steps forward in faith – *Do whatever he tells you*
- Jesus gives instructions – *Fill the jars and draw some out*
- The miracle occurs in the hands of the servants – *They fill them to the brim*
- Only a few know what really happened and they come to faith – *Mum and disciples*
- Jesus goes on a journey – *Down to Capernaum*

And it is here that we find the little phrase at the end of the story: 'What Jesus did here in Cana of Galilee was the first of the signs' (2:11). That phrase comes up once more in the Gospel, and then never comes up again: 'This was the second sign Jesus performed after coming from Judea to Galilee' (4:54).

My twenty-year adventure of discovery in the Gospel of John started here. Just a very gentle nudge; maybe this is a literary device. John is full of those little touches. They are signposts for us inside the story that help us to read the narrative better. I wondered whether these two stories belong together. First sign – second sign. So that is where we will go next.

Second Sign: The Healing of the Royal Official's Son

The second sign is the story of The Healing of the Royal Official's Son, in 4:43–54. Why don't you pause now and read it through a few times? We will walk through this story with the same questions. My suggestion is that you stop at each question, reread the scripture and answer it yourself before reading on.

Where Does the Story Happen? (4:46)

Cana. We've walked back there. There are lots of one-room houses made of mud bricks and a simple door. There are stone houses. Some are quite large, built around an open courtyard, with several rooms and servants doing the cooking. People sit up on the flat roofs, where it is cooler, talking. Some women are sitting together weaving wool.

Who Is There? Who Has Come Back to Cana? (4:6–8; 43)

If you read back in chapter 4 you will see that Jesus and his disciples have travelled from Judea to Galilee, stopping off in Sychar, a Samaritan village, where many in the village came to believe that Jesus is the Messiah. They stayed a few days and then headed on for Cana. They are probably staying at Nathanael's again.

How Does the Story Start? Who Starts It? (4:46)

A royal official. A very significant person. He has heard that Jesus has come to Cana. He is well briefed in his job. He is from Capernaum and has heard all the stories about Jesus and the healings that keep happening. He has walked along the main road. It is at least twenty miles and all uphill. But he is desperate. His son is so sick. He's dying. He has some people with him. Of course he has, he is a royal official. But by the end of the story he is simply called the father.

What Does He Ask Jesus? (4:47)

What everyone in his position would be asking: 'Please come and heal my son.' He comes to Jesus on behalf of someone else: his son.

How Does Jesus Respond? (4:48)

Very reluctantly. It's a massive rebuff. Jesus tells him off. 'Unless you people see signs and wonders . . . you will never believe.' You have this annoying desire to see miracles. Why do you have to have a healing before you will believe anything?

Now, let me ask you. Have you ever said that to anyone who has asked you to pray for a family member who is sick? I don't think so. I have never said it. I don't think I ever will. I say, 'Of course I will pray. What is his name? I will write it in my prayer journal. Let's pray now.'

What Does the Father Do? How Does the Royal Official Respond to That? (4:49)

He steps forward. He doesn't go into a rage. He doesn't go off in a sulk. He doesn't retreat. He steps forward in faith. 'Please will you come down. My son is so sick.'

What Happens Next? (4:50)

Jesus gives instructions. He completely changes tack. He stops being difficult and starts telling him what to do. Go away. Walk away from me. Walk home. As you go back home you will find that your son lives.

How Does the Miracle Happen? (4:50)

The miracle happens in the feet of the father and his retinue, in their willing obedience of faith. The man takes Jesus at his word and departs.

What Is the Outcome? (4:51)

Back home, the boy suddenly recovers. Nobody there knows that Jesus had anything to do with it. As far as his mother is concerned, if he has a mother, the boy just opens his eyes and shakes his head. He jumps out of bed and requests lunch. Imagine the joy. Imagine the shock. For that family, it is joy unspeakable. A terrible sense of impending doom and loss becomes a moment of abundant joy that will last all their lives. He will forever be the boy who came back to them.

Who Knows What Really Happened? (4:52–3)

Only the father. He puts it all together. What time did that happen? Yesterday. One in the afternoon. That was the time. That was the time we started walking back. Not knowing. Only believing. No Jesus with us. Just his word in our ears. Go away. Off home. That was the time. He and his household believe.

How Does the Story Finish? (4:54)

There is no mention of a journey in this story. Although someone went to find out what happened to the son.

*

The storyboard is the same.
- A significant person comes to Jesus – *The father*
- He asks Jesus to help someone else – *My son is sick*
- Jesus is reluctant – *Unless you people see signs and wonders you won't believe*
- He steps forward in faith – *Please will you come down*
- Jesus gives instructions – *Go*
- The miracle occurs in the feet of the father – *The man departs*
- Only a few know what really happened and they come to faith – *He and his household believe*

These stories have the same storyboard. There are some slight variations – Jesus is not a machine. He is a person. Even when we are doing the same things, we often do them slightly differently. But there is a consistency about our actions that reveals our personhood.

I'm in here somewhere. I am an embodied living soul. You can't see me. There is a physicality to me that tells you something about me. But often the outward appearance is not a good indicator of the inner substance. As you get to know me, as you spend time with me, as you see how I do things and as you see how I respond, you see the patterns. You see the consistency of who I am. As you see the patterns, you meet the person. We all love a puzzle. We all have this hard-wired ability to recognise patterns. We have this incredible ability to assemble data and make sense of it. That is how we make friends. Relationships form as we discover each other. That is what we are seeing here. We are not just seeing two miracle stories and two happy families. We are seeing a person. Someone we can know. Someone we can follow. Someone who can become our friend.

This is the way John has arranged his Gospel. He has chosen the stories carefully and prayerfully. They are written to reveal Jesus in such a way that we can know him and become a close friend. We all have stories in our family that we tell again and again. They sum up who we are in our quirky little ways. If you know those stories you can work out what we are really like and what matters to us.

And here came the next gentle nudge: are there any more? Are there any more stories like this in the Gospel of John? There are two more. There are developments and interesting variations, but these two stories follow this storyboard in every way. We will look at them in the next chapter.

This is your challenge, if you choose to accept it: to encounter Jesus in this beautiful house that is the Gospel of John.

5

Two More Signs

The Feeding of the Five Thousand

The third story that follows that storyboard of the first sign and the second sign is The Feeding of the Five Thousand. You can read it in 6:1–21. As before, maybe you could pause now and read it through a few times. We will follow the same set of questions so we can take in the whole story.

Where Does the Story Happen? Where Are They? (6:1)

The far shore of the Sea of Galilee. It's not Cana, but we are close by.

Who Is There? (6:2–3)

Jesus and his disciples. Plus a huge crowd who have invited themselves along.

How Does the Story Start? Who Starts It? (6:5–6)

There is an interesting difference from the previous two stories. This time, the person starting the story is Jesus. It is Jesus who sees the need and asks the question. So far, we have had a mother and a father. Now we have the Son.

What Does He Say?

'Where shall we buy bread for these people to eat?' It's not his own needs he is concerned about, but the hunger of the people who have been listening to him all day.

How Does Philip Respond? (6:7)

Very reluctantly. 'It would cost more than any of us can earn in six months. We don't have that kind of money.' Both the request for help and the reluctance to respond are here in the story. Because Jesus starts this story by voicing the need, the reluctance and the push-back are from someone else, from Philip.

Who Responds to Philip's Reluctance? (6:8–9)

Andrew. How does he respond? He steps forward with something. Or rather, with someone who has something. The reluctance creates opportunity for faith to be expressed. Andrew still has questions – how far will this go? But it is the response of faith. The same elements are present in the story. There is a request to help others. There is a reluctant response. And then someone steps forward with some faith.

What Happens Next? (6:10)

Jesus gives instructions: get everyone to sit down. Get it all organised. We get a lovely little eyewitness detail – there is plenty of grass in that place. John knows that some of his readers will be saying, 'Very unlikely to get five thousand men to sit down in the dust.' He wants the doubtful reader to know that the crowd do what Jesus tells them to do. They all sit down. It is all fine. There is plenty of grass. This is yet another detail that communicates to us that this is not a made-up story. This is eyewitness narrative. Someone was there, remembering who said what, counting the loaves, counting the men and looking at the grass.

How Does the Miracle Happen? (6:11)

It does not appear from the story that the five loaves are made into five thousand loaves and placed in a huge pile. There is still a significant element of hiddenness and understatement happening.

It would appear that it is as they give out the bread that the multiplication occurs. It is in the hands and the feet of Jesus and the disciples that the miracle happens. The story doesn't mention explicitly that the disciples get involved in the distribution. But the maths of mass catering can help us here. Anyone who has been to a party where there was only a single buffet station knows how long it can take to feed a few hundred people. This is a larger operation, running into thousands. I am fairly sure the disciples are involved in the breaking and therefore the multiplying of the bread. This detail is confirmed in the other Gospels (Mark 6:41; Matt. 14:19; Luke 9:16).

Imagine being part of that. Imagine being given half a loaf and five hundred plus people to feed. How would you handle that? How much would you give to start with? Imagine the strange and fearful joy of seeing that bread in your hand never diminish, no matter how much you break it. In the prayer of Jesus and the hands of Jesus and his disciples, the breaking of bread is the multiplying of bread.

What Is the Outcome? (6:12–13)

An abundance. A shortage is turned into a massive surplus. People take it home with them for tomorrow's lunch.

Who Knows What Has Really Happened? (6:14)

Here is another development from the first and second story. Everyone sees this one. It's much more public than the first two. This time, everybody knows it was Jesus.

How do they respond? Not well, which may be partly why Jesus was so reluctant and hidden with the first two. The people want to make him King by force. If you can multiply bread and feed thousands by breaking it, what might you do with the Romans when you get your hands on them?

In 63 BC the Roman general Pompey had conquered Jerusalem. Twenty-three years later, the Romans deposed the ruling dynasty and installed Herod the Great as their puppet King. Just before the birth of Jesus, Judea was made into a Roman Province with Samaria, called Idumea. Nobody likes being ruled by an empire with orders given in far-off places enforced by a privileged elite held in power by an invading army. It just means taxes. But the Jewish people also had an almost spiritual dislike of the Romans. Their whole identity rested on the story of the Exodus, when God set them free from pagan rulers and gave them a land where they could rule themselves with God as their King. There were numerous conflicts and Jewish–Roman wars. Perhaps Jesus was the answer? He might be able to win the war.

How Does the Story Finish? (6:15–21)

Jesus withdraws from the crowd. He will become King. But he will become King by the laying-down of his life, not by the taking-up of arms, miraculous or otherwise. The crowd have seen the sign, but they haven't seen the sign. They have seen what happened. They haven't understood what it means.

The disciples leave as they came, by boat. It is dark, but they are used to night-time fishing. Yet conditions are poor, with rough seas and a strong wind. They make very slow progress. Jesus isn't with them when they leave, a fact that the crowd notes (6:22). However, after his time alone with God up the mountain, Jesus decides to cross the sea by miraculous means. Setting the boundaries for water is an act of Creator God, which Jeremiah points out to those who do not see what God is doing and who turn aside from God (Jer. 5:21–3).

Crossing water by miraculous means is something we see with Moses, Joshua, Elijah and Elisha. Moses leads God's people through the waters to escape from an army that is trying to recapture them and use them for their own purposes. But by leading his people across the sea, God defeats the army and saves his people (Exod. 15:19). The psalmist associates this crossing of water by miraculous means with God's rule coming (Ps. 66:5–7) and God shepherding his people (Ps. 77:19–20). Joshua crosses water by miraculous means in order to lead God's people into their new life and new land (Josh.

3:7–17). It is a massive step forward into their new life. In all the Gospels, The Feeding of the Five Thousand and The Crossing of the Sea mark a significant turning point and the start of a new phase of Jesus' ministry.

It is not entirely clear quite why Elijah decides to do the crossing the water thing. Perhaps he doesn't fancy using the boat. What it does show is the kind of person he is and the relationship he has with God (2 Kgs 2:7–8). Elisha notes this and on his return journey looks to the parting of waters to demonstrate where he now stands in relation to God (2 Kgs 2:13–14).

The experience for the disciples is mysterious and rather frightening. But at least they don't have to row any further.

Can you see it? Can you see the storyboard? More to the point, can you see Jesus?

The Raising of Lazarus

The final story that follows this pattern is The Raising of Lazarus. You can read it in 10:40–11:54.

Where Does the Story Happen (11:1)

Bethany, a short walk from Jerusalem. The location of these four signs is Cana in Galilee, Cana in Galilee, Lake Galilee and finally Bethany. John the author is very precise with his geography.

When Herod the Great died, the Romans split his kingdom into five. The two Jewish areas were each ruled by one of Herod's sons: Herod Archelaus in the south over Jerusalem, Judea and Samaria, and Herod Antipas in northern Galilee. Not long after, the Romans got rid of Archelaus and made Judea into a Roman Province with a governor. At the time of Jesus this was Pontius Pilate. Day-to-day management of many things was handed to a local council led by the High Priest. At the time of Jesus this was Caiaphas. He and Pontius Pilate collaborated for more than ten years.

For the authorities based in Jerusalem, a man doing signs in Galilee is annoying and needs investigating, but it is not the end of the world. And anyway, it is not under their political control. A man doing a powerful sign in Bethany is very dangerous. Bethany is an hour's walk from Jerusalem and is a convenient place for wealthy Jews to live near but not in Jerusalem. The danger of a powerful sign in Bethany is not because it represents a direct threat to the position and power of the authorities – there is no indication that they are troubled by the thought of Jesus and his followers overthrowing them in a popular uprising. The danger is much more that if the people were to grow too excited about the appearance of a messianic figure then the Romans would clamp down and everyone would suffer (11:47–50). The plot to get rid of Jesus is to make sure that this does not happen. In the Gospel of John, it is the raising of Lazarus that triggers the arrest and death of Jesus (11:53).

Who Is There? (10:40–2)

Another interesting development in this story. Jesus isn't there – at least not to start with. Jesus is having time out with his disciples up north. He has gone back to his roots. He has taken the disciples back to where it all began – John baptising them all in the Jordan. He and the disciples are in what John describes as another Bethany, on the other side of the Jordan (1:28). He is two days' walk away from Bethany near Jerusalem. John loves these little word plays and symmetries. Jesus is in Bethany and also not in Bethany.

Who Starts the Story? (11:1–2)

Two sisters, whom Jesus loves: Martha and Mary. This is a family whom Jesus is especially close to (11:5). These stories are all started by significant people. So far, we have seen a mother, a father, a Son, and now two sisters. Almost a family. John the author loves these little details and connections.

What Do They Ask? (11:3)

'Lord. the one you love is ill.' A message that is pretty high on emotional content. But we are also back to the indirect method of communication. This is deferential. The sisters state the facts but do not make a direct request, which is so Middle Eastern. Translate that into English in my culture and it's an urgent, urgent, urgent request.

How Does Jesus Respond? (11:4–17)

Jesus is once again strangely and deliberately reluctant. He seems positive about the outcome of Lazarus' illness, but he stays where he is for two days. Is that what you would do? Is that how you react to very urgent messages from people you love about their relatives who are sick and need your help?

Those who are good at maths can work out when Lazarus died. Jesus is two days' walk from Bethany but stays two days before he sets off, and when he gets there Lazarus has been dead and in the tomb for four days. Therefore, Lazarus dies the same day that the messenger arrives up north to tell Jesus that Lazarus is sick. It wouldn't have made any difference if he had set off immediately. Except that being dead for four days is significant. The Jewish understanding of death was that the soul remained with the body for three days. After four days, you weren't just bodily dead. You were gone. You were completely dead.

Jesus knows that Lazarus is dead. After the two days of deliberate delay, Jesus tells the disciples that they are setting off for Bethany. They have one of their discussions where the disciples repeatedly don't understand what Jesus is talking about.

First, they are puzzled and worried about Jesus wanting to return to Judea as his life is in danger. They understand what might happen if he crosses the border. Jesus makes one of his cryptic remarks about day and night. Walking in the day is fine because there is light. It is only at night that you stumble in the dark. Apart from him assuring the disciples that there will be no night-time walking, this is probably a metaphor that means that those trying to kill him are stumbling about in the dark, but he is walking in the light because he is walking with God. Therefore, let's not worry about what might happen.

Then Jesus says that Lazarus has fallen asleep, and the disciples think he means that Lazarus is sleeping and point out that he will recover more quickly if they let him sleep. Once they discover that Lazarus is in fact dead, Thomas decides that Jesus' purpose must be that they are all going to die, presumably at the hands of those who are trying to kill Jesus, and he gets a bit dramatic about this. You will be glad to know that we hear no more of their conversation over the next two days. Their misunderstandings are all a bit painful, because they are so familiar.

How Do the Sisters Respond to Jesus? (11:18–37)

They step towards him. When Martha hears that Jesus is coming, she goes out to meet him. Mary, when she goes to meet him, falls at his feet. They affirm him and express faith. They both say that if Jesus had been there, Lazarus would have been healed. Their much-loved brother would not have died. There is terrible grief. But there is faith. Martha goes as far as to say that God will answer Jesus' prayers even now. But when Jesus suggests that resurrection is a possibility, she steps back to the safe ground of her Jewish faith. The resurrection will happen on the last day at the end of the age. Resurrection now is not what she expects.

In first-century Judaism there was a range of views about resurrection from death. These ranged from no resurrection at all through to a new bodily existence in a new age when God defeats evil, puts everything right and dwells with his people again (Dan. 12:2–3; Isa. 26:19; Hos. 6:2), which is where Martha seems to stand. This view was often associated with a political position of the defeat of Rome, the Empire being one of the dark powers that God was going to deal with.

In reply, Jesus personalises resurrection life to himself. Those who believe in him will be raised to life, even if they die. It will be as if they never die. He questions Martha on this, and she agrees with at least part of it. She affirms Jesus as God's new King, whom they were expecting to come. Like King David, Israel's greatest King, the Holy Spirit would come on him in power (1 Sam. 16:13). That is why Mary calls Jesus 'Messiah'. The Greek word *Christ* and the Hebrew word *Messiah* both mean 'anointed one' or 'one covered' – in Jesus' case, covered in the Holy Spirit. We are left guessing as to how she thinks that Jesus coming as anointed King is connected to the resurrection from death at the end of the age. But she is grieving. She does not want to discuss the finer details. She goes back inside.

Everyone is grieving. Jesus himself is deeply moved. Martha sends Mary out to meet him. She is weeping, and Jesus weeps with her. What does that tell us?

First, that Jesus approaches all these signs with an almost anti-fanfare. He does not arrive in the village with lots of excitement, cutting across the grieving process and confidently proclaiming his plan to bring Lazarus back to life. This is the same in the other Demonstration stories. All Jesus does in The Wedding at Cana story is speak privately to the servants. He plays no visible part in the process of the miracle actually happening. With The Healing of the Royal Official's Son, he sends everyone away from him. The miracle occurs as they go, not because he comes. Even the breaking of bread and its multiplication happens in a quiet, almost hard-to-see manner. There are no trumpets or triumphant tweets in any of these stories.

Second, Jesus is not a magician or a superman. His humanity is real. He never says, 'I've got this sorted. I've got the power.' In the Gospel of John he says the opposite. He does not have authority over death independently from God his Father. He can do nothing by himself (5:19). We are peering into the mystery of what it means to be Word made flesh. No surprise that there has been a lot of arguing about this over the years. It's hard to get your head round. It was finally resolved, as far as it can be resolved, at the Council of Chalcedon in AD 451, which declared that Jesus is 'perfect in Godhead and perfect in Manhood, the distinction of natures being by no means taken away by the union, but rather the property of each nature being preserved, not parted or divided into two persons, but one and the same Son'. Basically it is saying that Jesus is both God and man. He is truly God. He is fully man. But his being God does not combine with his being man to produce a superman with special powers.

Third, Jesus does not know the end of the story. When you and I pray for the sick and the dying, we don't know the end of the story. Jesus doesn't know either (5:19). He is in the story. He doesn't have our perspective of knowing what happens next. He is taking his time on this one. He seemed so confident a few days ago (11:4, 11). Has that certainty diminished now he has is near the tomb? Or is it important that he fully join his friends in their grief before gently helping them step into resurrection life?

Fourth, even God working in great power does not take away the sorrow and pain of loss. Being God does not mean that Jesus escapes from sorrows. Being God does not mean a pain-free life. We already know this (Isa. 53:3). Jesus genuinely and completely enters into grief. As a pastor also filled with the certainty of Christian hope of resurrection life, I too am deeply (and personally) aware of how important it is to grieve in response to death and not to rush glibly into proclamation of resurrection as if that takes away all the pain.

What Happens Next? (11:38–43)

Jesus gives instructions. He tells them to roll away the stone. As in The Feeding of the Five Thousand we meet reluctance, this time in the disciples. This story has reluctance on both sides. Jesus delays in Bethany by the Jordan. Martha is very reluctant about moving the stone. Lazarus has been dead for four days and in their climate the process of decomposition will be well advanced. The smell will be terrible. But Jesus calls her back to believing. As in the first sign, the glory of God is going to be revealed to those who believe.

How Does the Miracle Happen?

The same combination as before: faith in Jesus leads to obedience. The miracle happens through people doing what

Jesus tells them to do. People participate in the miracle, even though it is Jesus who does it. That is even more obvious in this case because Jesus speaks out loud in public. But Jesus works through their obedience. It's the same relationship that he and the Father have. The obedience of Jesus is the means by which the Father works. Our obedience is the means by which Jesus works.

What Is the Outcome? (11:44)

It's abundance. Lazarus is called out of death and comes back to life. It is impossible to imagine the feelings in the family. From life to death to life again.

How Does the Story Finish? (11:45–54)

As with the other signs, there is a group of people who believe. But the plot to get rid of Jesus rapidly gathers pace. For the authorities, this is all too close to home. The Sanhedrin meet and Caiaphas, the High Priest, persuades them that it is better that one man die than they lose the whole nation, even though they all know that they have no legal basis for such an action. Jesus knows of the plan, so as with the third Demonstration story, he goes on a journey to get out of the way.

*

It is the same storyboard but in a more developed and complex form. But what a strange collection of stories these are. They belong together. But they do look pretty random:
- Reality is changed by pouring in and drawing out of jars
- Healing happens by walking away
- Bread is multiplied as people are fed
- A dead son of a loved family is called back to life

I sat and looked at those for a long time. I had another question. Where had I seen those stories before?

Coming Together

Bringing these four stories together, the storyboard looks like this:

Narrative	2:1–12	4:43–54	6:1–21	10:40–11:54
The location of the story	Cana of Galilee	Cana of Galilee	Shore of Lake Galilee	Bethany and Bethany
A significant person comes to Jesus	Mother	Father	Son	Sisters
To ask Jesus to help someone else	'They have no more wine'	My son is sick	'Where shall we buy bread for these people to eat?'	'Lord, the one you love is ill'
Jesus appears reluctant	'Why do you involve me?'	'Unless you people see signs and wonders . . . you will never believe'	'It would take more than half a year's wages'	'When he heard that Lazarus was ill, he stayed where he was two more days'
Which causes someone to step forward in faith	'Do whatever he tells you'	'Sir, come down before my child dies'	'Here is a boy with five small barley loaves and two small fish'	'I know that even now God will give you whatever you ask'
Jesus gives instructions	'Fill the jars with water . . . Now draw some out'	'Go'	'Make the people sit down'	'Take away the stone'
The miracle occurs in the obedience of others	'So they filled them to the brim'	'The man took Jesus at his word and departed'	'There was plenty of grass in that place, and they sat down'	'So they took away the stone'

Only a few know what happened and they come to faith	'His disciples believed in him'	'So he and his whole household believed'	'After the people saw the sign Jesus performed, they began to say, "Surely, this is the Prophet"'	'Many of the Jews who had come to visit Mary, and had seen what Jesus did, believed in him'
Jesus goes on a journey that separates him	'After this he went down to Capernaum'		'Jesus . . . withdrew again to a mountain by himself' They saw Jesus approaching, walking on the water	'He withdrew to a region near the wilderness, to a village called Ephraim'

Four stories that belong together. As we look through the window of each story, we start to see that there is a person there. A person whom we can know. I'm making a friend, a friend like I have never had before. John's Gospel is this holy place. It's a sacred space. It is a space where the Word and the Spirit work together to make God known. Not just to make God known in the informational sense whereby I could give a description of God, but making God known in the relational sense whereby I find I have a friend in God.

There are so many features here that draw me to Jesus.

There is the complete absence of showing off. He does the most powerful miracles, and yet in the first two, most of the people who benefit have no idea it was anything to do with Jesus. The master of the banquet gives the credit to the bridegroom. Even when Jesus chooses to do the signs in a much more public way, he does not need to show off how great he is. Jesus does not try to build his reputation using powerful signs.

There is the engaging of others in the miracles. Jesus is so empowering. He knows what it is like to walk in obedience to his Father and

55

to listen to his Father and to work with his Father. He knows that he is not the power behind the miracle. He helps his disciples to step into that space too. As his obedience creates the opportunity for the Father to work, he encourages others into obedience that also creates the opportunity for the Father to work.

The reluctance and delay are probably the most unusual and striking features of these stories. But it is very compelling. Need in others can be used in a controlling way. Jesus uses reluctance and delay to safeguard his freedom. He does not respond immediately to need. He waits and responds to God. Too often we become enmeshed in other people's needs and we are no help to them or to ourselves. Need, even desperate need, is not the engine of faith and obedience to God.

Jesus' ability to recognise and respond to the negative effects of these signs is also very attractive. Sometimes the good things we do give rise to a very bad response in others. Our actions reveal the darkness. Jesus is not thrown by this. He does not seek or need others' approval and praise. He can cope when people respond badly.

His empathy and vulnerability are deeply compelling. We struggle to understand how Jesus can be weeping with Mary one minute and then calling Lazarus to life the next. We assume that Jesus performing signs would overrule any grief he might feel at Lazarus' death. But that is not the case. Jesus is vulnerable throughout. He is vulnerable in feeling and participating in the grief at death and he is vulnerable in doing the sign. He doesn't suddenly become a triumphant wonder worker celebrating his great success. After all, death is still real. Lazarus himself will die again.

The signs all point beyond themselves. They point to the great miracle – the cross. We saw this at the very first sign. Part of Jesus' reluctance which he expresses to his mother is this: 'My hour has not yet come.' We have to read on to find out what he means.

6

Jesus Is Elisha

Connecting the Stories

These four stories are the stories of Elisha. They are all in 2 Kings 4–5, one after the other.

In the Elisha story, it is not wine in the jars. It is oil. But it is the pouring in and the pouring out that does it. A family in need are saved (2 Kgs 4:1–7). There is a related story, with oil in a jar in the Elijah narratives (1 Kgs 17:7–16) but it doesn't have the same level of correspondence as the Elisha story.

It is not a royal official's son who is healed by walking away. It is a royal official himself who gets healed by walking away. He's called Naaman. He comes to Elisha and he gets angry because Elisha won't come out and do the healing 'magic' over him. Elisha tells him what to do: 'Walk away from me. Go and do what I tell you and you will find your healing there.' Naaman has to be persuaded to do it (2 Kgs 5:1–19).

Barley bread is brought to Elisha and he says to set it before 100 men and it will feed them. His disciples say that is ridiculous. That will never work. The request and the reluctance are the other way around in this story. Exactly the same as it is in The Feeding of the Five Thousand. Elisha says, 'Give it to the people to eat. For this is what the Lord says: "They will eat and have some left over"' (2 Kgs 4:42–44).

And then there is a son in a family that loves Elisha and they have a little guest room for him to stay in their house. The son in this family dies. Elisha is away up country, and they have to send for him. When he finally gets there, the loved son is brought back to life (2 Kgs 4:8–37). Again, there is a related story in the Elijah narratives (1 Kgs 17:17–24).

There is a phenomenal level of correspondence between the Elisha stories and the Jesus stories. We'll take just one: the multiplying of bread.

> A man came from Baal Shalishah, bringing the man of God twenty loaves of barley bread baked from the first ripe corn, along with some ears of new corn. 'Give it to the people to eat,' Elisha said.
> 'How can I set this before a hundred men?' his servant asked.
> But Elisha answered, 'Give it to the people to eat. For this is what the Lord says: "They will eat and have some left over."' Then he set it before them, and they ate and had some left over (2 Kgs 4:42–4).

There are ten points of correspondence: (1) A prophet suggests (2) that everyone can be fed (3) from not very much (4) but his disciples are sceptical and reluctant. (5) Barley bread (6) is brought to the prophet (7), who gives instructions. (8) He gives the bread to them. (9) Everyone eats and (10) there isn't just enough; there is bread left over.

Ten points of correspondence in three verses. It is the same story. Jesus is being Elisha and John has seen it.

What of the other stories? How much do they correspond? Maybe you would like to look at that yourself:

- The Wedding at Cana in John 2:1–12 corresponds with The Olive Oil in 2 Kings 4:1–7
- The Healing of the Royal Official's Son in John 4:43–54 corresponds with The Healing of Naaman in 2 Kings 5:1–19
- The Raising of Lazarus in John 11:1–54 corresponds with The Raising of the Shunammite's Son in 2 Kings 4:8–37

There are fourteen points of correspondence between the Jesus story of The Wedding at Cana and the Elisha story of The Olive Oil: (1) A woman influential in the prophet's life brings (2) a desperate need (3) to the prophet's attention. (4) The prophet's first response is to push back (5) using a Middle Eastern idiom. (6) There is something available in the house. (7) The prophet then changes tack and gives instructions. (8) His instructions are followed by the servants. (9) Jars are gathered or have been gathered from the neighbours. (10) The jars are filled and (11) reality is changed. (12) Further instructions are given that conclude the story and (13) show that the need has been met by God's provision. (14) Only a few people know how this was done.

There are eleven points of correspondence between the Jesus story of The Healing of the Royal Official's Son and the Elisha story of The Healing of Naaman: (1) There is a prophet in Israel/Samaria with (2) a God-given gift to heal. (3) The royal official comes (4) to the prophet with (5) a desperate disease (6) believing that the prophet can heal. (7) The request to heal does not go down well. (8) The prophet is asked to heal. (9) The prophet doesn't actually do anything but tells the official to walk away from him and obey his instructions to receive his healing. (10) It is in the act of obedience that the healing occurs and (11) it is only those in the household who know the whole story.

We have already seen that there are ten points of correspondence between the Jesus story of The Feeding of the Five Thousand and the Elisha story of Feeding the Hundred.

There are sixteen points of correspondence between the Jesus story of The Raising of Lazarus and the Elisha story of The Raising of the Shunammite's Son: (1) The son of a family that (2) the prophet loves and stays with (3) falls ill. (4) His mother, or sisters who seem to be acting as mother, (5) send for the prophet. (6) The prophet is away from the family home but (7) the message reaches him. (8) There is a Middle Eastern discussion regarding the severity of the situation. (9) The sister/mother (10) falls at the prophet's feet (11) in deep distress. (12) The prophet comes to the dead son. (13) The prophet prays and (14) acts in faith. (15) The dead man is raised to life. (16) The relatives take charge.

This is how John has written his Gospel. There are four stories all connecting with each other inside four more stories that all connect with each other. It is the story of Jesus sitting inside the story of Israel.

Eight stories all interacting with each other create a space. We can immerse ourselves in this space just by reading the stories and recognising the relationships they have with each other. This biblically rich and deeply connected environment accomplishes two things simultaneously. First, it creates a dynamic three-dimensional structure that enables us not just to see what happened, but also, by seeing through what happened, we can see the person standing inside the stories. We can get to know Jesus. Second, it creates a safe space for the inner imaginative process that takes place when we read the stories. The Jesus that we see, the Jesus that we become friends with, is the real Jesus. He is the Word made flesh.

When we get to know another person, we do so by internalising their stories and making sense of the consistency of the patterns we can see in their behaviour and responses. However, people often aren't what we first expect them to be. We can easily make the wrong assumptions about people or misjudge what they say or do. We attribute thoughts, motivations and character traits to people that then turn out not to be true. Either our evidence was incomplete or our assessment was wrong. What is needed to correct this failing, which we all have, is a rich feedback loop from the other person. We try out our understanding of who they are, and we can then tell whether we have the correct insight. We see more of the person which forces us to re-evaluate our thinking. Or the person themselves challenges our conclusions directly. Friendship deepens through a series of guesses and course corrections.

To get the true view of who another person is, we need many stories. And we need to combine our observations from all those stories until we can arrive at a consistent, balanced, integrated understanding of the person. People often appear contradictory to start with. That is often because they are. But more insight from more observation can often help us see the deeper issues and character traits that explain the apparent inconsistencies.

John has created a space for us to know Jesus, relationally and personally. There is danger in that enterprise because the person reading the Gospel might recreate Jesus in their own imagination and in their own image. To be honest, most of us do this anyway. We tend to view and describe Jesus in terms that look very similar to our own outlook and beliefs. This Jesus is a great comfort to us. And we can be both shocked and affronted when someone from another culture or another age tries to tell us that Jesus might not be so conforming to our view of the world.

John has determined not to try to control the development of our understanding of Jesus and our relationship with him. In that he is wise. No one should seek to control the relationship of one person with another. It always ends badly. However, John does understand that you and I are likely to misunderstand Jesus. The disciples of the incarnate Jesus do that all the time. To create safety for us, John has created a space incredibly rich in truth. He knows that with the help of the Holy Spirit, as we immerse ourselves in the truth of God's Word, we can be led into all truth (14:25–6; 15:12–15).

Invitation

7

Come and See

Meetings and Meals

The story immediately before the first sign has four quick scenes within which the same things happen. They are in two parallel pairs. Scene one leads to scene two and then scene three leads to scene four in the same way. It is where the first disciples meet with Jesus. You can read the story in 1:35–51.

Where Does the Story Happen? (1:28)

Bethany on the other side of the Jordan where John is baptising. We do not know for sure where this is. Although the traditional under-standing of the location is Al-Maghtas, about 20 miles east of Jeru-salem, Carson is his book makes a compelling case for an area of wilderness much further north, called Batanea. This correlates much better with the details in the Gospel, particularly Jesus withdrawing here for safety later in his ministry (10:40). Al-Maghtas is too close to Jerusalem and would not put him beyond the reach of the authorities. Batanea bordered the eastern shore of Lake Galilee and the northern part of the Jordan River and is referred to as Bashan in the Hebrew Bible. In the Exodus story of Israel coming into their new life and new land, Bashan marks the transition, where they ceased to wander in the desert and started to take the land (Deut. 1:1–8). As John the author notes, this is the place where, for Jesus too, it all began.

Who Is There? (1:35, 40–1, 43–5)

John who baptises. We shall meet him in more detail in Chapter Sev-enteen. He sees himself as one sent by God to prepare God's people

63

for the coming of their new King. We know from the other Gospels that he calls people to repentance and baptises them in water as a sign that they are entering into a new life with God. Going into the water is seen as a 'crossing over' into a new way of living, just as Israel crossed over the Red Sea to be set free from slavery and crossed over the Jordan to enter the new land. John who baptises is there with two of his disciples. We quickly get to know the name of one: Andrew. But we never learn the name of the other. But we are going to meet him again. In scene two, Andrew introduces Jesus to his brother Simon Peter. In scene three we meet Philip who persuades his good friend Nathanael to meet Jesus, which happens in scene four.

How Does the Story Start? (1:36–9, 41–2, 43–7)

The story starts when John who baptises points out Jesus as the Lamb of God who has come to take away the sins of the world, something he has said before (1:29). This time two of his disciples take a look for themselves. They don't do very much; they just follow Jesus, who turns and speaks to them. Jesus starts the conversation by asking a question, one that you would ask two men who are silently following you: 'What do you want?'

The other three scenes have exactly the same elements; the stories are written in parallel. In scene two, Andrew acts like John who baptises. He introduces Simon to Jesus who starts the conversation, this time with a bold statement instead of a question. In scene three, the story is sparse. Jesus finds Philip. Jesus acts like John who baptises. Jesus points himself out and starts the conversation. 'Follow me,' he says, which is that wonderful combination of invitation and challenge that we saw before. In scene four, Philip acts like John who baptises. He invites his good friend Nathanael to meet Jesus. Jesus starts the conversation with Nathanael, using a very confident opener, very similar to his meeting with Simon Peter.

What Happens Next? (1:39, 42, 47–8)

First, food and conversation, especially in the first scene with Andrew and the disciple with no name. This is the Middle East. When you invite people to your home, cooking happens. I have many Iranian friends. I can't visit them without eating a meal. They never take no for an answer. Visiting their home means eating together. This is the first thing Jesus does in the Gospel – invite some people round to his home to be with him, to spend time with him and to get to know him. It is food and friendship. The next thing they all do is go off to a wedding together.

Second, what happens is what we have already seen. Those who spend time with Jesus invite others to do the same. This is what leads to the subsequent scenes in this story. Andrew invites Simon. Philip persuades Nathanael. This is how friendship starts. People meet and start talking, either spontaneously or because someone who knows them both brings them together, either by suggestion or invitation.

Third, what happens next is that Jesus appears to have a gift. He knows things about people.

Jesus can see what kind of person Simon is going to become. 'Your life is going to change so much I am going to give you a new name. I am going to call you Peter' (1:42). 'You are going to be strong, stable, weight-bearing and foundational. Others' lives are going to be built on you. You are going to withstand the forces that come against you to knock you over. You are going to be a shade and refuge in the heat of the day. You are going to be a safe place for those who are lost and lonely.'

For first-century Jewish people, names are much more than labels. Names are strongly connected to identity. Giving Simon a new name is a lot more than giving a nickname to a new friend. It is a powerful prophetic statement about who Simon is going to become. He is going to be a Peter. Does Simon immediately become this person? It would appear not. Later we are going to hear of his fearful denials of Jesus (13:36–8; 18:17–27) and his need of restoration (21:15–19). Is he eventually changed into this person? That takes us outside the scope of this book. But it would appear so. Jesus is good at seeing what other people can become.

With Nathanael, Jesus jumps over all the questions that are in Nathanael's mind with a life-giving statement to him of huge affirmation: 'Here truly is an Israelite in whom there is no deceit'

(1:47). 'In you, Nathanael, is truth. You have tremendous integrity. You are a man who refuses to bend the truth even slightly for your own advantage. You will have nothing to do with the lying and the trickery and the manipulation of truth that is happening all around you. You are a man whom God has chosen, a man whom God loves.'

Nathanael doesn't dispute the conclusion; he just wants to know how Jesus knows. It would appear that men from Nazareth don't normally do things like this (1:46). Jesus moves on in the gift: 'I saw you while you were still under the fig-tree before Philip called you' (1:48). This is evidently something that was true. It would appear that Nathanael was sheltering under a fig tree when Philip spoke to him. But Nathanael's response is so strong that it suggests there is more meaning in that statement than just location. We'll come back to that when we look at the Old Testament roots to this story.

Is Jesus highly intuitive, or gifted by God in how he does this? Probably both. The striking thing is that the knowing of Simon and Nathanael leads to so much good in their lives.

How Do They Respond to Jesus? (1:49)

We don't know what Simon made of Jesus giving him a new name and speaking a new identity over him. But we can see that he took the name and became a close friend and follower of Jesus. Nathanael, however, is extravagant in his response. He declares Jesus to be Son of God and King of Israel. Meeting Jesus has been a powerful experience for him. He is not alone in this. In this story everyone is getting connected with Jesus, starting to see who he is and being excited by their relationship with him.

What Does Jesus Do? (1:50–1)

Jesus receives what Nathanael says. Son of God and King of Israel is who he is. There is something beautifully incongruous about this. Normally, kings in Israel don't invite you round to their house and rustle up a late lunch. Kings of any country aren't known for opening their homes to ordinary people.

In response to Nathanael's belief in him, Jesus opens up not just his home but also his heart. He deepens their conversation very quickly. Because we read this story from the other side, with lots more information than Nathanael had at the time, it is hard for us to register the speed at which Jesus is moving forward his relationship with Nathanael. But Jesus reveals himself to him in very bold terms: 'Very truly I tell you, you will see "heaven open, and the angels of God ascending and descending on" the Son of Man' (1:51).

Nathanael is going to see heaven open over Jesus. Nathanael is going to see the power and presence of God coming down where Jesus is, down being the traditional direction of travel from heavenly reality to earthly reality. And Nathanael is going to see all the sins, failings, pressures, pains and prayers of the earth being carried up to heaven in and through the person of Jesus, up being the traditional direction of travel from earth to heaven. This is such an open hearted, extravagant and direct thing to be saying to someone you have only recently got to know.

*

This story has a storyboard. It has been deliberately formed from several parallel scenes with similar characteristics. Combining their features creates the storyboard:

- Someone points to Jesus and people are drawn to him – *There is the Lamb of God*
- Jesus starts a conversation – *What do you want? You will be called Peter. Follow me.*
- People connect closely with Jesus – *They spent that day with him*
- Meals happen that create space for relationships to grow – *An invitation to a Middle Eastern home includes food*
- Jesus shows that he knows something about another – *Here is a true Israelite. I saw you under the fig tree*
- This profoundly affects that person – *Nazareth! Can anything good come from there?* changes to *Rabbi, you are the Son of God.*
- People recognise who Jesus is – *We have found the Messiah. We have found the one Moses wrote about. You are the King of Israel*
- Jesus opens up his heart and quickly deepens the conversation – *You will see heaven open on me*

- Those who have met Jesus invite others to meet Jesus – *The first thing Andrew did was to find his brother Simon. And he brought him to Jesus*

So, what of the story immediately before the second sign?

The Woman at the Well

The story immediately before the second sign is a single story with several sequential scenes. These are not in parallel but move swiftly from one to the next, creating a dramatic and moving story. By the end, a whole village comes to meet with Jesus. You can read it in 4:1–42. We will walk through it with the same questions. You might want to stop at each question, reread the scripture and answer it yourself before reading on.

Where Does the Story Happen? (4:1–6)

A town in Samaria called Sychar. It is a place with a long history. The town well is called Jacob's well because it is near the plot of ground that Jacob gave his son Joseph.

Who Is There? (4:7–8)

Jesus and the disciples. John the author makes a point of it being lunchtime, and the disciples have gone off into town to buy food. Who wants to sit by a well, hungry and hot in the middle of the day, when the other option is poking around the shops of Sychar in the shade? And with a large group of men, who can agree on what lunch should be? But then, very unexpectedly, because it is not the normal time for this, a woman arrives on her own to fetch water.

How Does the Story Start? (4:7)

Kenneth Bailey in his book, *Jesus through Middle Eastern Eyes*, tells us the social conventions of the time.[1] When the woman arrives, Jesus, being a man, should withdraw from the well at least 20 metres and turn his back on the woman. We are mystified and perhaps even a little angry at such social norms that seem demeaning to women. But, as Bailey points out, it is also protective and respectful. It gives women protection from difficult men in social settings.

But Jesus steps over the social conventions that should keep them separate. He introduces himself in the kindest and gentlest way possible. He asks her to help him. Jesus catalyses the conversation and starts the story by asking his opening question: 'Will you give me a drink?'

What Happens Next? (4:8–18)

What happens next is a very deep conversation. It lasts until the disciples return with lunch. Depending on how far it is from the well to the town and how long it has taken to buy and prepare the food, we are looking at up to an hour, perhaps twice that.

The woman's first move is to challenge Jesus for stepping over the social conventions. But she must be intrigued. Otherwise she could simply stare Jesus down and refuse to speak to him at all. Jesus ignores her question about conventions and instead he invites her to ask him for a drink. If she asks him for a drink, it is living water that she will get. The woman somewhat sarcastically points out the impracticalities of this proposal. Jesus doesn't even have a bucket. She uses the history of the well to challenge Jesus' credentials. Their father Jacob dug and left them the well. A real well, still in use, with proper water. Is Jesus greater than Jacob?

Jesus sidesteps the challenge of his credentials and majors on the differences in product. Water even from their great father Jacob's well will give only temporary relief from thirst. Living water is a permanent thirst quencher, and to make matters easier, the new well will be located within the woman. At this she is possibly persuaded. But much more likely, she tests Jesus by calling his bluff. OK – give me some, then.

But the conversation on receiving an internal, and eternal, living water supply suddenly takes a strange and unexpected turn. As with Simon and Nathanael, Jesus shows that he knows. The full dysfunctionality of her life and the extent of her pain, rejection and shame are laid bare in a few brief moments. She has had five husbands and the man she has now is not her husband. Ouch.

How Does She Respond to Jesus? (4:19–20)

She does acknowledge Jesus' gift. He must be a prophet. But she desperately wants him to stop talking about her. It's all too painful and difficult. And he is a man, which makes it very problematic, because her relationships with men have been so hurtful. Rather than revisit all her disasters and agonies with this interesting but scary stranger, she attempts a diversion. Let's discuss religious politics. Who has got the right place for worship?

What Does Jesus Do?

I am a pastor. For more than thirty years I have led the same church in the north of England. It will not surprise you that one of our core activities is worship. We have a worship pastor and an incredibly gifted worship team who inspire us greatly. What never ceases to delight me is that the most important teaching Jesus ever gave on what worship is and how it is to be done is given here, at this well, just before a late lunch, to a woman whose name we don't know, who appears to have an exceptionally painful past and is still undecided about who Jesus is. This is just like the conversation with Nathanael. Engaging in open-hearted, self-revealing, high-trust conversations is apparently what Jesus likes to do. Worship is not going to be about place or even about format. Worship is going to be about the deepest part of your inner life connecting with God. Worship is going to be in the Spirit. God is seeking people who are seeking him from the deepest part of themselves. And worship is not about ritual; it will come from the place of truth. You will not be going through the motions; you will be pouring out your heart.

Something good always happens to us when someone shares their heart openly with us. Jesus opening his heart moves the woman. She gets near to where Nathanael was after his experience of Jesus showing that he knows. She expresses confidence that there is a Messiah coming who will explain everything, which opens the door for Jesus to say, 'It's me.'

This is an amazing sequence of events. First, Jesus steps over the terrible patriarchal social conventions and relates to the woman with equality, dignity and respect. Second, he engages her in interesting conversation for a lengthy period. Third, he shows that he knows. And fourth, he opens his heart to her, giving her one of the most profound insights into worship that you will ever hear. The healing transformation that all this has on her is extraordinary. She goes back to her village and begins inviting everyone else to meet him: 'Then, leaving her water jar, the woman went back to the town and said to the people, "Come, see a man who told me everything I've ever done. Could this be the Messiah?"' (4:28–9).

What is thrilling about this is the way that the woman is able to face her past without any shame. Her story has been so dysfunctional and difficult. She has had repeated, painful failings of committed relationships with resulting feelings of rejection and shame. Most of us try to hide the worst parts of our lives. Not only are we ashamed, but talking about it just brings back our pain. This is different. Jesus has taken the woman to a completely new place. She can face her past with freedom and without regret. Her story has been reframed and she has been healed. She says to her neighbours, 'Come, see a man who told me everything I've ever done.' That is not a woman hiding in shame. The pain of the past has gone. What went wrong in her life is still part of her story. But her freedom from the shame has become the reason to invite others to meet Jesus.

The story moves on. The disciples, after they have recovered from the shock of finding Jesus talking with a woman on their return with the lunch, try to get Jesus to eat. 'I've got other food,' he says. This turns out not to be a secret pizza delivery, but simply the energy that comes from conversations like the one he has just had. 'These people are ready to come to faith,' he says. 'Someone else has done the hard work here.' Sychar proves his point. Many believe in him when they see the dramatic life-giving change in the woman. They urge Jesus to stay with them, which he does for two days. They get to hear Jesus, they get to know him, they do lots of eating. Many more believe. Jesus isn't just the Messiah of Israel. He is here to save the world.

*

This story has a storyboard:

- Someone points to Jesus and people are drawn to him – *Jesus does this himself by stepping over the social norms*
- Jesus starts a conversation – *Will you give me a drink?*
- Social conventions are set aside – *Jesus speaks to the woman on his own*
- People connect closely with Jesus – *I can see that you are a prophet*
- Meals happen that create space for relationships to grow – *The delicious irony here is that it is lunchtime, but the delay in the meal happening allows the relationship to develop.*
- Jesus shows that he knows something about another – *You have had five husbands, and the man you now have is not your husband*
- This profoundly affects that person – *He told me everything I have ever done*
- People recognise who Jesus is – *We know that this man really is the Saviour of the world*
- Jesus opens his heart and quickly deepens the conversation – *True worshippers will worship the Father in Spirit and in truth*
- Those who have met Jesus invite others to meet Jesus – *Come, see a man who told me everything I've ever done*

These two stories belong together. They are starting to build a picture of what it means to become a friend and follower of Jesus.

So are there any other stories in John that have this storyboard? We will need to dig a bit deeper.

8

Going Deeper

I Know You

This one took more time to find, because, like the story of The Feeding of the Five Thousand, some of the roles have been reversed. You can read the third Invitation story, The Anointing for Burial, in 11:55–12:11.

Where Does the Story Happen? (12:1)

We are six days before the Passover festival begins. Jesus has come to Bethany, the village where Martha, Mary and Lazarus live. They are his close friends, who live in a prosperous village less than two miles from Jerusalem. It would appear that becoming a friend and follower of Jesus is for everyone regardless of gender, economic background, social standing or religious leanings.

Who Is There? (12:1–4)

Martha, Mary and Lazarus are all there, as are Judas and, we can safely assume, all Jesus' close disciples. They have been withdrawn from the public eye in the wilderness in a village called Ephraim. It is highly likely that they travelled together to Bethany.

How Does the Story Start? (12:2)

It's a meal again. Of course. This one is a dinner given in Jesus' honour. Martha is serving. She is so practically minded and loves doing things to bless people. It is likely that she either is a very good cook or has a very good cook. Lazarus is reclining at the table with

Jesus and the others, enjoying the meal together. What joy, what happiness, what celebration there must be. For a brief period, all the conflict that Jesus is having with the religious authorities and the growing hostility that is swirling around him can be left outside and good friends can enjoy time together, eating and talking over a lovely meal.

What Happens Next? (12:3–6)

Mary has disappeared. She has form on this, of course – not helping with the catering (Luke 10:40). But she is back now. Carrying something. And suddenly social conventions are radically set aside. Mary takes half a litre of pure nard perfume and pours it out on the feet of Jesus. A pint of pure perfume. This isn't just something from her make-up bag. This is a savings plan. It is worth a year's wages. In today's terms maybe around £30,000 or US$36,000. Thirty thousand pounds poured out on Jesus' feet: 'Then Mary took about half a litre of pure nard, an expensive perfume; she poured it on Jesus' feet and wiped his feet with her hair' (12:3).

It is not just the pouring-out of the perfume that is a massive step over the social conventions. Mary lets her hair down. She crouches or lies on the ground at the feet of Jesus and she lets her hair down. Culturally, this is huge. A first-century Middle Eastern woman would only let down her hair in the presence of her husband. This is almost an act of betrothal. Mary is saying, 'I love you like a wife loves her husband. I give myself to you like a wife gives herself to her husband.' She takes her own hair and she gently wipes it on the feet of Jesus. It is a moment of great intimacy.

And the whole house is filled with the smell of nard.

Most people are totally shocked by this and are not very happy. Matthew reports that the disciples are all 'indignant' (Matt. 26:8). In our story in John, Judas speaks up for them. It is a worrying sign when Judas is your spokesman. 'Why wasn't this perfume sold and the money given to the poor?' This sounds very reasonable, doesn't it? For many years I was privileged to be a trustee of a charity we established to care for asylum seekers and refugees. It has just won the Queen's Award for Voluntary Service. I am painfully aware of the financial pressures on charities. What could Action Foundation do with £30,000? It would keep the language school going for five months. Why this waste? This is dreadful.

It is good for us all to note that there are moments when sound financial reasoning can take us in the wrong direction. Calm and calculating analysis can betray us.

John the author lets us know that Judas' apparent love for the poor is really because he pays himself commission. In appearing to be generous, Judas is actually being shockingly greedy and deceitful. A £30,000 gift could have earned him maybe £3,000. His heart is in such contrast to Mary's. Mary is not seeing what she can get from the situation. What Mary has done is not even like giving to a good cause. This is something else entirely. This is deep devotion to Jesus and the complete abandonment that comes from sacrificial overflowing love. She is, after all, a friend and follower of Jesus. Complete self-giving because of sacrificial love is what he does. She is only following him.

How Does Jesus Respond? (12:7–8)

"'Leave her alone," Jesus replied. "It was intended that she should save this perfume for the day of my burial'" (12:7). Jesus speaks up and protects her. He receives her devotion, and he attempts to explain her purpose. This perfume was being saved for his death.

This is the moment of knowing. Except it is the other way around. Mary knows. Mary knows where Jesus is going. Mary knows that Jesus is preparing himself for his death. She knows that he is getting himself into the mental and emotional space where he could go through with it. Mary loves him. She so loves him. She takes her life savings and she pours it out on his feet. She is telling Jesus, 'I know what you are doing. I know where you are going. I know what you are facing. And I am so with you.'

Money doesn't matter any more. Savings don't matter any more. Good works don't matter any more. Someone else will have to look after the poor at another time. The poor will still be there next week and will still be poor. But Jesus is not going to be here next week. Jesus is going to be on the cross next week.

She is talking to Jesus. No words. It's all in the action. She is saying to Jesus, 'I know you have got to go through with this. I know you have got to suffer. I know you have got to die. I am just so with you. I am pouring this out on you so that you will know that I am with you. I can't be with you in your sufferings. But I am with you. I can't be with you in your death. But I am with you. I am as a wife to you. Even when everyone turns on you, and spits on you, and beats you and kills you, you will still be able to smell the love of the woman who let down her hair and wiped your feet and took the public censure that followed.'

The whole house is filled with the beautiful smell of nard. And from then on Jesus is surrounded by the beautiful smell of nard. Wherever Jesus goes, the smell of nard goes with him. A week later he is dying on the cross. To breathe when you are being crucified, you push down on the nails through your feet and pull your chest up on the nails through your wrists. Then you can take a breath. As Jesus gasps some air into his lungs, there is the nard. The lingering smell of nard comes through the smell of blood and sweat and death.

In this story, Mary is not starting out as Jesus' friend and coming to faith; she is a close friend expressing faith. In doing so there is this lovely role reversal with Jesus. She steps over the social norms towards Jesus. She knows him and she knows what is ahead for him. In her devotion to him she stands with him and acts extravagantly to affirm him.

*

THIS STORY HAS A STORYBOARD:

- Someone points to Jesus – *Mary is already a friend and follower of Jesus. She does not need him to be pointed out to her*
- Mary starts a conversation. It is a conversation without any words – *She took a pint of pure nard and poured it on Jesus' feet.*
- Social conventions are set aside – *Mary lets her hair down*
- People connect closely with Jesus – *She wiped his feet with her hair*

- Meals happen that create space for the relationship to grow – *Martha served while Lazarus was among those reclining at table with him*
- Mary shows that she knows something about Jesus – *It was intended that she should save this perfume for the day of my burial*
- This profoundly affects that person – *Jesus goes to the cross knowing her devotion*
- People recognise who Jesus is – *Mary is saying, 'You are as a husband to me'*
- Jesus opens his heart and quickly deepens the conversation – *You will always have the poor among you, but you will not always have me*
- Those who have met Jesus invite others to meet Jesus – *A large crowd . . . found out that Jesus was there and came*

So, are there any other stories like this? I looked for the meal.

Who Serves Who?

There are five scenes to this story of The Last Meal. You can read it in 13:1–14:31. It seems quite long, but it isn't really. John has put in lots of spoken word. He is doing this because he wants you to be there and experience it as a live event. He wants you to hear the interactions and feel the vibe. People-to-people interaction is what friendship and disciple-making are all about.

This story is the same people at one meal. We will look at the first two questions for the whole story and then we will look scene by scene with the other questions. As with the first Invitation story, John the author is giving us a depth of insight into Jesus by layering the stories and repeating things from different angles.

The story is set in a dramatic context of Jesus knowing, but this time knowing about himself. He knows it is time. He is going to the Father. No more time for disciple-making after tonight: 'Jesus knew that the hour had come for him to leave this world and go to the Father. Having loved his own who were in the world, he loved them to the end' (13:1).

Where and When Does the Story Happen?

We know we are in Jerusalem; we just don't know where. A deliberate veil is drawn over exactly who is providing the place to eat and how they all got there. The narrative jumps from the end of chapter 12 as if they have been teleported in. We don't get much help from the other Gospels, who also describe the arrangements for the meal happening in a somewhat mysterious manner (Matt. 26:18–19; Mark 14:13–16; Luke 22:7–13). We do know from John it is just before the Passover festival and it is evening.

Who Is There?

Jesus and his disciples are having what will turn out to be their last meal together. But only Jesus knows this. As we read on, we find that Judas Iscariot, Simon Peter, Thomas, Philip and the other Judas are all there and have something to say. It is at this meal that the disciple with no name gets something of an identity: the disciple whom Jesus loved (13:23).

Scene 1: Washing the Feet

What Happens Next? (13:2–5)

In the first scene, Jesus behaves like Mary with her nard at that infamous dinner. He acts rather than speaks. And, like Mary, his actions speak louder than any words ever could. We have the best seats in the house. We get to see what Jesus is thinking. The disciples only get to see what Jesus does, and that is shocking enough. The surprise for us is even bigger. What Jesus does is because of what he knows: 'Jesus knew that the Father had put all things under his power, and that he had come from God and was returning to God; so he got up from the meal' (13:3–4).

The man who knows he has come from God. The man who knows he is returning to God. The man who knows that everything in the cosmos is under him. That man gets up from the meal, strips to his undergarment, wraps a towel around himself, pours water into a basin and washes his disciples' feet. It is hard to imagine the full shock of this moment. Culturally, for fairly obvious reasons, washing feet is a task you either do yourself or it is done by a slave or very menial servant. Perhaps with all the cloak-and-dagger arrangements, menial servants have not been supplied. What is not allowed is that leaders do menial tasks. Jesus does what he did to the woman at the well, and what Mary did to him at the dinner. He steps straight over the social conventions. It appears to happen in strained silence, until he gets to Simon Peter.

How Does Peter Respond? (13:6–9)

Peter refuses. He doesn't have space in his head for Jesus to do this. He looks to him as his teacher. He calls him 'Lord' (13:13). Lords are not allowed to get their hands on dirt like this. Teachers do not do this. It is demeaning and completely wrong. It undermines everything that leaders and teachers are meant to be. But Jesus is busy turning everything upside down, because what is a given for Jesus is his authority. Everything is under his power. Jesus doesn't need to be protected from serving in order to be leading. For him, serving is to become what leading means.

So, for Jesus, Peter's refusal is a deal breaker. Either receive the feet-washing or it is the end of their relationship. Peter comes straight back with typical Middle Eastern directness: you had better wash my hands and do my hair as well. Peter is saying with typical wholeheartedness, 'I want to be completely part of you.' Don't you love someone who is all in?

What Does Jesus Do? (13:8–17)

First, he affirms Peter. You are clean. Mostly. You just need a bit of attention to one part. Let me do that.

Second, he shows that he knows. He knows that one of the disciples, whose feet he has just washed, is not clean. Serving is something we do for everyone. Even for people who are going to let us down and cause us pain.

Third, he shares his heart. He calls them to action. This is how you are to live with each other. For Jesus, disciple-making is both information and replication. It is what we see in the first Invitation story. Jesus invites Philip to be with him and follow him. Philip then replicates Jesus. He goes and invites Nathanael to be with Jesus. A disciple is not a stagnant recipient. A disciple gets in the flow. A disciple first receives but then gives. Jesus has washed our feet. We all wash feet now.

Scene 2: The Knowing of Betrayal

What Happens Next? (13:18–22)

As we have seen, Jesus knows. He knows his friends. He knows that one of them, who has shared all the meals they have had together, is turning against him. Someone who has eaten the bread is lifting up the heel, another one of those vivid Aramaic expressions. Jesus has mentioned betrayal before. It is not someone on the edge. It is someone really close in (6:70–1).

Jesus wants everyone at the meal to know that he knows and that he is not taken by surprise. When a close friend and follower turns in this way, it can rock everyone and raise questions about the leader. Jesus wants the coming betrayal to actually strengthen the convictions of the others. He uses the moment to teach an important principle. Jesus knows that he is sent from the Father. Therefore, he does not have to take betrayal personally. How others respond to him reveals how they are responding to God. The disciples are about to step into that space themselves. This is a vital lesson for them to learn.

Then Jesus just says it: 'One of you is going to betray me.' As Frank Morison points out in his book, *Who Moved the Stone?*, the betrayer is not informing the authorities about Jesus' location, which is fairly well known and largely predictable.[1] The betrayer is revealing Jesus' state of mind. The authorities are plotting to arrest Jesus but are hesitating on the timing. With the insights that Judas brings to them, they decide to immediately start the process that leads to Jesus' crucifixion. Betrayal is always from people who are close to us. Only someone in close relationship with me can know enough of me to really expose me. If I can't be betrayed, I don't have friends and I haven't been making disciples. Thank God, betrayal is not common. It's usually only one or two. So when Jesus says it straight, the other disciples are completely at a loss. What on earth does he mean?

How Does Peter Respond? (13:23–6)

Not unnaturally, Peter wants to know who it is. The disciple whom Jesus loved is sitting very close to Jesus. He could find out. Peter nudges him. 'You ask him.' The beloved disciple leans back on Jesus. It is such a profound moment of contrast. Touching intimacy and deep friendship with Jesus to discover brutal betrayal of Jesus. It would appear that the disciple whom Jesus loved keeps quiet about what he hears and now knows, because even when Judas leaves everyone else is still confused (13:28–9).

What Does Jesus Do? (13:26–30)

There is something so poignant about this. Jesus gives the betrayer some bread that has been dipped in the dish. Even in the moment of separation, Jesus is graceful. You can serve a betrayer and be kind to a betrayer. But you can't keep them as a close friend and follower. The time has come for Judas to leave. Jesus does not start a pity party. 'I gave so much to him and now look at what he is doing.' He doesn't take the victim role: 'These terrible things are all happening to me.' He knows that his discipleship of Judas is at end and that Judas must be freed to do what he thinks he must do. 'Get on with it quickly,' is what Jesus says. And Judas goes. Their relationship is finished now.

There is more than human dynamics at work. We've seen God at work in the other stories. The knowledge of the numerous husbands of the woman at the well, the new name for Simon and seeing the heart of Nathanael have all come to Jesus as a working of God in him. But here, with Jesus' knowing and releasing of Judas, the spiritual activity is tragically going in the opposite direction. Judas making up his mind gives room for Satan to come into him. Judas goes out. 'And it was night,' says John. It is. In every respect.

Scene 3: The Knowing of Denial

What Happens Next? (13:31–4)

Jesus knows exactly what is happening. Judas' betrayal will trigger his crucifixion, which is him being glorified. In John, the crucifixion is not humiliation; it is glorification. Jesus tells the disciples he is going away, and they cannot come. At least not yet. It is another opportunity for disciple-making. With Jesus moving into glory through the cross, they are to step into the space he leaves and love each other. In his absence, the love they have for each other will be how everyone else will know that they are Jesus' disciples.

How Does Peter Respond? (13:36–7)

He doesn't get it. Where is Jesus going? Why can't he follow now? He is heart and soul for Jesus. When everyone else was walking away that time, didn't he say that he had nowhere else to go but Jesus? Hasn't he already given so much? If required, he will give his life for Jesus.

What Does Jesus Do? (13:38)

Jesus shows that he knows. Yes, he is Peter, the great Rock of their community. But truth must be told. His great pronouncements of sacrifice are not going to happen. There is still substantial weakness and fear in Peter that he will have to face. He is going to deny that he even knows Jesus, not once, but three times. Disciple-making always involves helping others see and work through their weaknesses as well as celebrating and affirming their strengths.

*

These stories are all about friendship, discipleship, meals together, knowing each other and shared life. But what next? Here is an invitation to a home that is of a completely different order.

9

The Ultimate Invite

In My Father's House

You can read this part of the story in 14:1–31.

Scene 4: In My Father's House

What Happens Next?

Jesus can see that this is all very troubling for the disciples. He has redefined what it means to lead. Leaders serve. They wash feet. He has confused and upset them by telling them about the imminent betrayal. He has been pretty straight with Peter that he will soon find out that he is not as strong as he thinks he is. Jesus knows he needs to lift their gaze. 'Trust me,' he says. 'Trust God and trust me.' And then he invites them all back to his Father's house.

Now, before we talk in more detail about 'my Father's house', we need to do what we did before: look at the Old Testament sitting underneath these stories. 'My Father's house' is not a new idea that Jesus has just come up with. It certainly isn't a Victorian English idea full of sentimental, wishful nonsense. But let's note for now the enormity of this invitation. The first Invitation story opens with the lines, 'Where do you live?' 'Come and see.' Jesus has just taken that to a whole new level. Jesus is bringing in what he spoke about to Nathanael: the vision of Jacob's ladder, of heaven and earth being joined together in him. He is inviting them to his true home, his Father's house.

'My Father's house'. The dwelling place of God. An invitation to live where God lives. With rooms that are going to be made ready. It's not going be a place where we feel awkward and uneasy and secretly think that we don't belong. Apparently, it isn't quite finished yet, which makes it sound like all the building projects I have ever been involved in. But that's in hand. It will be a place prepared for us, that we will like, where we will feel completely at home. This is Jesus again opening his heart to his friends.

This is such an enormous invitation. Everything good that you love about spending time with people: friendship, meals together, knowing each other, loving each other deeply and laughing together will continue. But at the Father's place. All of that brought into the tangible presence of the holiness of God. With God there. Jesus will come and get us. Nathanael, the truest man of highest integrity – he is invited. The woman at the well, with her story of freedom from all her brokenness and shame – she is invited. And everyone in between. No racial, gender or past constraints. Getting there isn't a problem. Jesus isn't just sorting the accommodation; he is making the transport arrangements as well. 'I'll come and get you,' he says. 'You know the way.'

How Does Thomas Respond?

He is struggling. 'We don't know where you are going. This is all very difficult, Jesus. How can we know the way?' And bless him, he doesn't know the way. He isn't being awkward. He doesn't know what Jesus is talking about. We have the best seats in the house. We don't have to scratch our heads in bewilderment as Thomas does. You probably know Jesus' answer to Thomas' question.

What Does Jesus Do?

'Jesus answered, "I am the way and the truth and the life. No one comes to the Father except through me."' (14:6).

You don't need a ticket or a map. There isn't a list of qualifying achievements to complete. There isn't a language you have to learn, or a preferred colour of skin, or money that you have to earn, or brave deeds that must be done. 'It's just me,' says Jesus. 'That's the way – me. Knowing me. I'm the way to get there. I'm the truth as to what is there. I'm the life that you will share. Just me. Nothing more needed.'

And then, as if that weren't enough, Jesus speeds round the next bend of this extremely fast-moving conversation. 'You already know the Father and you have seen him' (14:7). 'Going to my dad's place is not going to be meeting a stranger. You have already seen him. Because you know me, you will know him.'

How Does Philip Respond?

At one level, this is hilarious. 'What we need, Jesus, is for you to show us the Father. That will be enough for us.' OK. Just give me a minute on that one. Where did I put the key for the cupboard where I keep the Holy Creator God?

It's funny, but it is also important. Philip's desire to touch and see God is one that we all share. Philip's problem is our problem too.

How Does Jesus Respond?

Well, bringing our Father in heaven out of a cupboard for everyone to see is not going to happen. There is no need. What Philip has not been able to grasp yet is that Jesus and the Father are one. I'm not sure I have completely grasped it myself. The words Jesus speaks are the Father's words even though Jesus speaks Aramaic, uses local idioms and presumably has a northern accent. The works Jesus does are the Father working. As we have already mentioned, theologians call this 'perichoresis', the mutual indwelling of the persons. The Father is so in Jesus and Jesus is so in the Father that whatever Jesus says and does is always both of the persons. They are so together as persons they are one. One God.

Amazingly, Philip, as a follower of Jesus, is also going to do the works of the Father. That is what Jesus' friends and followers do. They replicate both the heart and the actions of Jesus. Friends and followers of Jesus are going to do even greater works than Jesus. They are going to be greater because Philip isn't Jesus. And neither am I. It is a tremendous thing that the incarnate Jesus did the works of the Father. But he is one with the Father. What is even greater is that fallen humanity like Philip will do the Father's work. It's not greater from the point of view of comparing the works we do with the works Jesus did. It is greater in the sense that God does something even greater to do his works through us. How on earth will that happen? Because Jesus is going to the Father. His going to the Father is essential, not just for the Father's house to be finished, but also for God to do his work through the likes of us. And that is because Jesus being glorified with the Father through his death is not just the King coming into his kingdom (Dan. 7:13–14). Once Jesus ascends to the Father, the Spirit of Jesus will come to us and that will enable us to live in friendship with the Father and to do the works that reveal him.

Scene 5: Sending My Spirit

All of this presents a problem. How can we be friends with Jesus if he is no longer with us? Aren't we back to the absent God? It's all very well for the friends of Jesus in the flesh. But what about us? Aren't we back to where Philip is coming from? How do we know God when Jesus returns to being with the Father in the heavenly dwellings?

Jesus says that it is better for us that he goes.

There is more opportunity for us to know God now than there was to know God then. There is something better than Jesus in the body. We have Jesus in the Spirit.

First, as we have already seen in Chapter Two, all of us have been called into covenant relationship with God. And covenant friendship with God means obedience to God. Not crushing, condemning, guilt-ridden, shamed obedience. Not self-righteous, boastful, holier-than-everyone else obedience. Not self-willed, trying-hard, squeezing-the-life-out-of-you obedience. But joy-filled, life-giving, faith-building, God-revealing, God-glorifying obedience. Obedience happens within me because God is rewriting my heart and my mind and my will and forming everything within me into the likeness of Christ. That is what he promised to do.

Second, we have seen that Jesus says, 'You won't be doing this on your own. God will come, the Spirit will be sent, I will return. The world can't see this. The world doesn't know the Spirit. But you will know the Spirit. The Spirit is not a power. He's a person. He is going to be living in you. I am going to be with you. I won't leave you abandoned and bereft. The world won't see me. But you will. Because I am going to be alive, you will be alive' (14:16–19, 21, 23, 26–7). The way things are going to be has already begun. The invitation to the friendship with God in the Father's house starts now with the sending of the Spirit. This is 'realised eschatology'. We experience now in part what we will experience in an eternal fullness yet to come.

Jesus walked alongside Simon. The disciple whom Jesus loved leant back on Jesus. We walk with Jesus by the Spirit. We lean back on Jesus in the Spirit. The Father and the Son will come in the person of the Holy Spirit. God comes and makes his home with us. The coming of the Father and the Son by the Spirit replicate the actions of the incarnate Jesus with his disciples. We will know him, and that will be life-giving to us (14:15–20). We will see that we are loved (14:21). He will be at home with him (14:23). And he will teach us (14:26).

'Peace,' Jesus says to them. 'Don't be troubled. I am going away, but I am coming back. It's all good. You should be glad, really, that I am going to the Father. The Father is greater than I am.' The incarnate Jesus is of necessity submissive to the Father. His human nature is led by and submits to his divine nature. He loves the Father and does exactly what his Father commands (14:31). Once Jesus has returned in glory to the Father, this delicate constraint in their relationship as Father to Son is no longer in operation. Happy days for everyone.

Coming Together

Bringing these four stories together, the storyboard looks like this:

Narrative	1:35–51	4:1–42	11:55–12:11	13:1–14:31
The location of the story	Bethany on the other side of the Jordan	Sychar of Samaria	Bethany near Jerusalem	Jerusalem
Someone points to Jesus and people are drawn to talk to him	John who baptises	Jesus	*Mary is already a friend and follower*	*The disciples are already friends and followers*
Jesus/Mary starts a conversation with either speech or action	'What do you want?'	'Will you give me a drink?'	'She poured [perfume] on Jesus' feet and wiped his feet with her hair'	'So he got up from the meal, took off his outer clothing, and wrapped a towel round his waist'
Social conventions are set aside		Jesus talks to the woman on his own	Mary pours out the perfume and lets down her hair	Jesus washes the feet of the disciples
People connect closely with Jesus	'So they went and saw where he was staying, and they spent that day with him'	'I can see that you are a prophet'	She 'wiped his feet with her hair'	'Leaning back against Jesus, he asked him, "Lord, who is it?"'

Meals happen that create space for relationships to grow	'They spent that day with him'	'His disciples had gone into the town to buy food'	'Martha served, while Lazarus was among those reclining at table with [Jesus]'	'The evening meal was in progress'
Jesus shows that he knows something about another	'You will be called [Peter].' 'Here truly is an Israelite in whom there is no deceit' 'I saw you under the fig-tree'	'You have had five husbands, and the man you have now is not your husband'	'It was intended that she should save this perfume for the day of my burial'	'He who shared my bread has turned against me'
This profoundly affects that person	'Nazareth! Can anything good come from there?' changes to: 'Rabbi, you are the Son of God'	'[He] told me everything I have ever done'	Jesus goes to the cross knowing the deep devotion of Mary	'As soon as Judas took the bread, Satan entered into him'
People recognise who Jesus is	'We have found the Messiah'	'We know that this man really is the Saviour of the world'	Mary is saying, 'You are as a husband to me'	'Jesus knew that the Father had put all things under his power, and that he had come from God and was returning to God'

Jesus opens his heart and quickly deepens the conversation	'You will see "heaven open and the angels of God ascending and descending" on the Son of Man'	'True worshippers will worship the Father in Spirit and in truth'	'You will always have the poor among you, but you will not always have me'	'My Father will love them, and we will come to them and make our home with them'
Those who have met Jesus invite others to meet Jesus	'The first thing Andrew did was to find his brother Simon . . . And he brought him to Jesus'	'Come, see a man who told me everything I've ever done'	'A large crowd found out that Jesus was there and came'	'Everyone will know that you are my disciples'

In this set of stories, we discover what it means to be a friend and follower of Jesus.

It means being like Andrew and the disciple with no name, who are invited by Jesus to spend time with him. Disciple-making happens in the context of coming to my house and having a late lunch with me and talking for the remainder of the day. The first thing and the last thing that Jesus does in this part of the Gospel is to offer hospitality and make friends.

It means being like Simon Peter, who is given a new name by Jesus. Disciple-making means stepping towards a new identity, a new purpose and a new heart.

It means being like Philip, who is called by Jesus to follow him. This is that incredible blend of high invitation and high challenge. I get to be friends with Jesus. But I also get my life changed, which is what a disciple-making relationship is. The call from Jesus is to 'me'. It is to relationship, friendship and being with him. But the call is to 'follow me'. The call is to change into the likeness of Jesus in character and values. The call is to engage in the mission of Jesus.

It means being like Nathanael, who had all that was good in him recognised and affirmed by Jesus. Disciple-making is where you discover that Jesus knows you, that he sees what others don't see. He appreciates the person that you are, and he values what you do when others aren't watching.

It means being like the woman at the well. It means being given dignity, equality and respect. Disciple-making is not an opportunity to crush or control. It means being given the time you need to work through the issues that you have and the questions you need to voice. It means being known. But the knowing of everything that has gone so badly wrong so many times is not a condemning, shaming knowing. It means you discover that you are able to reframe your story and find that you are free. You are no longer condemned to go round the abusive cycle again. The power and the pain of your past have fallen from you. Your past is no longer determining your future. With Jesus it has become a signpost to your healing.

Disciple-making is inviting your brother, your friends and your community to come and join the party. This is not a closed clique or a self-help group or a meet-my-needs session. Disciple-making is finding yourself being caught up in the mission of Jesus to save the world. You go off to get some lunch, and when you get back you find that Jesus is busy talking to someone that you might well have struggled to speak to.

It means being like both the woman and Nathanael, being caught up into exciting revelation of what God is doing and who Jesus is and seeing that the house of God is coming on the earth.

It means becoming like Mary, deeply devoted to Jesus. Money doesn't matter any more. Even good works to help the poor will have to wait. Social conventions can be set aside. Love, devotion and worship are to be poured out at the feet of Jesus, despite what everyone else thinks or says. She is not giving as a benefactor, which is how many people give, when they finally get round to it: 'Let me help you with this good work that you are doing.' It is the other way around. Mary does not pour out her perfume as a helpful partner in the good work he is about. She is pouring out her love because he is going to his death. The giving is from her heart. In other people's eyes she is wasting it. But not in Jesus' eyes.

It means becoming like Jesus. Blasting to pieces the accepted wisdom on leadership. It means completely rewriting the rules on what leaders are and what leaders do. Disciple-making is getting your hands dirty. It is getting your hands on matters that others would prefer to keep at arm's length. Or maybe two arms' length. It is washing everyone until they are clean.

It means having people so close that they can betray you. It means serving and loving those people but also recognising the end of the relationship and releasing them to do what they think is best. Judas has to be released to follow his own heart, and at that moment not even Jesus can help him.

It means having the courage to put on the table the weaknesses that still lurk within people. 'Peter, you are not going to lay your life down for me today. Please stop making the grand statements. You are actually going to say you don't know me.' It means people letting you down and even pretending that they don't know you. And then being prepared to put all that right and carry on.

But. Disciple-making is not the goal. Disciple-making is the means. The goal is that all of us get invited into the house of God to become priests of God dwelling in God's house on earth.

10

Back to the Beginning

What part of Israel's story sits underneath these four Invitation stories?

We are going back to the beginning, to the start of the story of Israel. John the author drops a big hint. Nathanael is going to see heaven open and the angels of God ascending and descending on Jesus. This is a reference to a well-known Old Testament story called Jacob's Ladder. In the second Invitation story Jesus meets the woman at Jacob's well. There is nothing specifically in the Old Testament about Jacob digging a well. But Jacob was head of a very prosperous sheep-herding family. Wells were part of their business and essential to their prosperity. So it would be completely in order for a well to be attributed to him. There is something in her community's history that has preserved the understanding that Jacob dug the well that she has come to use. The town the woman is from is likely to be an ancient settlement found half a mile south west of the current village called Askar. It is just west of Joseph's tomb and a quarter of a mile from what is generally agreed to be Jacob's well. So it is to Jacob that we will dig in. We will start with Jacob's ladder, but as we will discover, there are many other features of Jacob's story that sit underneath the four stories we have been looking at.

To understand the story of Jacob, we need to read Genesis 25–50. To understand that you need to read the stories of his father Isaac and his grandfather Abraham which are in Genesis 12–24. I would encourage you to do this.

Jacob was from a very dysfunctional family. His father, Isaac, had a favourite son, which was not Jacob but his slightly older twin brother Esau. Isaac and Esau loved hunting, but Jacob was a quiet lad who liked being at home. Jacob also had problems with his mother, who was over-involved in his life. The name Jacob means 'one who deceives', because he came out of the womb grasping the heel of his brother. 'To grasp the heel' is an idiom that means 'to trick or to deceive'. Deception and manipulation are a habit that Jacob can't get rid of. In fact, he exploits it. There are two stories of him deceiving his brother and father.

He persuades his brother Esau to give him the birthright of the firstborn. This is a position of power. The firstborn son would become judicial head of the family on the father's death. In an era without courts and only scanty process of law, this carries a lot of authority. There is also an economic gain: the estate could be divided unequally, with the firstborn getting a double share. To be fair, Esau is weak. But Jacob exploits that.

Later, Jacob conspires with his mother to deceitfully obtain his father's blessing. In the West, we can struggle to understand the significance of this. But the blessing was real and concrete. To describe it in modern financial terms, the father's blessing is a big bank transfer. The blessing is for heaven's dew and earth's riches. An abundance of grain and new wine will be his. Nations will serve him, and he will be lord over his brothers. There is nothing left for Esau. Understandably, when Esau discovers the deception, he is foaming mad. He plans to kill Jacob, as soon as his father dies. Which is why Jacob, again under mum's orders, ends up fleeing for his life to his uncle. And on the way, God meets him. Asleep in the desert, all alone, the heavens open, and he sees a vision. You can read it in Genesis 28:12–15.

When Jacob awakes, he realises that God is there. Unknown to him, this is a place where heaven and earth join. He calls the place Bethel, which means 'house of God'. He sets up a pillar, which signifies that this is God's house. He worships God by pouring oil on top of it. And he commits to giving God a tenth of everything that God gives to him.

In summary:
- The house of God is where God appears. God is present with his people. God speaks his covenant love over his people.

- The house of God is not somewhere in heaven to which Jacob was taken. It is a place on earth to which God comes to be with his people.
- Blessings are spoken by God. God repeats the covenant promises made to Jacob's grandfather Abraham. All the nations of the earth will be blessed through Jacob. To Jacob, God promises, 'I will be with you, to watch over you and to bring you back.'
- Jacob responds in worship. Oil is poured out in sacrifice and Jacob gives back to God in a free and rich way from that which God has given to him.

Greg Beale, in his book *The Temple and the Church's Mission*, demonstrates that this is early Jewish temple theology and temple building.[1] Although the building aspect is confined to a pillar and an altar, all the ingredients we see here are found later in Moses' Tabernacle and Solomon's Temple.

Jacob's grandfather Abraham also built temple spaces, including one in Bethel. The story has the same ingredients. He pitches his tent (missing in the Jacob story, as he was running for his life). God appears to him and speaks covenant blessing over him. He builds an altar and calls on the name of the Lord. It is here that we find another significant association with these temple spaces: trees. The great tree of Moreh is where God speaks to Abraham and he builds an altar (Gen. 12:6–7). The great trees of Mamre are at Hebron, where Abraham builds another altar after God meets with him (Gen. 13:18). And the thickets on Mount Moriah trap the ram that is then sacrificed by Abraham as a God-given substitute for Isaac (Gen. 22:13).

Jacob returns to Bethel much later in his life. God calls him back and commands him to build a new altar. Jacob makes everyone in his now very extensive household give up all their foreign gods and worship the Lord. Jacob builds an altar and pours out a sacrificial drink offering and an oil offering. And nearby there is an oak tree which they name the Oak of Weeping because they bury his wife's nurse under it (Gen. 35:1–15). Beale concludes that the presence of trees next to worship sites where humans experience God's presence might well evoke the tree of life in the Garden of Eden.[2] In exile, after the destruction of Solomon's Temple, Ezekiel has a vision of a new temple. Life-giving water flows from the temple and there are a great number of trees, whose leaves are for the healing of the nations (Ezek. 47:1–12).

It is at Bethel that Jacob is given a new name. He will no longer be Jacob, one who deceives. He will be Israel. God has spoken this to him before, at another very significant encounter. Jacob is returning home because God has told him to go. Even after all these years, he is still very fearful of Esau. And out of that fear, he is still being deceptive. When he learns that Esau is coming to meet him with 400 men, he sends multiple gifts and his whole family out ahead of him (Gen. 32:6–23). Jacob himself hangs back. But God meets him and wrestles with him all night. God eventually gets Jacob to the place where the only thing Jacob can do is cling to God alone. The man who from his very birth has reached out to grab things for himself now holds on to God alone. It is there that he gets his new name from God: Israel.

There is a lot of theological discussion as to the meaning of the new name: Israel. It is a theophonic name, which means it describes something about God. Daniel is a similar theophonic name which means 'God judges'. Israel probably means 'God fights for us', which makes sense in the context of the story where the name was first given.

Now we are in a position to begin to see how the four stories in the Gospel come together with the Old Testament story of the Patriarchs underneath.

Simon meets with Jesus. He gets given a new name, a new identity: Rock. After the resurrection, Simon Peter meets with Jesus. He gets given a new job: Shepherd. Rock and Shepherd are how Jacob describes what God is like when he blesses his son Joseph:

> *because of the hand of the Mighty One of Jacob,*
> *because of the Shepherd, the Rock of Israel,*

because of your father's God, who helps you,
because of the Almighty, who blesses you
(Gen. 49:24–5)

Jacob meets with God and embarks on a very long journey, ending up with a new name. He gradually moves from Jacob, the one who reaches out to grasp things through deception and trickery, to become Israel, someone who clings to God alone. It is God who will fight for him. Simon too has a journey to go on. He will become all that God intends him to be. Jesus can see that he will take on the likeness of Jacob's God. He will be a Rock who shepherds.

Nathanael is sitting under a tree. He is sitting in the presence of God. He is in all probability meditating on Scripture and praying. There is so much deception and trickery and failure that is happening in the nation. Don't forget that this is the time of John who baptises. The nation is polarised. The authorities are deceitful and corrupt. But many ordinary people are getting serious about God in a new way and are getting ready for their new King. There are plenty of Scriptures that Nathanael could be studying and praying through when Philip comes to find him and takes him to Jesus. Psalm 118. Psalm 84. Psalm 32. Psalm 26:4–8. Psalm 120:1–7. We will never know. My favourite possibilities are Psalm 92:12–15 and Psalm 52:

> *You who practise deceit,*
> *your tongue plots destruction;*
> *it is like a sharpened razor.*
> *You love evil rather than good,*
> *falsehood rather than speaking the truth.*
> *You love every harmful word,*
> *you deceitful tongue!*
> *. . . But I am like an olive tree*
> *flourishing in the house of God;*
> *I trust in God's unfailing love*
> *for ever and ever.*
> *(Ps. 52:2–4, 8)*

Nathanael looks up at his fig tree, a sign of God's presence and blessing as he prays these psalms. And then he meets this man Jesus, who says to him, 'I saw you under the tree. You are not like all the deceitful people you see around you and the deceitful people in power in our nation. You are a true man of God. You will flourish in God's house. God will fight for you. Here is a true Israelite, in whom there is no deceit. You are not a Jacob.' And when Nathanael responds, Jesus opens his heart. 'The fig tree was just the beginning. You are going to see Jacob's ladder open up on me. The house of God is going to be renewed. You might feel like Jacob, all alone in a desert place. But the house of God is coming on the earth in its fullness.' Bethany beyond the Jordan, which is where John places this story, becomes a Bethel, a house of God.

Mary acts like Jacob and Abraham. As she worships at the feet of Jesus, she pours out the offering of fine oil upon him. Like Jacob, she is being a priest, pouring out the oil on Jesus, the pillar of God's house. In doing this, she follows Jacob in his encounter with God at Bethel. She is free from all financial constraints. She isn't worrying about the money. She worships with great abundance and freedom. She has been blessed. From the blessing she has received she blesses. She puts Jesus and worship of Jesus before everything else, even the vital responsibility of caring for the poor. First of all, she blesses Jesus. Bethany is Bethel.

We can see now why at the final meal with the disciples, Jesus' invitation is to the house of God. The meal is interrupted with the delayed feet-washing. As we have seen, Jesus is using this as a metaphor for redefining what leadership means. But foot-washing is also the normal Middle Eastern welcome to a house and to a meal. Abraham washes the feet of the three visitors who come from God. He rests them under one of the great trees of Mamre while the meal is being prepared. He discovers that this is none other than God who has come to visit him. The visitors announce to him and to Sarah, his barren wife, that Isaac, the child of promise, will be conceived by God's Word (Gen. 18:1–15).

Foot-washing is also what happens to priests. As the priests in Israel enter God's house their feet are washed. 'Aaron and his sons are to wash their hands and feet with water from it. Whenever they enter the tent of meeting, they shall wash with water so that they will not die' (Exod. 30:19–20).

In the Tabernacle of Moses and in Solomon's Temple, basins are prepared so that the priests can be clean. Jesus knows that he is going to welcome his disciples into his Father's house. They are priests of God, welcomed into the presence of the living God. This great tradition of Israel being a priestly nation, standing in the presence of God on the earth, which goes right back to Jacob and Abraham, is now being worked out in everyone who is a disciple of Jesus.

The blessing that God speaks to Jacob at Bethel is now spoken by Jesus to the disciples.

Genesis 28:15	John 14:18, 13, 3
'I am with you'	'I will not leave you as orphans; I will come to you'
'And will watch over you wherever you go'	'I will do whatever you ask in my name'
'And I will bring you back to this land'	'I will come back and take you to be with me'

So, what about the woman at the well?

There are three stories of women at wells in the stories of the Patriarchs. Each one connects.

In Genesis 24, Abraham sends his trusted servant to find a wife for his son Isaac from among his own relatives. God has called to him to live in the land of Canaan, but in order for their covenant relationship with God to remain intact, Isaac cannot marry into a family that worships idols. The servant goes to the land where Abraham came from and, very wisely, goes to the well where the women come to fetch water. He prays. He asks the Lord, 'When I approach a woman and ask her to give me a drink, if she agrees, may she be the one that you have chosen to marry my master's son'

(Gen. 24:1–67). It's a great prayer and a great question. The same one that Jesus asks.

In Genesis 16, a woman called Hagar is fleeing from Abram and Sarai. This is before they have an encounter with God and he gives them new names as well, the ones we know them by: Abraham and Sarah. Hagar, Sarai's servant, flees because her life has become a misery with them. She is ill-treated and rejected. God finds her sitting by a well in the desert. He hears her story. He speaks to her tenderly and affirms her. He sends her back to her community. Hagar is so transformed by this encounter she gives God a name: 'She gave this name to the Lord who spoke to her: "You are the God who sees me," for she said, "I have now seen the One who sees me"' (Gen. 16:13).

She obviously tells this story quite widely, because the well gets a new name as well. It is called Beer Lahai Roi, which means the Well of the Living One who sees me. This is the very experience of the woman at the well in our story.

Finally, in Genesis 21, Hagar and her son have to move out from Abraham and Sarah's extended family. Abraham, the father, is naturally upset, but God tells him that he will look after them. But her journey does not go well, and she runs out of water while wandering in the desert. She puts the boy under a bush and moves away. She doesn't want to watch him die. She sobs. God comes to her. He speaks faith to her. When she opens her eyes, she sees a well of water (Gen. 21:19). Our woman at the well is also a woman in some difficulty, probably excluded by many in her community. She needs a well of life-giving water, and Jesus helps her to open her eyes and see it.

Isaiah the prophet lives at a time when God's people have turned away from God. God speaks to them and says that he is going to send them out of the land. Jerusalem, and the house of God in Jerusalem, are going to be destroyed. However, Isaiah is a prophet of great hope. He sees a time when the house of God will be restored and, instead of being confined to one city of a small nation, all the nations will be blessed by God's house. In Isaiah 54 he sings a beautiful song of the restoration of God's people. This song is based on Jacob's story of discovering the house of God at Bethel.

In his dream, God speaks this to Jacob: 'Your descendants will be like the dust of the earth, and you will spread out to the west and to the east, to the north and to the south. All peoples on earth will be blessed through you and your offspring' (Gen. 28:14). Isaiah uses the same words in his song about what is going to happen to God's house when it is restored:

> *Enlarge the place of your tent,*
> *stretch your tent curtains wide,*
> *do not hold back;*
> *lengthen your cords,*
> *strengthen your stakes.*
> *For you will spread out to the right and to the left;*
> *your descendants will dispossess the nations*
> *and settle in their desolate cities.*
> *(Isa. 54:2–3)*

Isaiah puts that promise made to Jacob inside a song about a desolate woman who gets healed. The image Isaiah uses of Jerusalem is of a woman who has been cast aside. He says, 'Sing, barren woman.' He promises that the children of the desolate woman will be more than she who is married. He sings that she will not suffer disgrace and she will forget the shame of her youth. He says that the Lord has called her like a wife forsaken and grieved in spirit who has been cast off. He promises that the Lord in everlasting love will have compassion on her. She will be rebuilt. He invites her to come to the waters for free. As she comes to God and listens to him, God will make an everlasting covenant with her because of the love God has for his new King. Nations not known as belonging to God will come running. They will seek the Lord while he may be found, and they will call on him while he is near (Isa. 54:1–55:13).

As a poetic song about the story of The Woman at the Well, it doesn't get any better, or clearer, than that. The story of the woman is an enactment of the restoration of God's house as written by Isaiah while reflecting on Jacob's encounter with God at Bethel.

Underneath this set of four stories in the Gospel, we find the story of the family that became Israel and the vision that they were given of

God's house extending across the whole world. We see Jesus gathering and inviting us into God's house. Friendship and meals become discipleship and change of heart, life and name. Disciples become priests. And I don't mean a recognised role within the church. I mean those who are standing on earth, maybe even wandering in the desert, who suddenly find that they have been washed clean and that they are being welcomed into the very presence of the Living God who sees them and dwells with them.

Provocation

II

The Challenge

Closing Down the Temple

What we have been discovering I found so exciting. It wasn't just the first sign and second sign stories that belonged together. The stories immediately before the first sign and immediately before the second sign also worked together in the same way. What next? What about the stories immediately after?

The story immediately after the first sign is Closing Down the Temple. You can read this in 2:13–24. We are going to immerse ourselves in the story. The drama and the action are vivid. There is lots of detail. There is depth to the characters and passionate interaction between them.

Sometimes we can read the Bible like we are miners. We think our job is to shift all the rubble to one side so we can go back up to the surface with a bit of gold that we've extracted. That's not what we are doing here. We are more like ramblers. We are trying to climb a hill and see the panorama of the story before us. Then we can understand how the whole landscape fits together.

As before, a good way of using this book is to simply read the questions and then just go straight on and read my answers. But my great hope is that this book will help you get immersed into the Gospel. So, better still, stop after each question. Go back and read the story again. Take in the view. Then answer the question yourself before moving on to read my answer. My aim is that as you repeatedly reflect on the story, you will begin to see for yourself the richness of all it contains.

Where Are We and What Time Is It? (2:13–14)

We are in Jerusalem. It is near the Passover. We have walked up to the Temple. If you read to near the end of the story you will see that the Temple is still in the process of being rebuilt. Like all good building projects, it is over time and over budget. It was King Herod who started it. He loved a lavish project. But he didn't finish this one. So far, it has taken forty-six years (2:20). That gives the reader a steer on the year. We are somewhere between AD 26 and 29, depending on what year they actually started, which we don't know.

In Jesus' day the temple was deeply corrupt. Don't think of it as just a large church. The Temple was a religious city state that had tremendous power and exerted huge influence. Think Parliament, the Vatican and Premier League football rolled into one. All in the hands of just a few ruling families.

Many Jewish groups had abandoned Temple worship and spoke against it. Judaism wasn't one big happy family in the first century. There were lots of groups and sects with conflicting agendas and different theological interests. The Qumran community, which gave rise to the Dead Sea Scrolls, lived out in the desert and despised the Temple. Many others had withdrawn from Temple worship. But Jesus didn't withdraw. He stepped into the Temple and engaged directly with the issues.

Who Starts the Story? (2:15)

Jesus. This is not an angry reaction. This is a considered and deliberate response to the terrible problem of corruption in the Temple. Even though Jesus is upset, he isn't letting his emotions just carry him along. He has chosen the time and the means to express his outrage. He makes a whip. Imagine that. He makes it himself. He is walking through the crowds at the market on the way into the city. He stops and buys several cords of rope. Judas has to pay for it. Andrew has to carry it. Jesus looks stony faced. He's not saying very much. They go and sit in the Temple courts. Jesus wants the rope. He's been in the Scouts. He knows his knots. There he is, lashing it all together. Imagine the conversation among the disciples. 'What is he doing? Unless I'm mistaken, that looks like a whip.'

What Does Jesus Do? (2:15–16)

He gets up on his feet. He is cracking his whip. He is shouting. He is throwing tables over. He is scattering money. He is untying sheep. He is driving them out, loudly and vigorously cracking the whip over them. People start to resist. Jesus confronts them with raw anger: 'Get out, get out of here. This is wrong. This is so wrong.' He smacks his hand onto the side of a bullock. He gets a whole herd of them moving off. People scatter before them. He cracks the whip again.

There is another side to Jesus. He has strength of conviction and passion in his indignation.

With a powerful prophetic action, Jesus brings the Temple, or at least part of it, to a standstill. His message is this: God is coming to close you down because you have turned God's gift upside down.

For the Jewish people, the Temple is the place of God's presence on earth. The Temple is the place where God meets with them. The Temple tells them: God is with us; God is among us; the actual presence of our eternal creator God is here with us. The Temple is the place of God's forgiveness. The Temple sacrifices are God saying, 'I forgive you; I accept you; I cleanse you. Even though I am high and holy, I receive you.' The Temple is a physical, tangible reality that speaks of God's love. But the ruling families have taken the gift of God and turned it into a way of making money. They have turned God's presence to personal gain. Jesus' prophetic action speaks of God's impending judgment upon them, when the Temple will not be temporarily stopped, but permanently destroyed.

How Do the Disciples Respond? (2:17)

The disciples are in difficulty. What can they do? They look for a Bible verse. They remember one: 'Zeal for your house will consume me.' That is a quote from Psalm 69:9, where the writer calls on God to judge his people. The people he expected to understand and support him have turned against him. It is the psalm of a man who is rejected because he takes a stand. Not a bad choice for this moment. But although it might explain how Jesus feels, it doesn't really explain why Jesus is doing this. His disciples simply don't understand. John admits that it took the passing of time, the resurrection of Jesus from the dead, some lengthy reflection on Scripture and remembering what Jesus said for the disciples to finally understand what happened on that crazy day (2:21–2).

How Do the Authorities Respond? (2:18)

Because all organisations are made up of humans, they are always at risk of going wrong. When organisations become corrupt, they can be very difficult to change and dangerous to challenge. I don't know if you have ever challenged an organisation about its values. I'm not just talking about customer service failings like your broadband speed or your utility bill. Have you ever challenged an organisation about what it really stands for? I've done it a couple of times in my life. It is not an easy experience. You can't do it without being challenged back.

The authorities recognise that this is a prophetic action. They don't simply arrest Jesus for criminal damage and inciting a riot. They demand to know his authority to do prophetic actions. If he has authority from God, he has to prove it. You can hear the disciples breathing a sigh of relief. We might just get away with this. We've got loads of signs. Hundreds of healings. Which one do you want? But that is not exactly how Jesus answers them.

What Does Jesus Say? (2:19)

The reply Jesus gives is deliberately provocative. He says something they just don't understand: 'Destroy this temple, and I will raise it again in three days' (2:19).

This is not an explanation. It is a prophetic statement that Jesus knows they are not going to understand. You want an explanation? You want to know where my authority lies? Well, how about the crucifixion and the resurrection? See what you make of that. It's much easier for us to know what he means, from the best seats in the house. Much more difficult to understand him if you happen to be the Deputy Manager for Money Changing on duty in the Temple on that particular day.

This has to be one of the best remembered sayings of Jesus. You find this 'destroy and raise up' statement in the mouth of his enemies and his friends. It comes up in Jesus' trial (Matt. 26:61). The authorities use it to accuse him of being a false prophet. When you find the same statement being attributed to someone both by their supporters and by their detractors, it gives it tremendous credibility.

What Does It Mean?

First, it means that God is going to judge the corrupt Temple and it will be no more. God's judgment is coming on the Temple because of the failings of the leaders and their corruption of God's gift.

Second, it means that Jesus is the new Temple (2:21). We will discover, when we get to the Old Testament underneath these stories, that Isaiah, Micah and Ezekiel all see a new and glorious Temple being built that will heal the nations and spread over the whole earth. Jesus takes all that to himself. 'Forget this structure here, I am the Temple. My death and my resurrection are the true and full expression of all that the Temple stood for. Destroy this temple and I will rebuild it in three days. This physical temple in which we are standing is just a picture that pointed to me.' This is a bold theological step.

Third, he is announcing himself as a temple builder. In being the person who will build the new Temple, he is proclaiming himself to be the new King. It is kings who build temples. No one else does it. Jesus' coming is an act of great hope – God's prophetic purpose is going to be fulfilled in him. There is going to be a righteous King who will build the house for God, which is what God had promised to King David.

How Do People Respond? (2:20)

There are many who simply reject him. The ruling elite are very disparaging.

Others in the city see all the healings and believe. But Jesus doesn't trust them, and he does not entrust himself to them. He can see what's in their hearts. They like the miracles, and for now they love him. But Jesus knows that when the challenges of discipleship and the call of the cross become real, they will fade away (2:23–4).

The Healing at the Pool

The story immediately after the second sign is The Healing at the Pool. You can read the story in 5:1–18. We are going to dive into this story and have a good look around. We rightly think of Jesus' healing ministry as something that is both a blessing for the person who is healed and a demonstration of God working. It might be a surprise to you that healing can also function as prophetic challenge. Stay with me. This is something Jesus does in all the Gospels.

Where Are We and What Time Is It? (5:1–5)

We are in Jerusalem again, at one of the festivals. We are not at the Temple, but similar to the Temple, we are in a well-known public place. The Pool of Bethesda is a cross between a day-care centre and a healing shrine. Sick people gather, believing that the water has some kind of healing power that they can access. This is a strange, superstitious idea. Sadly, it is not working for this man (5:5–7).

Who Starts the Story? (5:6–7)

Jesus takes the initiative again. The man does not send for Jesus. He doesn't know who Jesus is. He only finds out later when they meet again (5:14). On their second meeting he pays a lot more attention, but on this first meeting he doesn't know him. He does not ask Jesus to heal him. He does not ask for prayer. He does not approach Jesus. Jesus goes to talk to him and begins by asking a question: 'Do you want to get well?' (5:6).

Too much psychologising has been done over this question. People have said things like, 'You have to want to get well before Jesus can heal you.' This is well meaning but can be cruel. We have several chronically sick people in our church community. When you are chronically sick, you have to adapt your life to your limitations. In a church like ours, it also means you have been prayed for many times and nothing has happened. The problem with proposing that Jesus is asking the question in this way is that it suggests the chronically sick are getting in the way of their own healing. You are not well because you don't want to be well. That is very cruel.

Jesus is not tackling the psychology of the chronically sick. He is simply taking the initiative. He goes to the pool. He picks the man out from all the sick people there. He does not heal anyone else. He's looking for someone to do something for him. The man seems to be the sort of person he is looking for. He opens the conversation with a question. Jesus is also being respectful. He is thinking ahead. As we are going to discover, Jesus plans to enlist this man in his project to challenge the authorities. He is just making sure that the man is happy with being enlisted by being healed.

The man's answer is most revealing. He doesn't mention Jesus or faith or God or prayer. It's a bit of a sad, superstitious answer: 'Sir . . . I have no one to help me into the pool when the water is stirred. While I am trying to get in, someone else goes down ahead of me' (5:7).

The man does not ask Jesus to heal him. The man has no expectation whatsoever. This story is different from the classic healing ministry of Jesus where people bring the sick to him, or the sick themselves request prayer, and Jesus prays for them. This is not a response to a request for healing. Jesus is doing something dramatic, something prophetic. This is the same as going into the Temple and making a whip. Something is about to happen.

What Does Jesus Do? (5:8–9)

In the Temple, Jesus scattered the market and overturned the tables for changing money. This too is an overturning. The challenge is more subtle but is actually even more provocative. Jesus deliberately overturns the authorities' teaching on Sabbath regulations.

The Jewish law says don't work on the Sabbath. The Sabbath is a day for rest. But the detail of what that means is a matter for interpretation. Jeremiah says don't carry your load (Jer. 17:21). But even then, what constitutes a load is not specified. The idea of a mat as a load has been added later as an interpretation. It is an attempt to understand and apply that scripture. This is what Bible teachers do.

Neither do the Scriptures say that healing is a work that should not be done on the Sabbath. The authorities believe that and teach that. In their teaching, healing is seen as a work of creation. They teach that as God rested from his creative work on the seventh day and made it a Sabbath, we therefore should rest from healing on the Sabbath. The synagogue leader says this in the Gospel of Luke: 'There are six days for work. So come and be healed on those days, not on the Sabbath' (Luke 13:14). By healing on the Sabbath, Jesus is deliberately provoking the authorities. He is provoking them to re-examine their position both on healing and on Sabbath.

Jesus is revealing how upside down their teaching has become. He is not challenging the scripture. He is challenging them. Just as he overturned their greed in the Temple, he is overturning their petty, pointless, narrow, oppressive rules.

As in the Temple, they've turned something good from God into something bad. The reason God created the Sabbath was so that we have time for rest and recreation in our lives. In the process, we are saved from being addicted to work and we are saved from the endless pursuit of money. God knows that we need all these good things in our lives. The Sabbath is here to serve us and do us good. But the way the authorities are teaching it has turned it the other way up. They've made it into something oppressive, something petty and something legalistic. Their teaching about rest isn't restful any more.

Jesus tells the man to carry his overturning of their Sabbath teaching into the city for all to see. 'Then Jesus said to him, "Get up! Pick up your mat and walk." At once the man was cured; he picked up his mat and walked. The day on which this took place was a Sabbath' (5:8–9).

How Do the Authorities Respond? (5:10–16)

There is nothing in this story about the disciples' response. But there is plenty about what the authorities think. They understand it perfectly as a direct challenge to their authority. When the authorities see this man, all they can see is the mat-carrying. That's all they can think about – the infringement of their regulations and the undermining of their authority (5:10). They completely miss the wonderful joy that a man who has been disabled for thirty-eight years is now walking.

There is an immediate investigation. Sabbath law has been broken. But why and by whom? I can imagine the man clinging to his mat, unwilling to put it down. After thirty-eight years of lying on that mat, and probably being carried around on it, for him to walk and carry it is all part of his healing. His healing happened in response to a single command. 'Get up! Pick up your mat and walk.' Carrying the mat isn't an optional extra. It is part of the healing process, part of his empowerment. The man, in his reluctance to put down his mat, explains that he is just doing what he has been told, and he refers the authorities to one who gave him the command to carry it.

There is a bit of a delay in the investigation, because to start with the man does not know who it was that told him to do this. But then Jesus finds him at the Temple and tells him to sort his life out. The man discovers that it was Jesus who healed him, and he tells the authorities. They are pretty angry: 'So, because Jesus was doing these things on the Sabbath, the Jewish leaders began to persecute him' (5:16).

We will soon come on to the Old Testament that lies underneath these stories. But as a foretaste, this is what Isaiah thought of that:

> *The Lord says:*
> *'These people come near to me with their mouth*
> *and honour me with their lips,*
> *but their hearts are far from me.*
> *Their worship of me*
> *is based on merely human rules they have been taught.'*
> *(Isa. 29:13)*

What Does Jesus Say? (5:17)

Jesus says something that makes their blood boil: 'My Father is always at his work to this very day, and I too am working' (5:17).

This is a very shocking thing to say. This is not conciliatory. This is not an explanation.

The Jewish authorities teach that healing was a work that God rested from on the Sabbath. If you are sick on the Sabbath, come back tomorrow. However, they also teach that God never rests from his work of judgment. So, when Jesus says, 'My Father is always at his work to this very day,' they would agree with that. God is always at his work of judgment. God never gives up being against evil. God never stops being against sin. God never rests from rooting out corruption. God never says, 'I don't care about sin today.' No.

So far so good in what Jesus is saying. He then says, 'I too am working.' And their blood boils over. He calls God 'my Father'. He says his work is God's work. He is saying that the healing isn't just a healing. God is working to this very day in judgment. I am working in judgment too.

When we think of judgment we tend to think of punishment. That isn't wrong. The idea of justice includes the principle that there are consequences for people who do things that cause harm. But judgment is a bigger idea than just punishment. It is also about revealing what is happening. Before we can get to consequences, we must first get a clear view of what is going on. We have to reveal reality, especially the deeper attitudes of people's hearts. Then, as well as consequences, judgment is about putting things right. Justice is about punishing the offender. But it is also about healing the hurting, releasing the oppressed and rebuilding society to live in a healthy and righteous way. God's judgment includes all these elements: (1) revealing what is happening; (2) just consequences for those who deliberately and knowingly cause harm; (3) rebuilding everything to be good.

It is the work of revealing that Jesus is doing in this story.

Jesus is not afraid to find out what is in the hearts of the authorities. He is not afraid to press the buttons that expose their inner thoughts and feelings. He knows that in order to rebuild the right principle of rest in our lives, he must first reveal the terrible distortions of Sabbath teaching that have placed such a burden on people. The irony of this story is that the load the authorities are forcing the people to carry by their distorted teaching is so much greater than the mat Jesus told the man to pick up. Jesus plans to throw it all down.

What Does It Mean?

First, it means that God is going to judge their corrupt teaching. The Temple is the holy place, the place of encounter with God. The Sabbath is the holy time, the time of encounter with God. Both need to be demolished and rebuilt in the right way.

Second, it means that Jesus is the new Sabbath. He is the holy time of meeting with God. When we go to Jesus, we go to rest from our work.

Third, it means that Jesus is the restoring of God's Word. When the new King comes and the new Temple is built, which we looked at in the previous story, the teaching of God's Word will not be abandoned. The nations will come to hear God's Word. Isaiah saw that too (Isa. 2:2–3).

How Do People Respond? (5:18)

'For this reason they tried all the more to kill him; not only was he breaking the Sabbath, but he was even calling God his own Father, making himself equal with God' (5:18). This is tragic. They just can't see it. They just won't accept it. What Jesus is saying does not fit with their worldview. Things that challenge our worldview tend to cause very bitter arguments. This one is no exception.

Conclusion

I was really excited. Here are two stories that are working together. As we look at them both we begin to see Jesus. We are seeing another side to him. It's dramatic and passionate. There is a love for justice and truth that is compelling him to take a prophetic stand. As we look at the stories, we can see the person.

The shape of the stories is this:

	2: Closing Down the Temple (2:13–24)	5: The Healing at the Pool (5:1–18)
Where and when?	Jerusalem Near Passover The Temple	Jerusalem One of the festivals Pool of Bethesda
Jesus takes an initiative	Makes a whip	Finds the paralysed man
Jesus does a prophetic action	Drives out the animals Turns over the tables	'Get up! Pick up your mat and walk'
The disciples and others do not understand	Look for a Bible verse Don't understand until later	

The authorities do not like it at all and challenge Jesus	Recognise this as a prophetic action and demand a sign of Jesus' authority	Because he is doing these things on the Sabbath, they begin to persecute him
Jesus' response is very provocative	'Destroy this Temple, and I will raise it again in three days '	'My Father is always at his work to this very day, and I too am working'
What it means is that God's judgment is coming. It speaks of Jesus being God's new King. There will be a new Temple, a new Sabbath rest and a new people of God	1. God's judgment is coming on the Temple 2. Jesus is the new Temple, the holy place of encounter with God 3. Jesus is the new King who will build the new Temple	1. God the Father is judging 2. Jesus is co-working with God in providing a sign that enables the judgment of God to come 3. Judgment is first about revealing what is happening 4. The Sabbath regulations need to be demolished and rebuilt 5. Jesus is the new Sabbath, the holy time of encounter with God
Most people reject him. Those who do respond positively, either Jesus doesn't trust them or they are afraid to make themselves known	Many reject him The ruling elite are disparaging People love the signs, but Jesus doesn't trust them as they haven't understood the signs	They try all the more to kill him

The question now is: are there any more stories in John that have this shape? I found two more.

12

Signs of the King

The Healing of the Man Born Blind

The third story that has the same narrative structure as Closing Down the Temple and The Healing at the Pool is the story of The Healing of the Man Born Blind. You can read it in 9:1–41. It is a classic story with several fast-moving scenes, some punchy dialogue and an unexpected twist. Like The Raising of Lazarus, this story enriches the storyboard that we have discovered with more details and deeper insights into the characters.

Where Are We and What Time Is It? (9:1)

It looks like we are still in Jerusalem, although that is not explicitly stated. The story happens as Jesus 'went along'. There is one detail later in the story that gives it away. The man is sent to the Pool of Siloam and is expected to know where that is and to be able to get there on his own. The Pool of Siloam is in Jerusalem. Unusually, there is no specific time check, but more on that later.

Who Starts the Story? (9:2–5)

It would appear from later dialogue that this man is quite well known in Jerusalem. By the end of the story we know he is something of a character. He certainly exhibits a great deal of strength and clarity of mind when under investigation. However, at the start of the story he is the blind man who is always there. Beggars on the street are often not noticed by those passing by. After his healing, some have difficulty to say for sure that it is the same man. Apart from the difficulty of accepting that a man born blind can see, it would appear that they don't have a sufficiently strong memory of his appearance to be certain that it is him.

It looks like the disciples are simply walking past him and ignoring him. It's what we all do. It is Jesus who 'saw' him. It is Jesus who draws the disciples' attention to him. It is Jesus who starts the story.

Even when he is pointed out, the disciples are not interested in the man himself. They want to turn the man's plight into a theological discussion. This is also what we do. It is much more comfortable to talk theologically about people in need than it is to help them. Helping is generally messy and difficult. The disciples seem to share the commonly accepted view that sickness is caused by sin. But this man was born blind. This challenges their worldview and raises questions. Is it possible to sin in the womb? Maybe this sickness was inflicted on him because of his parents' sin? Jesus will have none of it. None of it at all. Sickness, certainly in this man, is simply an opportunity for God to work. Stop talking about sin. Start thinking about what God is doing.

The use of the word 'work' should immediately alert us. It was 'work' that Jesus was doing when he healed the paralysed man. The Father's work (5:17). The work of judgment. Jesus immediately confirms this to us. He pauses. And he puts everything that follows into the context of night and day, darkness, and light: 'As long as it is day, we must do the works of him who sent me. Night is coming, when no one can work' (9:4).

This is judgment language. The light shines in the darkness. The darkness doesn't get it and struggles against it (1:5). The coming of God's light reveals how dark the darkness of humanity has become. Some will come to the light, so their lives can be seen (3:21). Others just love the darkness and are determined to remain there (3:19–20). This is a judgment story. The light of Jesus is about to shine in the darkness of Jerusalem.

What Does Jesus Do? (9:6–7)

It's unusual. Jesus makes mud, using his spit. He then plasters it all over
the eyes of the man who is already blind. He is now a double-blind
man. He can't see with his eyes that aren't working. And then Jesus
does the same as he did with the paralysed man. He sends him into the
city. A blind man, with his eyes daubed in mud, gropes his way through
the city on his own to find the Pool of Siloam, where he washes off
the mud daubed over his eyes. This is not the normal treatment of the
deserving or even the undeserving poor.

But he does go home seeing.

How Do People Respond? (9:8–12)

The man's neighbours and friends are happily confused. There is a
fair amount of discussion as to whether it is even the same man. But
he insists, 'It's definitely me.' They want to know how on earth this
has happened. So he tells them. He certainly has the story clear in
his mind. He is a step ahead of the paralysed man. He knows Jesus'
name. 'Jesus put mud on my eyes and told me to go to Siloam and
wash. I went to Siloam and washed and then I could see.' It's not a
complicated story.

But it causes a right hoo-ha, as they say.

How Do the Authorities Respond? (9:13–34)

They take the man off to the authorities. And here we are again. The
unholy action of healing on the holy day is deeply troubling to them.
It is totally against regulations to heal on the Sabbath. So they have
an investigation.

They quiz the man first and hear his story. Mud, wash: see. Sim-
ples. And then THE row breaks out again. If you start by accepting
the healing, you have to conclude that God is at work and that this
man Jesus is possibly someone whom God has sent. A prophet even.
But if you start by insisting that Sabbath regulations have been broken, you cannot go there. I mean, God would never undermine our
Bible teaching, would he?

The Pharisees take the extraordinary step of asking the blind man his view on this conundrum. He is definitely leaning in the direction of God worked, Jesus is a prophet. This is probably the day after the healing happened. The man has had time to think. Jesus is more than just a name to him now. Jesus is starting to take shape in his mind, even though the man has never actually seen him. Not yet.

The authorities lean the other way. They want to discredit the healing and make the problem go away. They drag the parents in and pursue the 'are you sure this is your son' line of attack. The parents are afraid. Power of any kind makes most people anxious. They know that if they get this wrong there will be consequences. They confirm the son is theirs. They confirm that he was born blind. They have no further comment to make, Your Honours.

Now, it is well recognised that the Jewish authorities did not establish it as policy to exclude Christians from synagogues until many years later. For many years, what was to become 'Christianity' existed within Judaism. A group within Judaism was normal. There were many groups and sects within the Jewish faith in the first century. After the resurrection, for the Jews and the God-fearing Gentiles who came to follow Jesus, what was going on was simply the fulfilment of the Hebrew Scriptures. Following Jesus was still 'Judaism'. Jesus was God's new King, long promised to Israel. But after the fall of Jerusalem and the destruction of the Temple, Judaism had to be significantly reinvented. It was at this point that people identified as 'Christians' were formally excluded from Jewish communities and from Jewish worship and had to become something separate.

However, there aren't any Christians in this story. This is a story of how the Jewish authorities respond to a Jewish man. The authorities do have the power to exclude Jewish people from the worshipping community for not following regulations. As with all organisations, those in charge have sanctions over those who belong. Like all large institutions spread over a wide area, the way those sanctions are applied in practice vary with local context and the character of the leaders holding the power. It would appear that the synagogue leaders in Jerusalem have decided to use their powers to attempt to suppress support for Jesus and his teachings. The blind man's mum and dad know that and are worried about it.

Having not got very far, they drag the blind man back in and try to bully him to adopt their stance, which is what people of power with fixed opinions and clear agendas always do: 'Give glory to God by telling the truth . . . We know this man is a sinner' (9:24).

But they have picked the wrong man. Or maybe Jesus has picked the right one. There is some brilliant dialogue, of the kind that always happens when people in power, who are fixed in their view of the world, are confronted by some data that contradicts them, but such is the power of their worldview within them that they are forced to deny the facts, bully the people involved and try to suppress the situation to stop it getting out of hand. The interchange between them and the seeing man is hilarious. Except it is so tragic (9:25–33). They chuck him out of their community. If not bodily, then certainly spiritually. 'You are not part of us. You are not welcome at our worship.'

What Does Jesus Say? (9:35–41)

Jesus leads the man to believe in him. The seeing man worships. The blind can see.

Jesus summarises the story. It is very provocative – a judgment story. It is a story that reveals what is really happening: 'For judgment I have come into this world, so that the blind will see and those who see will become blind' (9:39).

Some Pharisees ask the obvious question: 'Do you think we are blind?' They are the best teachers in their community. They are at the top of their game. This is a bit like Premier League footballers asking Jesus, 'Do you think we can't pass?' Sometimes people ask questions so that they can write us off. They ask questions to trap us. If Jesus says, 'Yes, you are blind too,' they can just dismiss him. It is obvious they are not blind. They are the best Bible teachers around. If Jesus says,

'No, you are not blind,' then they can ask him to pay more attention to their teaching.

But Jesus gives a much deeper answer. Not one they are expecting. And, it would appear, one that they have no answer for. Jesus says, 'No, you are not blind. If you were blind, you would not be guilty of the sin that so besets you. You are not blind, and therefore you are responsible for where you have gone wrong with your teaching. If you were blind to the truth you would not be responsible for misrepresenting the truth. The problem that you have is that you claim to see everything clearly. You are not prepared to recognise that you might be wrong. The problem is that you are blind to your own blindness.'

This is where the story truly works. The man was a double-blinded man. He had mud blinding his blind eyes. He was blind to his own blindness. This is the Pharisees' problem. They cannot see their own blindness. They cannot see that their teaching on rest is not restful. And this is wilfully done. Even when challenged by Jesus, they won't reflect. They never say, 'We might have got this wrong.' When the prophetic challenge happens, they harden their position. They reach for the power that they have to stop Jesus' teaching that is threatening their position.

This a worldview challenge. We all have a worldview. We look at the world in a certain way. It is like wearing glasses. We look at the world through a set of assumptions, things that we hold to be self-evident. The problem is that when someone comes along who challenges our worldview, we can't see it, because we don't look *at* our worldview; we look *through* our worldview. When someone comes along and points out that our glasses are covered in mud, and the way we are looking at the world is wrong, we find it so difficult to accept. We are blind to our own blindness. This is not just the problem of the Pharisees. It is the human condition.

But what this story reveals is that they won't do anything about it.

Jesus is giving them an opportunity to re-examine themselves. But what he finds is that they are unwilling. They refuse him. They reject him. It is being revealed that those who can see are becoming blind.

The New King Comes

The fourth story that has the same shape as the other three in this set of stories is The New King Comes – when Jesus comes to Jerusalem as King. You can read it in 12:12–50. As before, we will dive into the story and ask all the same questions to help unfold its full shape. Then we can see how the stories work together. And we will see Jesus through the stories. We will be able to know him.

Where Are We and What Time Is It? (12:12)

The clock is ticking. The authorities have decided that the best course of action is to kill Jesus. He has been hiding from them in Ephraim, a village in the wild with good views in all directions (11:53–4). But he has come, as he always does, to the festival in Jerusalem. It is now five days before the Passover. Jesus is on his way into Jerusalem from Bethany. The authorities are looking for him (11:57).

Who Starts the Story? (12:12–14)

Jesus starts this one too. He sets off for the city. The crowd hear that he is on his way. They gather to meet him. There is a growing sense that God is going to do something great. All that God has promised through the prophets might finally happen. Jesus finds a young donkey. The other Gospels tell us that he gets the disciples to go and fetch it (Matt. 21:1–3; Mark 11:1–3; Luke 19:29–31). Sitting on a donkey is a hugely provocative act. Like making the whip. Like picking out the lame man. Like sending a double-blind man into the city. Some actions have massive symbolic meaning, way beyond their actual content. This is one of those. It's God's new King who will ride the young donkey (Zech. 9:9). God's rule is not going to come by the taking up of arms and the exerting of powerful force. The King is coming in gentleness and meekness. Sitting on a donkey.

What Does Jesus Do? (12:12–15)

A trip into Jerusalem to do some teaching is turned into an excited royal procession. The crowd start shouting and waving palm branches. They start singing psalms about the coming of the King. The one quoted is Psalm 118. It sings of the goodness of God, the deliverance of God and the victory of God. It is not specifically attributed to David, Israel's greatest King, but it is retelling his story. The one who was rejected has become the one on whom all hopes rest (Ps. 118:22).

How Do the Disciples Respond? (12:16)

They don't understand. They certainly don't understand how the King comes and the kingdom works. They probably don't even get the significance of the donkey. It is only after the death and resurrection of Jesus that they remember what happened, understand it and connect it all up with the Scriptures. From the best seats in the house, we get to see it and understand it. We get the helpful commentary as we are going along.

How Do the Authorities Respond? (12:17–19)

The people who have been in Bethany and are coming into the city are telling the story of Lazarus. Others in Jerusalem hear that Jesus is coming and are going out to try to catch a glimpse of him as he arrives. They meet. As a way of informing and exciting large numbers of people about Jesus, it is a perfect storm.

The Pharisees are totally cheesed off. Project Suppress the Teaching of Jesus is going horribly wrong.

What Does Jesus Say? (12:20–8)

As with The Healing at the Pool, the end of this story is woven into the beginning of the next. Some Greeks ask to see Jesus and his answer is very provocative: 'The hour has come for the Son of Man to be glorified. Very truly I tell you, unless a grain of wheat falls to the ground and dies, it remains only a single seed. But if it dies, it produces many seeds' (12:23–4).

We first discovered that Jesus has an 'hour' at the first sign – The Wedding at Cana. Part of Jesus' reluctance to engage with dealing with the lack of wine at the wedding was because his hour had not come, which he expressed very strongly to his mother: 'Woman, what is this to you or to me? . . . My hour has not yet come' (2:4).

We find out what his 'hour' is by reading on to this point. But it still leaves a puzzle. Why is not being time for his death a reason for his reluctance to do the sign at the wedding? What is the connection? We get part of the answer at The Feeding of the Five Thousand. When people see the multiplying of bread, they want Jesus to take up his powers and use them against their enemies. They want to make him King by force. What they can't see is that Jesus is going to become King by doing the exact opposite: giving up power and laying down his life.

The Romans have power because of military might and machinery of their government that is kept in power by the threat of violence. The Jewish authorities have struck a deal and have taken up their power alongside them by all the obvious means. Making money at the expense of the population. Creating regulations that oppress people and kept them in line. Having sanctions over people to expel them from belonging to the community, keeping them in check because of fear of exclusion. Demonising everyone that speaks against them. Bullying and threatening any who dare to challenge them.

But the way to defeat corrupt power is not by taking up power.

Jesus must fall into the ground and die. Only then will the true harvest come. The death of Jesus is not humiliation. It is his glorification. And it is his multiplication. Because those who follow Jesus will also not live for themselves. They will give themselves. Good things can grow from the laying down of their lives and the giving up of their power.

This is the way the nations will come to God and everything will be put right.

Bringing It All Together

Now we can see how these stories all work together.

	2: Closing Down of the Temple	5: The Healing at the Pool	9: The Healing of the Man Born Blind	12: The New King Comes
Where and when?	Jerusalem Near Passover The Temple	Jerusalem One of the Festival of Weeks Pool of Bethesda	Jerusalem Feast of Dedication/Lights Pool of Siloam	Jerusalem Near Passover The road to Jerusalem
Jesus takes an initiative	Makes a whip	Finds the paralysed man	Points out the blind man	Sits on a donkey
He does a prophetic action	Drives out the animals Turns over the tables	Get up, pick up your mat and walk	Makes mud with spit, puts it on the man's eyes. Sends him to Siloam	Receives the proclamation of the crowd as King
The disciples and others do not understand	Look for a Bible verse Don't understand until later	Nothing	His neighbours are confused and unsure it is him	Don't understand until later
The authorities do not like it at all and challenge Jesus	Recognise this as a prophetic action and demand a sign of Jesus' authority	Because he is doing these things on the Sabbath, they begin to persecute him	Hold an investigation and interrogate the man, his parents, and the man again Hold to their worldview that Jesus must be a sinner Bully the man Throw him out of their community	This is getting us nowhere

Jesus' response is very provocative	'Destroy this Temple, and I will raise it again in three days'	'My Father is always at his work and to this very day, and I too am working'	Leads the man to believe in him 'For judgment I have come into this world, so that the blind will see and those who see will become blind'	When the Greeks come: 'The hour has come for the Son of Man to be glorified' Seed into the ground
What it means	1. God's judgment is coming on the Temple 2. Jesus is the new Temple, the holy place of encounter with God 3. Jesus is the new King who will build the new Temple	1. God the Father is judging 2. What Jesus is doing is co-working with God in providing a sign to enable the judgment of God to come 3. Jesus is the new Sabbath, the holy time of encounter with God	1. God's judgment is coming 2. The blind will see 3. Those who claim that they can see, but can't, will become blind 4. The blind man is a metaphor He is blind to his own blindness	1. Jesus is the new King 2. The nations will come to him 3. He will be lifted up to reign by dying

Most people reject him	Many reject him The ruling elite are disparaging People love the signs, but Jesus doesn't trust them as they haven't understood the signs	They try all the more to kill him	The Pharisees ask, 'Are you saying that we are blind?' Jesus says, 'No. If you were blind you would not be guilty of sin. You claim to see and yet are blind to your blindness. You are responsible for this.'	Many leaders believe but are afraid of those who have the power to exclude them

13

The Songs of Isaiah

Underneath these stories of Jesus working with the Father to speak judgment to the corruption and idolatry of the leaders of Israel is the Prophet Isaiah. It isn't four stories this time. It is virtually the whole book. To make matters easier, we will focus on a few themes.

Isaiah lives and works in Jerusalem. It is no surprise that the four stories we have been looking at all happen in Jerusalem. Isaiah is a priest in the Temple. One day at work, he has a vision of God filling the Temple. The holiness of God is terrifying. It helps Isaiah to see how unclean he and the nation have become. He thinks he is going to die. But instead, God calls him. God sends Isaiah to speak his words of judgment and hope to his people. This comes with a paradoxical commission, because one outcome of Isaiah's message will be to reveal the blindness of the leaders and harden their hearts still further against God.

All the elements of the stories we have been looking at are found in Isaiah. Other prophets, like Micah and Jeremiah, also contribute. But in these stories Jesus is being Isaiah.

Isaiah opens with this theme of God's judgment coming on God's people. God's people, God's children, do not know God and have become corrupt from top to bottom (Isa. 1:1–6). Israel is under judgment. The sacrifices at the Temple are meaningless. The Sabbaths are worthless (Isa. 1:10–15). God wants justice for all. Sin will be fully dealt with. And there will be a straight choice between listening to and following God and resistance and rebellion (Isa. 1:16–20). Israel has sunk to the place where she is making money from being unfaithful to God. Corruption, deception, bribery and injustice to the poor have filled the land (Isa. 1:21–3). Isaiah sings:

When you come to appear before me,
who has asked this of you,
this trampling of my courts?
(Isa. 1:12)

Think of Jesus, standing in the Temple courts, with the whip in his hand. Furious at all the corruption. Knowing that God is going to deal with it. But without any power of his own in the institution. A prophetic voice speaking into the darkness and looking to God to bring change.

But then Isaiah sings of hope. He sees a new King coming. He sees the City, which represents the people of God becoming righteous and faithful (Isa 1:24–6). He sees the Temple being rebuilt. He sees God's house becoming the most influential thing in the world. He sees the nations gathering to it to hear God's word. He sees peace coming to the nations (Isa. 2:1–4). Isaiah sings:

The mountain of the Lord's temple will be established
as the highest of the mountains;
it will be exalted above the hills,
and all nations will stream to it.
(Isa. 2:2)

Think of Jesus, challenged by the authorities to give a sign of his authority, telling them that he will rebuild the Temple in three days. They don't get it. They don't realise that Isaiah was written about him. They don't realise he is seeing himself in this scripture. But it is what has happened.

Isaiah urges God's people: let's come to the light, let's walk in the light:

Come, descendants of Jacob,
let us walk in the light of the Lord.
(Isa. 2:5)

Think of Jesus, repeatedly saying, 'I am the light of the world. Come into the light while you still have the chance.' But, as Isaiah says, the land is full of superstitions, pagan customs and the making of money:

They are full of superstitions from the East;
they practise divination like the Philistines
and embrace pagan customs.
Their land is full of silver and gold;
there is no end to their treasures.
(Isa. 2:6–7)

Think of Jesus standing by the Pool of Siloam, looking at the people desperately clinging to the superstitious hope of the stirring of the waters that might make them well. Think of Jesus standing in the Temple courts, throwing all the money on the ground, turning the tables over.

Isaiah sees how people are trapped because those in power who are deliberately blind to the problem are using their power to keep everyone in line. He urges people to break free:

Stop trusting in mere humans,
who have but a breath in their nostrils.
Why hold them in esteem?
(Isaiah 2:22)

Think of the man with the mat, reporting Jesus to the authorities. Holding them in esteem. Think of the blind man who stands up to the authorities and gets thrown out for his pains. Think of the leaders who believe and yet won't make that public because they are afraid of what might happen.

Isaiah sings a song of God's vineyard. The vineyard is God's people. God has planted them and tended them and done everything for them. But the fruit is bad. There is economic injustice. The rich get richer. The poor get poorer. The people seek pleasure rather than God. Their lifestyles are self-indulgent. There is moral inversion. Bad things are called good. Everyone thinks they are an authority on everything. There is no humility. The courts are corrupt. There is no justice (Isa. 5:1–24). No wonder judgment is coming. God hates the injustices that happen when his people stop listening to him. Think of Jesus, along with many other voices, deeply troubled by all the corruption that he sees around him. In the middle of injustice, the religious life of the nation goes on. But for many their heart is not in it. It is just a lot of empty rules. Their hearts are far from God:

> *The Lord says:*
> *'These people come near to me with their mouth*
> *and honour me with their lips,*
> *but their hearts are far from me.*
> *Their worship of me*
> *is based on merely human rules they have been taught.*
> *(Isa. 29:13)*

Think of Jesus challenging the teaching of Sabbath regulations that have emptied the Sabbath of rest.

While at worship, Isaiah sees God. He is called from that place to go and speak God's word to God's people. But there is something very unusual about it. His speaking of God's word will bring fresh hope and fresh vision to people. But it will also have the effect of making the problem worse. When the light shines, the darkness will get even darker:

> *He said, 'Go and tell this people:*
> *'"Be ever hearing, but never understanding;*
> *be ever seeing, but never perceiving."*
> *Make the heart of this people calloused;*
> *make their ears dull*
> *and close their eyes.*
> *Otherwise they might see with their eyes,*
> *hear with their ears,*
> *understand with their hearts,*
> *and turn and be healed.'*
> *(Isa. 6:9–10)*

This is how the authorities' response to Jesus is described.

But it is not all bad news. Some people who are sitting in darkness are going to see a great light. They will rejoice. They will respond. They will see the victory of God. A child will be born who will be God's new King (Isa. 9:1–7).

> *For to us a child is born,*
> *to us a son is given,*
> *and the government will be on his shoulders.*
> *And he will be called*
> *Wonderful Counsellor, Mighty God,*
> *Everlasting Father, Prince of Peace.*
> *Of the greatness of his government and peace*
> *there will be no end.*
> *(Isa. 9:6–7)*

Think of Jesus, riding the donkey into Jerusalem. God's new King has come. The government is on his shoulders.

Isaiah's prophetic songs move effortlessly between these two great themes. The corruption, the injustice and the darkness that is going to be judged and demolished. And a new King who comes to build a new, glorious, just and righteous Kingdom where God will dwell. Both will happen. God will take a whip against his enemies who have grown so fat, in order to release his people who have suffered so much:

> *The Lord Almighty will lash them with a whip,*
> *as when he struck down Midian at the rock of Oreb;*
> *and he will raise his staff over the waters,*
> *as he did in Egypt.*
> *In that day their burden will be lifted from your shoulders,*
> *their yoke from your neck;*
> *the yoke will be broken*
> *because you have grown so fat.*
> *(Isa. 10:26–7)*

The victory against Midian was completely against the odds and was completely the work of God. All Gideon and his men did was lift up some lights (Judg. 7:7–25). The victory against Egypt was the same. Moses lifted up his staff (Exod. 14:15–31). God doesn't just assemble a bigger army to get his victory. He works through weakness. Think of Jesus lifting up his whip in the courts of the Temple. The full economic and religious power of the nation is against him. All he has is the whip in his hand.

But when God's new King comes, even in weakness, the nations will gather to him:

In that day, the Root of Jesse will stand as a banner for the peoples; the nations
will rally to him, and his resting-place will be glorious . . .
He will raise a banner for the nations
and gather the exiles of Israel;
he will assemble the scattered people of Judah
from the four quarters of the earth.
(Isa.11:10, 12)

Think of the Greeks coming, requesting to meet Jesus, and all this means to him. This theme of the expansion of God's people to include all the nations runs right through Isaiah. The nations will gather, and the world will be filled with the fruit of God. God's new King will be a light to the Gentiles. God's new house will be a house of prayer for all nations (Isaiah 14:1–3; 27:2–6; 42:1–9; 49:1–6; 51:4; 52:13–15; 56:6–8; 60:1–3; 66:18–21). Isaiah sings repeatedly of the nations coming to God and seeing his glory: 'And I, because of what they have planned and done, am about to come and gather the people of all nations and languages, and they will come and see my glory' (Isa. 66:18).

Think of Jesus, when he hears of the Greeks wanting to see him, immediately turning to everyone and saying, 'The hour has come for the Son of Man to be glorified' (12:23).

Isaiah sings of other signs that will show that God's new King has come:

Your God will come,
he will come with vengeance;
with divine retribution
he will come to save you.'
Then will the eyes of the blind be opened
and the ears of the deaf unstopped.
Then will the lame leap like a deer.
(Isa. 35:4–6)

Think of the stories that John has chosen and brought together. The blind man sees. The lame man walks. The new King has come. These signs will show it. The Prophet Micah, a contemporary of Isaiah, also speaks of this vision. The new King will come (Mic. 2:13), the new house of God will be built (Mic. 4:1) and the lame will walk (Mic. 4:6–7).

The Healing at the Pool is a prophetic sign that the new King has come. This healing is a provocative prophetic sign that the new Temple, the new dwelling of God on the earth, has come. The new Temple doesn't stand apart and use its privileged position to accumulate wealth and power to itself. The new Temple goes out to serve. It goes out to the superstitious, the needy, the weak, the lame and the blind. It brings the presence of God to them. God has broken out. God is on the streets. The lame are being gathered.

But not everyone will see it. Isaiah can see that blindness is endemic in the leaders of Israel (29:9–12; 42:17–22; 44:18; 56:10–12; 59:9–11). Isaiah sings of how blindness is a closed mind:

> *They know nothing, they understand nothing;*
> *their eyes are plastered over so that they cannot see,*
> *and their minds closed so that they cannot understand.*
> *(Isa. 44:18)*

Think of the picture of the man born blind, walking into the city with his eyes plastered with mud. He is what has happened to the authorities. Isaiah says that this blindness has come because of idolatry. God is no longer God to them (Isa. 44:19–20). The effect of this is the proliferation of taking advantage of others, not bothering to tell the truth, lack of integrity, empty arguments and lies, spinning a web of deception, violence, feet that are quick to rush into sin, the pursuit of evil schemes and no peace or justice in the nation (Isa. 59:1–8):

> *So justice is far from us,*
> *and righteousness does not reach us.*
> *We look for light, but all is darkness;*
> *for brightness, but we walk in deep shadows.*
> *Like the blind we grope along the wall,*
> *feeling our way like people without eyes.*
> *At midday we stumble as if it were twilight.*
> *(Isa. 59:9–10)*

135

But – there is also good news. When the new King comes, those who are blind will see:

> *I, the Lord, have called you in righteousness;*
> *I will take hold of your hand.*
> *I will keep you and will make you*
> *to be a covenant for the people*
> *and a light for the Gentiles,*
> *to open eyes that are blind,*
> *to free captives from prison*
> *and to release from the dungeon those who sit in darkness.*
> *(Isa. 42:6–7)*

Think of that man who has sat all his life in the dungeon of darkness. Suddenly, he can see. What a moment of joy that must be.

Isaiah captures this deep tension in his poetry. The blind see and rejoice. Those who refuse to see end up in darkness and shame (Isa. 42:16–17). There is more. But that is probably enough. Jesus has been reading Isaiah. Isaiah has prophesied about Jesus. John has chosen four stories that show Jesus as Isaiah. Some see. Others become blind. Jesus is speaking prophetically to power.

Contention

14

The First Arguments

A Night Visit

A pattern is now emerging in how John's Gospel has been written. The literary device of first sign and second sign leads us to read these stories alongside each other. They have the same narrative shape. The stories before the first sign and second sign also belong together and have the same shape, as do the stories after the first sign and the second sign. They form a repeating sequence:

Invitation	1:29–51 The First Disciples	4:1–42 The Woman at the Well
Demonstration	2:1–12 The Wedding at Cana	4:43–54 The Healing of the Royal Official's Son
Provocation	2:13–25 Closing Down the Temple	5:1–18 The Healing at the Pool

So now we will look at the story after the first Provocation story. You can read it in 3:1–15. This story is different. It's all dialogue, which does increase our insight into the inner world of Jesus. It helps us greatly in deepening our friendship with him because he speaks his thoughts and feelings with clarity and passion. However, because there is very little action in the narrative, we will have to approach it with a slightly different set of questions. We don't have the progression of the story to help us see the narrative shape. In my experience, it is these stories where most people give up reading. We just get lost in the arguments.

Because we are trying to get an overview of the whole Gospel, we won't be able to go to the depths. But I am hoping that you will be able to see more clearly what is going on in these stories and therefore be much less likely to get lost as you find out what Jesus thinks on some key matters.

Where Are We and What Time Is It? (2:23–4)

It would not be too big a jump to borrow the time and place from the end of the previous story. In John's Gospel Jesus goes regularly to Jerusalem to worship at the festivals. In complete contrast to the other Gospels, most of the action in John occurs in Jerusalem. The Passover is a huge international annual celebration where Israel gathers in Jerusalem to retell the Exodus story, enact the story through the sacrifice of the Passover lambs and restate their identity as the people whom God set free. In John there are three Passovers recorded. This is the first: 'Now while he was in Jerusalem at the Passover Festival' (2:23).

In the following sentence, which is a comment from John the author, we learn that Jesus knows what is in people's hearts and he doesn't entrust himself to them (2:24). In this story, Jesus does not entrust himself to the person who comes to see him – Nicodemus. So the author might want us to see this as a specific example of the general statement just made. Nicodemus comes at night, which means he doesn't want others to know. Although somebody does. They meet at someone's house while all is dark outside.

Who Starts the Conversation? (3:1–2)

Nicodemus. He is a teacher, a Pharisee and a leader – a member of the Ruling Council, no less. He is in the government. In the United Kingdom, think House of Lords or the Cabinet Office. In America, think Senator.

How Does the Conversation Start? (3:2)

Nicodemus makes an opening statement. He is affirming Jesus. He calls him 'Rabbi', which means 'teacher'. He is not blind to the possibility that Jesus has come from God. The signs that Jesus is doing seem to suggest this. Nicodemus is weighing the evidence, which

140

is what he has been trained to do. He is moving carefully towards a possible conclusion that God is with Jesus. This isn't belief like the blind man who sees and worships Jesus. It's exploratory.

When people start a meeting with that kind of speech, you always know that they have more to say. He is just preparing the ground with an affirming introduction. Nicodemus is a highly educated theologian. Nicodemus is on the Ruling Council. He has some questions – which he never gets a chance to ask.

How Does Jesus Respond? (3:3)

Jesus replies, 'Very truly I tell you, no one can see the kingdom of God unless they are born again' (3:3). This is totally surprising. If it had been me, I would have made much more effort to be conciliatory and honouring to Nicodemus. That is because important, influential and clever people impress me, and there is something in me that wants to impress them and connect with them. Jesus doesn't seem to be operating from that place at all. We are getting a good insight into how Jesus interacts with powerful people. He's very pleasant. But he is quite confrontational. What Jesus does is take charge of the meeting and reset the agenda on a topic of his choosing. He gets Nicodemus completely on the back foot.

He tells Nicodemus that what he needs is a completely new start. This is shocking. You can hear Nicodemus sucking all the air out of the room. Nicodemus knows what 'born again' means. When Gentiles, or people who are not Jewish, decide to believe in Israel's God they are described as being 'born again'. And Jesus says, 'That is what you need, Nicodemus.' Shocking.

How Does the Conversation Develop? (3:4–10)

Nicodemus is so wrong-footed, all he can do is try to pretend that he doesn't know what Jesus means: 'How can someone be born when they are old? . . . Surely they cannot enter a second time into their mother's womb to be born!' (3:4).

We'll see in a minute that this is a bit feeble, really. But it is obviously the best he can manage in the circumstances. Nicodemus is just not used to people talking to him like this. Jesus doesn't let him off. He hits him with the longer version: 'Very truly I tell you, no one can enter the kingdom of God unless they are born of water and the Spirit. Flesh gives birth to flesh, but the Spirit gives birth to spirit. You should not be surprised at my saying, "You must be born again"' (3:5–7).

'Nicodemus, you are telling me that you can see that God is working through me. Let me tell you, God wants to come and work through you. God wants to come and start a new life in you by water and Spirit. And that is going to be such a profound change in you that it will be like starting your life all over again.'

Nicodemus is reeling. He is nearly finished. All the clever questions and penetrating enquiry are gone: 'How can this be?' he asks (3:9).

In the notes of the meeting that we have, now written up in the Gospel, this is the only other sentence that Nicodemus says. Nicodemus the powerful man, the highly trained teacher and the member of the Ruling Council finds himself being teased in a hugely challenging way: 'You are Israel's teacher . . . and do you not understand these things?' (3:10).

What Does Jesus Mean?

'You', he says: this is Personal. 'Must', he says: this isn't an option. 'Be', he says: this isn't something to do. This isn't an action you can tick off or a skill you can master. Be is a state of being. A baby isn't an action, a skill or a behaviour. A baby is a human being. 'You must be a spiritual being, Nicodemus. For you to be a spiritual being as well as a human being, the Spirit of God has to blow right through your life. To become a child of God, you must be born of water and the Spirit. You must be born again.'

Let's tackle from this from three places: sociology, history and Scripture.

SOCIOLOGY
Jesus is describing a liminal space. A liminal space is the time between two realities. It is the time between 'what was' and 'what's next'. It is a place of transition, waiting and not knowing. Liminal space is where all transformation in our lives takes place,

if we learn to wait and let it form us. A baby, at birth, moves from womb to world. It's a big transition. Moving from not breathing to breathing. Not eating to eating. Not seeing to seeing. Not speaking to crying. There are many liminal spaces in life. Moving from working life to retired life or from single life to married life or from student to worker are all movements through a liminal space. Moving through a bereavement is to go through a particularly dark and difficult liminal space.

All liminal spaces are uncertain, confusing, dark and sometimes dangerous. There is loss of control. There is loss of certainty. The familiar landmarks of life disappear. We can see that happening to Nicodemus in just three sentences.

Becoming a follower of Jesus – being born again – is to go through a liminal space. To have God blow right through us is a massive change. To come alive as a spiritual being is a massive change. To have God take charge of our life is a massive change. Why do we resist God? Why do we resist being born again? Why do we resist the blowing of the Spirit in our lives? Because we don't like the liminal space. We don't like the loss of control. Like Nicodemus, we try to cling grimly to what is familiar. But liminal spaces have the potential for the greatest transformation we will ever experience. Which is why on a good day we all deeply desire them.

HISTORY

At the time of Jesus, the Jewish faith was very attractive to others. The Jewish people believed in One God. Everyone else was into this mad polytheism with multiple competing gods. The gods were often more flawed, violent and irresponsible than humans. Israel was different. Israel trusted in their Creator God who was a Just God, a Righteous God, a Loving God and a Father God. People from a pagan background did turn to faith in Israel's God. When that happened, those people were baptised. They were described as being born again.

This is where we see that Nicodemus is caught on the hop. Nicodemus is being difficult. He doesn't like what Jesus says. Why should a respected, highly educated teacher of the Jewish faith need to be born again? That is what the pagans need.

Jesus isn't teaching something new. This teaching is in the Hebrew Bible. Ezekiel, one of Israel's greatest teachers and prophets, foresaw a time when God would move among his people in a fresh way, in a way they had never experienced before:

> I will sprinkle clean water on you, and you will be clean; I will cleanse you from all your impurities and from all your idols. I will give you a new heart and put a new spirit in you; I will remove from you your heart of stone and give you a heart of flesh. And I will put my Spirit in you and move you to follow my decrees and be careful to keep my laws.
> (Ezek. 36:25–7)

A whole new life. Born again by water and by Spirit. Jesus is teaching Israel's teacher from Israel's Bible.

How Does the Conversation Finish?

Now that Nicodemus has gone quiet, Jesus has a couple more things he wants Nicodemus to know. And they are both about Jesus himself. After all, Nicodemus has come to find out more about Jesus. But Nicodemus needs Jesus to quieten his leadership and teaching abilities before he can hear Jesus. Strong leaders and gifted teachers can struggle to get to know people. Their heads are just too full of their own material. Now that Jesus has sorted that out, Jesus is not afraid to talk to Nicodemus about who he is. He doesn't hold back from being open about himself just because of who Nicodemus is. He wants Nicodemus to know that he is authentic. And he makes another really surprising statement about who he is.

AUTHENTICITY (3:11–13)

'I do know what I am talking about,' is what Jesus says. 'I am talking about stuff I know and stuff that I have seen' (3:11–12). 'The reason I know what I am talking about is because of where I have come from and the insight that I have': 'No one has ever gone into heaven except the one who came from heaven – the Son of Man' (3:13).

It's a bold disclosure.

This is for Nicodemus. But it is also Jesus talking to himself. When people come probing you and investigating what you are saying, it is good to remind yourself of where you have come from and how you know what you know. The thing about Jesus is that he never went to the recognised schools. He doesn't have an educational and professional CV. This constantly troubles the authorities. How does he know what he knows? The reason it is so troubling is because Jesus is so good. He is confident in how he handles Scripture. He has such depth to his knowledge. He has such authority to his teaching. But nobody knows who taught him. It is all very puzzling. Jesus begins to open up about this and reveal himself. He does have credentials – just not the ones they were expecting. He isn't just making all this up. Like any good teacher, he has also been a good learner – just not from someone the authorities have on their list of qualified people who can train teachers to teach.

SURPRISING STATEMENT – IDENTITY (3:14–15)
Jesus doesn't stop there. He has another surprising statement to make: 'Just as Moses lifted up the snake in the wilderness, so the Son of Man must be lifted up, that everyone who believes may have eternal life in him' (3:14–15).

Jesus describes who he is. This is a statement of identity. He takes one of the stories from the Exodus, the healing snake, and tells Nicodemus, 'That story is about me.' We should not be too surprised by this. We are getting very used to knowing Jesus by reading the Old Testament. But for Nicodemus, it must be very surprising. It has been one of those evenings.

The story of the healing snake comes at a point in the Exodus story where the people have become impatient and are grumbling. Again. Why are we on this wretched journey? There is no bread. There is no water. We hate the food (Num. 21:4–5). Keep those statements in mind. God judges his people and sends a mini plague of venomous snakes that bite them. The people repent and ask Moses to pray for them, which he does. And God says to make a healing snake and put it up on a pole: 'So, Moses made a bronze snake and put it up on

CALLED TO BE FRIENDS

a pole. Then when anyone was bitten by a snake and looked at the bronze snake, they lived' (Num. 21:9).

The sign of God's judgment, the snake, is lifted up on a pole, and when people look at it, they live. We have the benefit of knowing immediately what this is all about, because we know that God judged Jesus for our sin when he was lifted up on the cross so that we can be healed. But for Nicodemus, it must be so strange and surprising – which just goes to confirm how highly trained Jesus is. To see who he is and what he has to do from such an obscure story is remarkable. But once you have seen it, it all makes perfect sense.

These surprising statements are working at a number of levels. For Jesus, he is restating who he is. To be well versed in your identity is very healthy. For us, who know, it is exciting and revealing. We feel very drawn to Jesus. He is opening the door of his heart to us. For Nicodemus, it is very challenging. He is going to have to think about all this for quite a while. Like anything we don't understand, he will either have to break through into understanding, or he will just have to walk away.

Summary

In this story we see a number of dynamics and interactions.

1. PEOPLE STEPPING TOWARDS JESUS
Nicodemus starts by affirming Jesus. He does not make a belief statement. But he does make an affirming exploratory statement.

2. PEOPLE PUSHING BACK ON JESUS
Nicodemus does not reject Jesus or seek to stone him. But the questions he asks after Jesus' surprising statement are not exploratory or affirming. They are typical debating questions of someone who is trying to dismantle the other person's position.

3. JESUS CHALLENGING PEOPLE
Jesus challenges Nicodemus in three ways:
- Jesus makes three **surprising statements** that are also revealing of his **identity**: (1) you must be born again; (2) you must be born of water and spirit; and (3) the Son of Man must be lifted up like the snake in the desert. In all three, Jesus is using

the Old Testament with himself in the middle, drawing on both the Prophet Ezekiel and the Exodus story.

- Jesus challenges Nicodemus, who has really come to question Jesus in order to establish his **authenticity and credibility**. In the time of Jesus, as now, authenticity as a witness to events and credibility to teach were crucially important. If you could not establish your credentials to speak, then you could not be heard. Jesus understands this and states his credentials. Very boldly.

- Jesus makes a **directly challenging** remark about Nicodemus' teaching ability. Or lack of it.

*

We can now look at the story after the second sign. What is going on there?

No Interruptions

You can read this story of No Interruptions in 5:16–47.

Where Are We and What Time Is It (5:1)?

As with the story of Jesus meeting Nicodemus, we need to borrow the time and place from the previous story, The Healing at the Pool. The reason is that, just as Closing Down the Temple moves straight into the Nicodemus story, The Healing at the Pool flows very naturally into this one. With this story, the join is even closer. The concluding sentence of The Healing at the Pool is the opening sentence of this conversation. Although, we should probably start calling them arguments, because that is what they have become. We are in Jerusalem (5:1).

Who Starts the Argument (5:16–18)?

Some pretty angry people: 'For this reason they tried all the more to kill him; not only was he breaking the Sabbath, but he was

147

even calling God his own Father, making himself equal with God' (5:18).

In the previous story, Nicodemus is considered, open and reflective. We see that side of him again a bit later (7:50–1). These people are different. They are angry. We saw how Jesus didn't let Nicodemus do much talking. Jesus certainly didn't let him set the agenda. In this story, Jesus ups his game on that. He doesn't let them speak at all. We can feel the tension in the air. We can sense that people are drawing in breath and are about to speak. But Jesus doesn't leave a gap. It's a bit like some of those interviews we sometimes see on the news where the person trying to ask the questions just can't stop the other person from speaking.

How Does Jesus Respond? (5:19–23)

We saw with the Nicodemus story how Jesus spoke of his authenticity. He knows what he is talking about. He has credentials. In Jesus' response to these people's anger, we see a similar thing. But his first response is not about his authenticity. It's about his **authority**:

> Jesus gave them this answer: 'Very truly I tell you, the Son can do nothing by himself; he can do only what he sees his Father doing, because whatever the Father does the Son also does. For the Father loves the Son and shows him all he does. Yes, and he will show him even greater works than these, so that you will be amazed.
> (5:19–23)

Jesus knows that he is acting and teaching with great authority. He also knows why he has that authority. His authority does not come from his position. He has not been appointed by anyone. He does not have a defined leadership role in the organisation. Neither has he received a democratic mandate from the people. The authority of Jesus comes entirely from his relationship with the Father. Three times in this argument, with only him talking, Jesus draws back the veil on his relationship with the Father. Their relationship is not just close; it is filled with empowering authority.

	Father	Son	
5:20	Loves the Son	Can do nothing by himself	5:19
5:20	Shows him all he does	Only does what he sees his Father doing	5:19
5:20	Will show him even greater works than these	Does whatever the Father does	5:19
5:21	Raises the dead and gives them life	Gives life	5:21
5:22	Entrusts all judgment to the Son	Will be honoured as the Father is honoured	5:23
5:26	Has life in himself	Granted by the Father to have life in himself	5:26
5:27	Has given the Son authority to judge	Judges only as he hears	5:30

To have authority releases and empowers the individual to act on behalf of those in charge. Those who have authority know that the full power and the full extent of the resources of those in charge will be at their disposal should the occasion demand it. In the UK, police generally do not carry weapons. Their vehicles have blue lights. When stopping a car, they use the blue lights. Blue lights by themselves do not make cars stop. But most drivers do stop. That is authority in action. The power is kept in reserve. If the driver does not stop at the blue lights, then the full force of the organisation will be deployed to stop the car. Those who have authority given to them in this way act entirely in line with the wishes, requirements and purposes of those who sent them. An ambassador speaks as the government. The policewoman acts as the police chief. In the UK, the soldier acts for the Crown. The person with authority is not just fulfilling a task. They are representing and being the person who sent them.

Jesus opens his heart. It is a beautiful thing to see because Jesus is under pressure here. But he tells them clearly and directly that he does these things because he has authority. His authority does not come from blue lights. It comes from love – the love of the Father. There is the security of equality. The Son is not lesser than the Father. This is what causes his Jewish audience so much difficulty. By describing his relationship with God as Father–Son, Jesus is making himself equal with God (5:18). Jesus doesn't deny or soften that. He restates it multiple times. There is willing interdependency, a two-way trust. The Son can only do what he sees the Father doing. The Father could withhold, but he doesn't. He loves the Son and shows him all he does. The Father has given all judgment to the Son. The Son is Head of Judgment. The Father trusts the Son to do it. But the Son says, 'I only judge as I hear. I have been given responsibilities, but I am listening all the time to the Father.' Jesus isn't a bureaucrat just following rules and procedures. He is following the Father. There is endless affirmation. Jesus knows he is the Son. He is trusted. He is relied on. Jesus knows he is loved by his Father. He is affirmed. He is cherished. He is appreciated. He is highly thought of. And in that relationship of loving affirmation flows incredible empowering authority.

We are not used to authority flowing through relationships. We think more of relationships being close and kind and warm and intimate. This adds a whole other dimension to what can happen when we know God and live in his love.

The other question that we must consider is: how does Jesus know that this is who he is, and this is how his relationship with God would work out? Where does he get these ideas from that obviously affect him so deeply? We will consider this more when we look at the Old Testament stories that lie underneath.

How Does the Argument Develop? (5:24–30)

Having spoken of his authority, as with Nicodemus, Jesus makes the first of his surprising statements: 'Very truly I tell you, whoever hears my word and believes him who sent me has eternal life and will not be judged but has crossed over from death to life' (5:24).

Hearing Jesus' word and believing in the Father who has sent his Son is the step that brings the person into eternal life. Eternal life is not something that will happen in the future, at the end of the age. Eternal life starts in the present life. There is a judgment to come that this person will not face. They have 'crossed over'. By believing, they have moved from judgment and death into life.

This is the same sort of language as being born again. It is coming into a new life, a new state of being. Crossing over from death and judgment into a whole new life and state of being is the Exodus story: 'Then Moses stretched out his hand over the sea, and all that night the Lord drove the sea back with a strong east wind and turned it into dry land. The waters were divided, and the Israelites went through the sea on dry ground, with a wall of water on their right and on their left' (Exod. 14:21–2).

Israel was facing death at the hands of the Egyptian army. But through Moses hearing God and acting in authority combined with God working in power, the nation crossed over from death to life and escaped the judgment that was then inflicted on Egypt. Such was the power and excitement of this moment, moving from certain death into newness of life, that great songs were written to celebrate it that are still being sung (Exod. 15:1–21).

Jesus follows this surprising statement with another: 'Very truly I tell you, a time is coming and has now come when the dead will hear the voice of the Son of God and those who hear will live' (5:25). This is Ezekiel. In a vision, God brings the prophet into a valley filled with dry bones. God then tells him to speak to the bones. As Ezekiel speaks with authority, the bones come together; tendons, flesh and skin appear, and the breath of life enters into them. They stand up. A vast army (Ezek. 37:1–14).

In the time of Jesus, resurrection from the dead is not a central feature of Jewish belief. A whole section of Judaism doesn't believe in it at all because it has anti-Roman political associations and they are trying to get along with the Empire, not challenge them. Ezekiel's story is the main Resurrection story in the Hebrew Bible. Those who do believe in the resurrection of the dead see that as happening at the end of the age.

Jesus takes this great story and places himself in the middle of it. As with Nicodemus, Jesus repeats his surprising statement, but in a longer version (5:28–30). After the resurrection there will be a judgment of works. And he will be the judge. This is what makes the Exodus reference so important. Those who believe have already 'crossed over'. They will not be judged – at least not in this way.

How Does the Argument Finish? (5:31–47)

With Jesus still talking. Like the Nicodemus story, Jesus has some matters he wants them to know. He is anticipating their questions about his authenticity. And he is also challenging their practice. Do they really know the Bible as well as they say they do?

AUTHENTICITY — AUTHENTIC PERSONS
Authenticity as a teacher is significantly linked in Jewish culture to the testimony of qualified people. One of the most recognised and respected teachers of the time is Gamaliel. If Gamaliel says you are good, then you are good. He wouldn't say that unless he knows that you are.

Jesus has testimony from a qualified person (5:31–2). His hearers look at John who baptises as a qualified person (5:33–5). But Jesus has someone testifying for him who is even more qualified, has greater weight and is more up to date than John. His Father. Oh dear. This isn't going to go well. Fasten your seatbelts. But it does highlight the difficulty in having an argument about authenticity. At a human level, authenticity works in self-contained systems. People who have the power to authenticate others always authenticate others who are like them and who substantially agree with them. People who have been authenticated find it very difficult to listen to and hear from those who aren't inside their group of authenticated people, who are naturally teaching the complete truth. Arguments between people who are in different but self-authentic groups are usually very bitter and rarely resolved. Think of American politics.

AUTHENTICITY — AUTHENTIC METHOD
This is why Jesus makes some remarks about how to have a methodology to establish authenticity. How are we going to establish what the truth is and who is authentic? Answer: study the Scriptures. He obviously puts it negatively because he is in an argument, and this is what they are *not* doing. But it can equally be read as a positive instruction: 'You study the Scriptures diligently because you think that in them you have eternal life. These are the very Scriptures that testify about me, yet you refuse to come to me to have life' (5:39–40).

This makes what we are doing so exciting. We are reading the Gospel of John and the Hebrew Bible to discover Jesus and come to him and have life. Jesus says to them, 'You say you are authentic, but your methodology doesn't bear scrutiny. It isn't me you are going to have to answer to. It's Moses. He wrote about me and you claim to be following him and are basing your claim to authenticity on him' (5:45–7). This is an incredibly audacious claim. It makes me laugh, it is so bold. And yet it is so true. What it means for us is that, as long as we stick to the simple method of reading the Bible to find Jesus, we should be fine.

Challenge

Jesus says to Nicodemus, 'You are Israel's teacher, but you don't understand.' In this argument he goes quite a lot further in the challenge. 'You have never heard God's voice. You have never seen God. His word doesn't live in you. You refuse to come to me. You don't have God's love in your hearts. You accept praise from each other, but you don't seek praise from God.'

In an argument like this, it is actually kind to say what you really think. In situations like this we don't help other people when we think one thing but say something different. Jesus is very confident, clear and open hearted. As before, we are seeing a different side to him. But one that is very much part of him. People don't get killed for healing the sick and teaching about God's love. You get killed for challenging the powers that are ruling in the wrong way.

The Story So Far

These are complex and dense passages. But actually, they both follow a simple structure. By bringing them together in this way, as with the other sets of stories, we are able to see what is going on. The whole narrative of these two stories can be teased out into six categories of speech. They are overlapping and they do interact. But each part of the dialogue fits fairly easily into one.

People in the arguments come to Jesus in two ways:

1. STEPPING TOWARDS JESUS

This can be exploratory and affirming, as with Nicodemus. 'Rabbi, we know that you are a teacher who has come from God.' As we work through the other stories, we will find that, in a few cases, exploration turns to belief.

2. PUSHING BACK ON JESUS

This can be with questions, as with Nicodemus. He stops affirming Jesus and we see the real reason why he has come – to probe, examine and test him. It can also be outright opposition and rejection, as in the second story. They try to kill him. There will be much more of this as we look at the other stories in this group.

*

The next four categories are the ways Jesus responds to people:

3. SURPRISING STATEMENTS

As we have seen, Jesus uses the Exodus story and the prophecies of Ezekiel to say very surprising things to people. These things catch them off guard but speak strongly of his **identity**.

4. AUTHENTICITY AND CREDIBILITY

Jesus speaks strongly as to how he is an **authentic and credible** person. 'I do know what I am talking about. I am telling you what I have seen and heard. I am not just making this up. I am an authentic person who has been validated. It just happens to be John who baptises, the Father and the Scriptures who authenticate me.'

5. AUTHORITY

Jesus explains where his **authority** comes from. 'I don't have a human position or a recognised role. My authority comes from my relationship with the Father. I am speaking and acting entirely for him and he has empowered me to do this.'

6. DIRECT CHALLENGE

Jesus tells the truth. He tells people what he really thinks about their condition before God. They claim to know God and understand the Bible, but it would appear to him that neither of these are true. Because he loves them, Jesus wants them to know the truth.

*

Both these stories are made up of this beautiful weaving together of people responding to Jesus and Jesus responding to people. They are presented as live events with detailed dialogue. John the author wants us to hear and see first-hand the heart of Jesus. He knows that when Jesus is under scrutiny and pressure, he speaks of who he is in the clearest way.

The question is: how many more of these stories are there? It turns out that there are five more. It would appear that this aspect of Jesus is something that John is most interested in.

15

Bread and Water

The Bread of Life

The next story in this panel is found in 6:22–71. While the dialogue all flows together and the story can be read as a single argument, it also conveys the impression that this is an argument that happens over a period of time and keeps being revisited. You know that family row that is difficult to resolve because nobody will back down and it drags on for days, if not weeks. This is one of those.

Where Are We and What Time Is It? (6:1–4, 16–17, 22–4)

We are in Galilee, on the other side of the lake to the feeding of the five thousand (6:25). The disciples did set off for Capernaum (6:16–17), which is where the crowd head when they realise Jesus isn't still with them (6:24). They saw the disciples leave in the boat, but not Jesus, so it is all a bit confusing. We do know that some teaching was given in the Synagogue in Capernaum (6:59). Like the other two stories in this panel, we are borrowing the time from the previous story. The Passover is near (6:4).

Who Starts the Conversation? (6:25)

The crowd want to know more about how Jesus managed to get to Capernaum (6:25). After all, he didn't appear to go with the disciples and he certainly didn't come with them. The start of this story is a bit more like Nicodemus. The opening question is potentially **stepping towards** him and seems to be because of genuine interest in Jesus' travel arrangements.

How Does Jesus Respond? (6:26–34)

But Jesus starts by being **challenging.** He tells them straight. They have worked hard to find him because he met their needs so spectacularly. But they don't see the meaning of the sign that he did in feeding the five thousand. When it comes to effort, working for bread is one thing. They need to put more effort into getting the food that endures for eternal life, which he will give them. They need to see beyond the sign of multiplying bread to who he is and what he gives. God has set his seal of approval on him. He is an **authentic** person (6:26–7). It doesn't take much challenge from Jesus to reveal where the crowd is at. Like Nicodemus, they move straight into **pushing back** on him. It's not a humble enquiry. Their questions are coming from a place of testing Jesus. They are trying to catch him out: 'What must we do to do the works God requires?' (6:28).

This is tricky. It isn't a nice question. The Law of Moses is taught every week in Capernaum. Everyone knows what God wants you to do. If Jesus says give your tithe and love your wife, then he is just like all the other teachers. If he says something different, then he is in trouble for teaching against the Law. As in the story after The Healing at the Pool, Jesus moves to **authority** mode: 'The work of God is this: to believe in the one he has sent' (6:29).

The work they need to do is believe. This is clever. Jesus is calling them back to their roots, back to Abraham. Except that he also places himself alongside God in the middle of their story. When God chose his people, he began with one couple to whom he gave new names: Abraham and Sarah. God called them to be his friends and made a covenant with them. A covenant was a mutual, faithful commitment between two parties that was made with solemn promises sworn with an oath. A covenant marker was set up, often a pillar with the promises inscribed on them. The covenant was sealed in a sacrifice and celebrated with a meal, demonstrating that both parties had now entrusted themselves to each other. It was a very common practice at the time. God made Abraham and Sarah promises that they simply could not fulfil unless God worked. They were to have children, become a nation that belonged to God, be given a land to live in peace and prosperity, and through them everyone in the whole world would be blessed. You

157

can read the covenant story in Genesis 12, 15 and 17. Abraham, we are told, 'believed the Lord, and he credited it to him as righteousness' (Gen. 15:6).

Abraham didn't just believe in the sense that he thought God existed. Abraham believed in the sense that he gave himself completely to God, entrusting himself, his family and his whole future entirely into God's hands. This is covenant love, a mutual giving of self that brings God and humanity together as one. It is at the very heart of Jewish and therefore Christian theology.

When God saved Israel from slavery in Egypt and set them on the journey to their new land, it was because of the covenant he had made (Exod. 6:2–8). When God came to them at Sinai, the covenant was restated and renewed (Exod. 19:1–8). The Law was given in the context of covenant love. The Law was given to make clear how God's people were to live in the light of the covenant love they had received and the promises they had entered into to be God's people.

So what Jesus does here is take them back to basics. To belong to God, the 'work' is not this law or that law. The 'work' is to do what Abraham did – believe God. The 'work' is to entrust yourself completely to God and his Word. What Jesus does is include himself right at the centre of what it means to believe God. They are to entrust themselves and give themselves to him. This is exactly the same argument that the Apostle Paul makes in Romans and Galatians. Only he takes a bit longer about it.

Not unexpectedly, the people want a sign to prove Jesus' authority as one sent from God. They are still testing and **pushing back** on him. This is deeply ironic, given the sign that they have just witnessed of feeding thousands with five loaves. But that simply underlines that seeing miracles doesn't mean that you have seen Jesus. Perhaps, because bread is on their minds, they choose the example of manna in the wilderness. We are in the Exodus story again. Manna from God fed the people on their long journey through the wilderness. It was bread from heaven that kept them alive. Can Jesus match Moses? (6:30–1).

Jesus is comfortable with this. He takes them on, remaining in **authority**. 'Manna wasn't from Moses. It was my Father who gave it, and it is available now': 'It is not Moses who has given you the bread from heaven, but it is my Father who gives you the true bread from heaven. For the bread of God is the bread that comes down from heaven and gives life to the world' (6:32–3).

How do people respond? You can hear the sarcasm and the growing sense of them **pushing back** on Jesus: 'Sir . . . always give us this bread' (6:34).

This isn't someone praying an early version of the Lord's prayer. This is someone trying to reveal that Jesus is all hot air by calling his bluff.

How Does the Conversation Develop? (6:35–59)

Jesus gives it to them. He surprises, challenges and reveals his authority to them.

Jesus makes a **surprising statement**: 'I am the bread of life' (6:35). Jesus says, 'That story points to me. A new and greater Exodus is happening. You will need daily nourishment to go on the journey that God has for you. I am your bread. You will feed on me.' We will look at this more when we dive into the Old Testament that lies underneath these stories.

Jesus makes a **challenging observation**: 'You have seen me and still you do not believe' (6:36). He knows where they are at. He knows that their questions are not believing questions but unbelieving, **push-back** questions.

Jesus reveals his **authority**: 'All those the Father gives me will come to me, and whoever comes to me I will never drive away' (6:37). He and the Father are working together. We get the sense that Jesus knows this is not going well and that people are going to walk away. If you have come to feed and save people with eternal life, it is incredibly disappointing when they walk away. How could God's people turn away from God? But Jesus knows that is part of the story. In affirming his authority to keep safe all who come to him, he is speaking as much to himself as anyone (6:38–40).

The people don't get it. They can't see it. They start grumbling. They are Jesus' neighbours. They know his mum and dad. What is all this coming down from heaven nonsense? They **push back** on him (6:41–2). Jesus is very patient. He stays in the argument. He restates his authority, touches on his authenticity and makes the second of his surprising statements in this story.

Jesus reveals his **authority**: 'No one can come to me unless the Father who sent me draws them, and I will raise them up at the last day' (6:44). He and the Father are working together. Together they will gather God's people and raise them to life.

Jesus reveals his **authenticity**: 'No one has seen the Father except the one who is from God; only he has seen the Father' (6:46). 'I do know what I am talking about,' he tells them.

Jesus makes a **surprising statement**: 'I am the living bread that came down from heaven. Whoever eats this bread will live for ever. This bread is my flesh, which I will give for the life of the world' (6:51).

Jesus is so courageous. The argument isn't going well. The people can't see what he is saying. They are getting increasingly hostile. But he doesn't hold back. He reveals more about how he is the bread that gives life. The source of nourishment that is going to feed the world is his death on the cross. That is the food that will give eternal life.

We have such good seats on this story. We are looking at the story after the death of Jesus and the giving of his flesh to bring life to the world. We are looking at the story with the meaning explained to us. His body was broken to bring life to us. For the people who are in the story, it isn't surprising that the opposition to Jesus grows. It just doesn't make sense to them. They **push back** on Jesus: 'Then the Jews began to argue sharply among themselves, "How can this man give us his flesh to eat?"' (6:52).

And now we get to the **surprising statement** that surpasses all surprising statements so far:

> Very truly I tell you, unless you eat the flesh of the Son of Man and drink his blood, you have no life in you. Whoever eats my flesh and drinks my blood has eternal life, and I will raise them up at the last day. For my flesh is real food and my blood is real drink. Whoever eats my flesh and drinks my blood remains in me, and I in them.
> (6:53–6)

This is Ezekiel. It is a direct quote from Ezekiel, which in the original prophecy is equally emphatic and graphic. A sacrifice is prepared in Israel. God calls to the birds and wild animals:

> Assemble and come together from all around to the sacrifice I am preparing for you, the great sacrifice on the mountains of Israel. There you

will eat flesh and drink blood. You will eat the flesh of mighty men and drink the blood of the princes of the earth as if they were rams and lambs, goats and bulls.
(Ezek. 39:17–18)

Now for Jesus to take this scripture and apply it to himself is a bold theological step. But as we see in all these stories, Jesus takes many surprising scriptures from Ezekiel and applies them to himself.

What Does Jesus Mean?

We have to remind ourselves that the scripture Jesus is using is from where Ezekiel sees an apocalyptic vision. Ezekiel sees spiritual reality. The problem with seeing spiritual reality is that there are no words to describe it, because all our words come from our own, earthly, reality. So the way these visions are put into words is with symbols, metaphors and exaggerated language. The book of Ezekiel opens with a heavenly vision. He describes God appearing in immense clouds with 'flashing lightning' and 'brilliant light' (Ezek. 1:4). He sees a fire that is like glowing metal, in the middle of which are four living creatures that each have four faces and four wings (Ezek. 1:5–7). Spread out over their heads is a vault and a throne. On the throne is a figure like a man, who from the waist up looks like glowing metal, full of fire (1:22–7). These are all attempts to put into words that which is beyond words. After seeing this vision, and being called to be a prophet, Ezekiel is sent to the people of God who are living in exile in Babylonia. He has to lie down for a week (Ezek. 3:15). I have some sympathy with that.

We need to treat this vision of God's victory and sacrifice in Ezekiel 39 as a similar apocalyptic vision. Ezekiel is describing something that can only be put into words using images and metaphors. We need to look through the imagery to understand what he has seen.

Ezekiel sees a tremendous battle in which the enemies of God – Gog and Magog – come against God's people. On the mountains of Israel they are defeated. God's name will be known all over the world. The weapons the enemy has used will all be destroyed. The land will be cleansed. A sacrifice will be prepared in Israel for the birds and wild animals. They will eat the flesh and drink the blood of the sacrifice in which all the powers that stand against God have been defeated. God will restore his people. They will forget their unfaithfulness. He will gather his people from the nations and the long exile will be over. God will pour out his Spirit on his people (Ezek. 39:1–29).

As an understanding of the cross of Christ, this is pretty profound. Through the cross of Christ, God's enemies have been gathered and defeated. Through the cross of Christ, God's name is being made known all over the world. Through the cross of Christ, all the weapons of the powers of darkness are being picked up and destroyed. Through the cross of Christ, our lives are made clean. Through the cross of Christ, a sacrifice has been prepared that changes everything and defeats all our enemies. Through the cross of Christ, God is restoring us and pouring his Spirit out on us. Through the cross of Christ, the long exile is ended.

There are a couple of points that need a little thinking through. First, it would appear that we are cast in the role of the birds and wild animals because we are invited to drink the blood and eat the flesh of the sacrifice. That isn't very flattering to us. But it is just a metaphor, just as eating flesh and drinking blood are metaphors that convey a deeper reality. It isn't the only place where Jesus uses imagery about birds. If we can briefly jump out of John into Matthew's Gospel, Jesus tells a parable about the kingdom of God where he likens it to a small seed that becomes a tree that is so large that the birds of the air come and nest in the branches (Matt. 13:32). I am pretty sure Jesus does not mean that the expansion of God's kingdom work will lead to the building of aviaries and the keeping of pigeons. It's a metaphor used to convey spiritual realities.

The other complicated aspect is that the sacrifice in Ezekiel's vision is of the powers. Ezekiel sees that the enemies of God, mighty men and the princes are killed. And Ezekiel sees that their blood is like sacrificial blood. Jesus takes these two metaphors and puts himself in the middle. It would appear that on the cross, Jesus took all the darkness into himself, just as he took all sin upon himself. The sacrificial blood that was shed is both the defeat of God's enemies and nourishment for God's people. The Apostle Paul uses this language: 'And having disarmed the powers and authorities, he made a public spectacle of them, triumphing over them by the cross' (Col. 2:15).

We are more used to the cross being a place where Jesus took on all our sin so that we might have forgiveness. We are less familiar with the cross being the place where Jesus took on all the dark powers so that we might have victory. But both are wonderfully true. Jesus' blood was shed. Our sins are forgiven. The powers of darkness were defeated. And we are nourished in this.

How Does the Argument Finish? (6:60–70)

Many of his disciples can't accept this (6:61). They are offended. Jesus speaks again of his **authenticity**. He has come from heaven and will return. His words are life giving (6:62–3). He **challenges** them. There are some who do not believe. He knew this would happen (6:64). He affirms his **authority** and the fact that he and the Father are working together: 'This is why I told you that no one can come to me unless the Father has enabled them' (6:65).

This is a moment of profound change. Following the feeding of the five thousand, Jesus starts being much more open about the cross. It does not get the public vote. That is not the sort of Messiah that they want. They don't like the laying down of life. They don't understand that it is by giving his flesh that God's King will come. Many of his disciples walk away (6:66).

It is here that the Twelve make a brief appearance in the Gospel. Apart from when Thomas refuses to believe and is identified by John as one of them (20:24), this is the only point that the Twelve appear, with Jesus **challenging** them as to whether they want to walk away too (6:67). John wants us to know that even the Twelve are something of a mixed bag. Simon Peter makes a great statement that shows he is getting to know Jesus: 'Lord, to whom shall we go? You have the words of eternal life. We have come to believe and to know that you are the Holy One of God' (6:68–9).

Jesus has chosen them. But one of them will betray him.

Water Within

The next Contention story is found in 7:1–8:1. As before, I suggest that you live in the scripture for a while. Let it soak into you. Then see how the argument works, using the six categories of speech we have identified from the other Contentions. If you need to refresh your mind on these, you can find them on pages 154–5.

This is another argument that probably went on for several days. John has carefully edited the various strands together.

Where Are We and What Time Is It? (7:1–2, 9–10)

It is getting much more dangerous for Jesus. He deliberately stays up north. He is safer there. But the Festival of Tabernacles is near (7:1–2). Jesus loves the festivals. So he comes to Jerusalem secretly and not with his brothers (7:9–10). It is in Jerusalem that this argument happens.

Who Starts the Argument? (7:3–15)

His brothers are the first step. It must be strange for them, their brother being so well known and yet increasingly controversial. However, they are, as far as they are able, **affirming** towards him. Public figures should go to public places (7:1–4). But they are not believing. John helpfully clarifies that for us (7:5). They don't understand *how* Jesus is going to become a public figure. They are thinking of crowds, public speeches and signs. They are not thinking about death and the cross. So Jesus **challenges** them: 'My time is not yet here; for you any time will do. The world cannot hate you, but it hates me because I testify that its works are evil' (7:6). He stays behind in Galilee and comes to Jerusalem secretly by himself (7:9–10).

The leaders are looking for him. The people are divided. They are questioning of him. Some say he is good. Others think there is something deceptive going on. When he does begin to teach, the authorities' assessment of him is very like that of Nicodemus. In a strange sort of a way they are **affirming** of him: 'How did this man get such learning without having been taught?' (7:15). As we have seen before, the striking thing about Jesus is how good he is as a teacher, without having been to any of the recognised schools.

How Does Jesus Respond? (7:16–27)

Jesus reveals his **authority**. It isn't his teaching; it is God's word he is speaking (7:16). There is a fairly straightforward test to check that he an **authentic** person. 'Am I seeking personal glory? Am I trying to promote my own name and my reputation? Am I trying to be better known? Or am I seeking God's glory because he sent me? I am not doing this for me. I am doing this for him' (7:17–18). Jesus **challenges** them: 'Why are you trying to kill me? That is against the law' (7:19).

The people don't get it. They don't get Jesus and they don't get the threat that is rising against him. They **push back** on him. He must have some kind of demonic problem (7:20).

Jesus **challenges** them again. The threat to him is because he has exposed the corruption of both Temple and Sabbath. His healing on the Sabbath has made him an enemy of the state. But their Sabbaths are based on ridiculous regulations. If circumcision is permitted on the Sabbath, why not healing (7:21–4)? These few lines reveal a fascinating insight into the author. The author faithfully reports what Jesus said: 'Moses gave you circumcision.' The author does not edit the statement. But the author is also concerned for the educated reader, who knows that circumcision came from the Patriarchs, not from Moses. So he adds an extra clarifying comment. We suddenly see the author in the text, which is most unusual. He hides himself so well. But here he is, fastidiously accurate in his reporting and yet also smoothing over things that could cause unnecessary difficulties for readers.

This challenge sets off a bit of a discussion among the people. It is all a bit confusing. They are getting mixed messages from the authorities. In the end they **push back** on Jesus. They decide (1) they know where he is from; and (2) if he were the Messiah, they wouldn't know where he were from. They are mistaken in both these conclusions, but never mind.

How Does the Argument Develop? (7:28–39)

Jesus restates his **authority** in pretty bold terms: 'I am not here on my own authority, but he who sent me is true. You do not know him, but I know him because I am from him and he sent me' (7:28–9). This polarises the people. Some try to seize him. Their **pushing back** on Jesus is moving towards rejection. Others **step towards** him. They believe him. The chief priests hear this and try to arrest him. Jesus speaks again of his **authority**. He knows where he has come from. He also knows where he is going. Back to the one who sent him. He is very aware of what gives him authority. But the shadow of the cross is lying across his mind: 'I am with you for only a short time, and then I am going to the one who sent me. You will look for me, but you will not find me; and where I am, you cannot come' (7:33–4). He is a sent one. His authority does come from the Father. But he is sent to die.

Those listening simply don't understand. There are many Jews scattered across the Empire. Greek-speaking people are drawn to Jewish monotheism. Maybe Jesus is going to teach them. As we have seen so many times, Jesus does not engage with the misunderstanding. Instead, he makes his **surprising statement**: 'Let anyone who is thirsty come to me and drink. Whoever believes in me, as Scripture has said, rivers of living water will flow from within them' (7:37–8).

Very wonderfully, this is both the Exodus story and Ezekiel. They come together here. In the Exodus story, the people of God are in the wilderness. They are on their long journey towards their new land and new life. But, as is often a problem in deserts, they run out of water. The running out of water story comes immediately after the running out of food story and God giving bread from heaven. Yet again, the people grumble against Moses. 'Why have you led us out of Egypt? We had a better life there. We don't think God is with us any more.'

God tells Moses to take his staff and stand by a huge rock. God himself will stand with him: '"I will stand there before you by the rock at Horeb. Strike the rock, and water will come out of it for the people to drink." So Moses did this in the sight of the elders of Israel' (Exod. 17:6).

Despite their grumbling and unbelieving and forgetting all that God has done to deliver them, on their great journey out of slavery and to their new land, God provides life-giving water for them in the dry and dusty desert.

In Ezekiel, the prophet sees an extended vision of the rebuilding of the Temple. As with the vision of the great battle and the victory of God that we have looked at, this vision is not of something that was ever built in a physical sense. It is a metaphor that speaks of the glory of God dwelling among his people. A glorious temple space is beautifully placed right in the centre of their lives and their land. From this Temple, with God among his people, flows a river of water that brings life to the nations. 'The man brought me back to the entrance to the temple, and I saw water coming out from under the threshold of the temple towards the east' (Ezek. 47:1).

The river gets deeper and deeper. There are swarms of living creatures. When it empties into the sea, the salty water becomes fresh. There are large numbers of fish. Wherever the river flows, everything lives. Along its bank are trees whose leaves are for healing. This life-filled vision echoes the Garden of Eden, where we also find God and trees, and waters and life. Eden is a temple space too.

What Does Jesus Mean?

Rather surprisingly, the author pops up again. He wants us to understand this one: 'By this he meant the Spirit, whom those who believed in him were later to receive. Up to that time the Spirit had not been given since Jesus had not yet been glorified' (7:39).

Both the Exodus journey and the beautiful vision of Ezekiel have the water of life as a gift from God. The Temple and the Rock are the source. Both are Jesus. He invites us to himself. He is the Rock in the dry space. He is the glorious revealing of God in the garden space. He invites us to come and drink deeply from him. An unending, ever-deepening flow of life will come from him. Wherever the Spirit flows from within us, abundant life will spring up around us. Trees will grow and nations will be healed.

So, which story is it? Are we in the desert? Have we been released from slavery by the death of our Passover lamb who takes away the sins of the world, only to find ourselves struggling in a dry and lifeless place? Does our former life look so much better to us now that we wished we had never begun this journey? Do we feel that if we don't get some refreshment soon on this journey that God has got us on, we are going to be dead? Is the only thing we can see a huge rock that does not seem very promising?

Or are we living the dream? Are we living in a beautiful garden city? Is the very presence of God all around us? Does abundance of life fill every horizon? Is there an ever-deepening flow of God's life-giving power within us? Are we just pulling fish after fish from the water? Does everything look ordered, well designed, all in proportion to itself, with dazzling symmetries and incredible detailing?

The answer, of course, is both. Both are true. For us, the Exodus journey and the Ezekiel vision are both real. Bible teachers have a word for this. It is 'eschatology'. What that strange but important word means is this: our experience of Jesus now is a great foretaste of what is to come. But it lands in the middle of everything that has gone wrong. To follow Jesus is to live in this tension. We receive the outpouring of God's Spirit within us, bringing life all around us. And we are walking through a desert, to a country at which we have not yet arrived. With only God for company. And only God for the refreshment that will keep us alive.

As I look back over my journey with Jesus, there have been many moments when I have been excited, overwhelmed and indeed out of my depth, seeing the life that springs up when the Spirit of God flows. I have also felt, even at the same moment, that I am living in a spiritual desert and I might yet die if I don't get some refreshment from God. But what I am for ever grateful for is that even in the driest desert, the pure life-giving water of the Spirit of Jesus flows from the rock that is Christ and refreshes my soul with himself.

This tension that comes from following Jesus can be difficult to manage. This is probably why the author pops up – to make sure we understand this one. He knows how important it is that we get this.

How Does the Argument Finish? (7:40–52)

Some people **step towards** Jesus. They believe. Others are still **pushing back**. They still have questions about where the Messiah was born. The people are divided. The guards return without arresting him. Jesus has arrested them. The Pharisees are furious. Nicodemus tries to be reflective. But the mind of the authorities is made up.

16

Death and Life

You Will Die in Your Sin

The next Contention story is found in 8:12–59. As before, I suggest that you live in the scripture for a while. Let it speak for itself. Then dig into it and see how the argument works, using the six categories of spoken word that we have identified from the other Contentions. Remember that this has been written so we get to meet with Jesus and know him.

Where Are We and What Time Is It? (8:2, 20, 59)

As the story unfolds, we discover that we are at the Temple. The story opens with Jesus teaching in the Temple courts near where the offerings are placed (8:20). At the end of the story, when they start picking up stones to kill him, he slips away from the Temple grounds (8:59). However, this story has no time check. Unusually, there is no stated connection with any of the festivals, although it is possible that it happened close to the story in chapter 7, at the Festival of Tabernacles. More on that later.

Who Starts the Argument? (8:12)

Jesus starts this one. It's a variation from the stories we have seen so far. He makes one of his **surprising statements that reveal his identity**: 'I am the light of the world. Whoever follows me will never walk in darkness, but will have the light of life' (8:12).

This is from the Exodus story. In the Exodus, the people of God are delivered from slavery in Egypt by God's power and the sacrificial death of the Passover lamb. But having let them go, the Egyptians decide to pursue them and recapture them. Slave masters don't like letting slaves go free. To defend them from the Egyptians, God, who has been lead-

169

ing Israel through angelic presence, comes round the back of Israel and stands between Israel and Egypt. When God does this, he causes the Egyptians to be in darkness. But the people of God are in the light: 'The pillar of cloud also moved from in front and stood behind them, coming between the armies of Egypt and Israel. Throughout the night the cloud brought darkness to the one side and light to the other; so neither went near the other all night long' (Exod. 14:19–20).

God's people are in the light and God's enemies are in the dark. It is at this point that the waters of the Sea are parted. Because God's people are in the light, they are able to cross over to life. It is only after they have crossed over that the Egyptians discover what has happened. As the Egyptians try to pursue Israel into the sea, the waters return over them and they are drowned (Exod. 14:13–28).

The light of the world doesn't light up the whole world. The light of the world brings light to God's people. The world is still in darkness. Isaiah draws on this truth in one of his great prophetic songs (Isa. 60:1–3). Jesus is taking one of the big events of the Exodus story and using it to describe who he is.

How Do the Pharisees Respond? (8:13–20)

They **push back** on Jesus, asserting that talking about himself like this is not valid. He can't just proclaim himself as the Light of the World. Jesus' response to them is to affirm himself. He speaks of his **authenticity**. What he has to say is valid because of where he has come from and where he is going. Because of who he is, he has the perspective required to speak of himself in this way. He can testify to himself. Of course, there still needs to be another witness. In Jewish Law there have to be two witnesses for something to be true. As he has done before, Jesus refers to his Father as the other witness to his identity as Light of the World. There is a strong echo to the Nicodemus story in the way that the Pharisees respond to that. They either do not understand, or, perhaps more likely, pretend not to understand. They **push back** on him. If his Father is going to testify – where is he?

Jesus responds by being **challenging**. 'You just don't get it', he says. 'You don't know me or my Father.' This is very direct. Telling the most qualified teachers of the Bible in the nation that they don't know God is not for the faint-hearted. But no one seizes him because his hour has not come.

How Does the Argument Develop? (8:21–30)

Jesus makes another of his **surprising statements**: 'I am going away, and you will look for me, and you will die in your sin' (8:21).

The authorities who are arguing with Jesus are not really listening to him. They miss the warning. They get stuck on him 'going away'. They start speculating about whether Jesus is going to kill himself. So Jesus gives them the **surprising** warning again: 'I told you that you would die in your sins; if you do not believe that I am he, you will indeed die in your sins' (8:24).

The authorities **push back** on him again. They question him. Who is he to be saying things like this (8:25)? To answer, Jesus reveals more of his **authority**. He has been sent by God. He is saying what God has given him to say. He speaks what the Father has taught him. However, the authorities still don't understand (8:26–9). But some **step towards** him and believe in him (8:30).

What Does Jesus Mean? (8:31–6)

This warning is from Ezekiel. Ezekiel is called by God to be a prophet and to speak God's word to God's people. One of the aspects of this call is to be a watchman for Israel. A watchman, strangely enough, watches out and speaks up. A watchman looks for danger and gives people advance warning of trouble coming. Ezekiel is told by God to warn Israel of the danger of dying in their sins: 'But if you do warn the wicked person to turn from their ways and they do not do so, they will die for their sin' (Ezek. 33:9).

When Ezekiel gives this warning from God, he too encounters opposition and resistance. And he too restates the warning that God has given him, but louder and longer (Ezek. 33:12–16). Jesus is taking Ezekiel's warning and saying it with himself in the middle. People will die in sin unless they believe in him. The way out of being stuck in sin is belief in him. It looks like several people leave at this point. Because Jesus continues arguing with those who have stepped towards him and responded by believing in him, he makes his third **surprising statement**: 'If you hold to my teaching, you are really my disciples. Then you will know the truth, and the truth will set you free' (8:31–2).

Jesus is developing his warning. People are slaves to sin. Only by becoming his disciples and knowing the truth will anyone escape from slavery to sin and be free. To the people of God and the descendants of Abraham, this is a shocking thing to say. This is exactly the same as telling Nicodemus that he needs to be born again. His new followers **push back** on him. They are God's people, descendants of Abraham. The Exodus story is their story. They aren't slaves to anyone. Why would Jesus suggest that they need to be set free? Jesus develops his surprising statement further: 'Very truly I tell you, everyone who sins is a slave to sin. Now a slave has no permanent place in the family, but a son belongs to it for ever. So if the Son sets you free, you will be free indeed' (8:34–6).

It is here that we see Jesus bringing the two Old Testament stories together, Exodus and Ezekiel, and enfolding them together to make the new story that he is telling. Ezekiel's warnings show that there needs to be a new Exodus. There needs to be a new freeing of the slaves. As the slaves are brought into freedom, they will form a new family of God. Because:

1. Sin is a power, as Egypt was a power. Sin isn't just an action, something we do that is wrong. Sin enslaves us. We cannot free ourselves from its powerful grip. And as Ezekiel warns, if nothing is done, we will die in our sin.
2. Slaves to sin don't belong to God's family, no matter who their ancestors are.
3. The Son belongs to God's family.
4. The Son is free from sin.
5. The Son will work like God worked in the Exodus. The Son will set his people free. And then they will be free indeed.

How Does the Argument Finish? (8:37–59)

This is the classic argument of people with different worldviews. It's one long clash. Jesus repeatedly **challenges** them. They repeatedly **push back** on him. It doesn't finish until someone leaves. As with arguments of this nature, one line of reasoning runs quickly into another, which makes teasing it all out quite difficult. But this is broadly what happens.

Jesus **challenges** them. He is just saying what his Father has revealed to him. They are saying what they have learnt from their father. They **push back** on him: Abraham is our Father. Jesus **challenges** them: No, he isn't. Otherwise you would not be trying to kill someone who speaks the truth from God. You have a different father. They **push back** on him: God is our father. Jesus **challenges** them: No, he isn't. Your father is the devil. He is a murderer and a liar. And so are you. They **push back** on him: You are one of those dreadful Samaritans. And you are demonised. Jesus **challenges** them: No. You are dishonouring me and God. I'm not bothered, but he might be. Last warning with another **surprising statement**: If you listen to me and obey what I say, then you won't die. They **push back** on him: Now we know you are demonised. Everyone dies. Abraham died. Are you greater than him? Jesus affirms his **authenticity**. You can't blame him for taking a minute or two to do that. 'God glorifies me. I know him. I obey him. Abraham saw me coming and he was happy.' These are what make Jesus certain of his authenticity: his Father and Scripture. They **push back** on him. You haven't had your fiftieth birthday party yet mate! And you've had a chat with Abraham. Yeah. Yeah. Yeah. Blah. Blah. Blah.

Jesus surprises them: 'Before Abraham was born, I am!' (8:58), which is one heck of thing to say – on two counts. First, the claim to longevity. Second, the taking of God's holy name to himself. When God calls Moses to lead Israel in the Exodus journey he is looking after sheep in the desert. One of the many objections that Moses has to God's plan is that he does not know God's name. So God speaks his name to Moses. He takes the name 'I am'. In Hebrew, this is *Yahweh*. It speaks of God's eternal, unchanging existence. This name is so revered in Israel that it is never spoken out loud – until Jesus speaks it of himself. No wonder they pick up stones to stone him. At this point Jesus slips away.

The Shepherd and the Gate

The sixth Contention story occurs in 10:1–39. Because of all that Jesus says about shepherds, this passage is probably more familiar to you. Church leaders like this text a lot more than the one about dying in our sins. As you dig into it, you will find all six categories of the spoken word that we have been using to understand these stories. Let Jesus step out of the page as you meet with him.

Where Are We and What Time Is It? (9:40, 10:1, 22)

This story appears to follow straight on from The Healing of the Man Born Blind. That story finishes with Jesus talking with some Pharisees about the problem of being blind to their own blindness (9:40–1) and flows straight into, 'Very truly I tell you Pharisees . . .' We are in Jerusalem. Like several of the other Contentions, this argument takes place over a period of time. In the later section we learn that it is winter, and it is the Festival of Dedication. Jesus is walking in Solomon's Colonnade, part of the Temple Courts (10:22–3).

Who Starts the Argument? (10:1–18)

Jesus. He has taken the initiative. He has stopped just responding to the authorities' awkward questions. These arguments are going to happen. May as well get on with it. Jesus makes not just a surprising statement but a **surprising speech.**

What Does Jesus Say?

He sets the scene for his surprise with a metaphorical story (10:1–5). There is a sheepfold, a gate, some thieves and robbers, a shepherd and a gatekeeper. The shepherd knows the sheep. The shepherd talks to the sheep. They recognise his voice. The sheep follow the shepherd. They seem to know all about stranger danger. The metaphors are vivid. And the language is exaggerated: bad thieves, good shepherd. The Pharisees don't understand. Unfortunately for them they are in the story. Unlike us, who are reading about it afterwards, with quite a lot of help (10:6).

So, Jesus gives them the longer version of the **surprising speech**.

First, Jesus is the gate to life: 'I am the gate; whoever enters through me will be saved. They will come in and go out, and find pasture. The thief comes only to steal and kill and destroy; I have come that they may have life, and have it to the full' (10:9–10). This is a story with him in the middle. He is the means by which the sheep are saved or kept safe. The gate is something the sheep walk through. There is a coming in, a coming into safety. And there is a going out, a going out into good grazing. Both by coming in and by going out there is life.

This is the Exodus story.

When God's judgment comes on Egypt, Israel are saved. They are saved by coming in. Coming inside. Israel are brought in through the door and the door is closed. As instructed, they daub the door with the blood of their Passover lamb. By virtue of coming in, and staying in, behind the blood, they live. The angel of death 'passes over' them. There is no death behind the door. Israel are then brought out. They are brought out from slavery and death. God brings them, eventually, to a good place, where they come in. A new land that they can call home. When God made the covenant with Abram, that he fulfils in the Exodus, he promised Abram that he himself would provide the way out and the way in: 'But I will punish the nation they serve as slaves, and afterwards they will come out . . . In the fourth generation your descendants will come back here' (Gen. 15:14–15).

God is the gate. The way out and the way in. In Moses' song of victory following the defeat of the Egyptian army, Moses sings about Israel being brought in, to dwell in the presence of God:

> You will bring them in and plant them
> on the mountain of your inheritance –
> the place, Lord, you made for your dwelling,
> the sanctuary, Lord, your hands established.
> (Exod. 15:17)

When Moses is calling on Israel to love God with all their heart and soul and strength, he retells the Exodus story, complete with God bringing out and bringing in: 'Before our eyes the Lord sent signs and wonders – great and terrible – on Egypt and Pharaoh and his whole household. But he brought us out from there to bring us in and give us the land that he promised on oath to our ancestors' (Deut. 6:22–3).

The Exodus story, in summary form, is this: being brought in to safety, to be brought out from slavery, to be brought in to new life in the land.

Jesus takes the Exodus story and puts himself right in the middle of it. We have met all these ideas in the previous stories. Jesus is the way into the safe place where you are shielded from God's judgment. Judgment won't happen to you (5:24). He is the way out of slavery to sin. If the Son sets you free, you will be free indeed (8:36). He is the way into the new land of knowing God and enjoying God. If you come to him, streams of living water will flow from within you and water your inner world by his Spirit (7:38). Coming through Jesus will bring you out of death and into life (5:24). Jesus is the gate in the new Exodus. The way in and the way out.

Second, Jesus is the good shepherd: 'I am the good shepherd; I know my sheep and my sheep know me – just as the Father knows me and I know the Father – and I lay down my life for the sheep' (10:14–15). The qualities of the good shepherd that Jesus describes are extraordinary and highly sacrificial. The shepherd is going to lay his life down for his sheep. That is because of the great love he has for us and the depth of relationship he desires to have with us:

- The sheep listen to his voice (10:3, 16, 26)
- He calls his own sheep by name and leads them out (10:3)
- His sheep follow him because they know his voice (10:4)
- 'I know my sheep and my sheep know me – just as the Father knows me and I know the Father' (10:14–15, 27)

However. This is not a nice talk about the kindness of God and the pastoral ministry of the church. This is an argument that is going to get Jesus into a lot of trouble. There is an irony here of our favourite teachings being located in these difficult passages. But why does this teaching cause so much trouble? For Israel, the shepherd is not just someone who tends sheep (or cares for people). To shepherd in Israel is to rule. David, their greatest King, was taken from tending sheep to being shepherd of the nation. Their greatest King, the model of all kings to come, was shepherd to the people of God:

> He chose David his servant
> and took him from the sheepfolds;
> from tending the sheep he brought him
> to be the shepherd of his people Jacob,
> of Israel his inheritance.
> And David shepherded them with integrity of heart;
> with skilful hands he led them (Psalm 78:70–2)

So when Jesus calls himself the good shepherd, he is calling himself the good King. And he contrasts himself very strongly with all the other rulers of Israel who are failing very badly, calling them thieves and robbers (10:8). The rulers of Israel are not caring for the people. They are taking what they can get from their privileged position. They are not loving the people. They are exploiting their authority for their own selfish gain. True. But contentious.

What Does Jesus Mean?

This is Ezekiel. There are many references to God as shepherd of his people in the Old Testament: Isaiah, Psalms, Zechariah, etc. But in the way Jesus tells this story, particularly with the references to the failings of the leaders of Israel, we can see Ezekiel underneath.

Immediately after giving Israel the warning about dying in their sins, Ezekiel turns his prophetic gaze on the shepherds of Israel. They are not doing well. Ezekiel speaks strongly against them. They are thieves and robbers. They just take care of themselves. They are not caring for people. They are ruling harshly. God's people have not been gathered into a good place. They have been scattered and left to fend for themselves. The shepherds are exploiting the people and feeding off them. There is no justice. Not surprisingly, God is going to judge them and deal with them. You can read all this in graphic detail in Ezekiel 34:1–10.

The incredible remedy that Ezekiel prophesies to this terrible problem is that God himself will come and shepherd his people. God will gather them from the nations. God will search for those who are lost. God will heal those who are sick. God will bring them in to good pasture. God will shepherd the flock with justice (Ezek. 34:11–19). The way that God will do this is to send another David to them. A new King will come. He will save them. There will be one flock and one shepherd. Everyone will live in safety. The land will be blessed (Ezek. 34:20–31).

In retelling the Ezekiel prophecy with himself in the middle, Jesus is effectively placing himself into the story as God. Just to turn that particular screw another notch, Jesus concludes his shepherd speech by revealing more about his **authority**: 'The reason my Father loves me is that I lay down my life – only to take it up again. No one takes it from me, but I lay it down of my own accord. I have authority to lay it down and authority to take it up again. This command I received from my Father' (10:17–18).

Jesus and the Father are working together. He is the new Davidic King, come from God to shepherd God's people properly. But, as we have already seen, the new King comes by laying down his life. The route to glory is the cross. There are no selfish shortcuts to true power.

How Do the Pharisees Respond? (10:19–24)

We can see what the shepherd story means, that Jesus is talking about the crucifixion and the resurrection. But the authorities think he is mad. Or demonised. Or both. They **push back** on him (10:19–20). Some, however, are glancing back at the healing of the blind man. Is that really the work of a demonised man? It's all very difficult for them. Jesus doesn't fit their expectations of what a King is, and yet he does these amazing signs.

Time seems to pass after that. The second half of this story begins with some of the authorities **stepping towards** him. This is like meeting an excitable version of Nicodemus. It seems positive. But it might not be: 'The Jews who were there gathered round him, saying, "How long will you keep us in suspense? If you are the Messiah, tell us plainly"' (10:24).

How Does the Argument Develop? (10:25–38)

Jesus is not afraid to be **challenging** to reveal people's hearts. 'I've told you before, and you don't believe. I have done all these works, but you don't believe. The reason you don't believe is because you don't belong to me' (10:25–7). It is a pretty devastating critique. Jesus restates his **surprising statement** again. This time a short version: 'My sheep listen to my voice; I know them, and they follow me. I give them eternal life, and they shall never perish; no one will snatch them out of my hand' (10:27–8).

The sheep of Jesus listen to him, know him and follow him. This is eternal life. This is the death of death. Jesus' sheep are in Jesus' hand and they are safe and saved. Nothing can take them from him. Jesus restates his **authority**. He and the Father are working together on this. Ezekiel's prophecy is coming true. God will care for his people himself through his new King. The Father and the Son are one (10:29–30). Stepping towards him moves quickly to **pushing back** on him. They pick up stones. Not because of the good works, but because of his claims to equality with God (10:31–3).

AUTHENTICITY

Jesus' response to the threat of his imminent death is to reveal his authenticity. How will they know that Jesus is authentic? How will they know that he knows the truth and is teaching the truth? Jesus wants to talk about how we understand the Bible and how we use the Bible, because one way to test his authenticity is to test his words against Scripture.

It's a brave moment. There are men with stones in their hands all around you. They have no reservation about killing you. They think they are doing God's work. But Jesus wants to have a quick chat with them about how to use the Bible. OK, chaps. Just before we move to the whole stoning the blasphemer thing, let's just have a quick lecture on biblical interpretation. This is not who I usually have in my class for that topic. But establishing someone's authenticity is very important. In this moment, it is of life and death importance. Checking that we are using the Bible properly is hugely significant, especially if we are thinking of killing someone for misusing it.

Jesus has a quick lesson up his sleeve on why his use of Father for God and Son for himself working together as One is not a denial of monotheism. It is not blasphemy. It is biblical.

'Has it not been written in your Law, "I said, you are gods"? If he called them gods, to whom the word of God came (and the Scripture cannot be broken), do you say of Him, whom the Father sanctified and sent into the world, "You are blaspheming," because I said, "I am the Son of God"?' (10:34–6, NASB)

What Does Jesus Mean?

Well. This is the Exodus story and Ezekiel 34 being brilliantly used with Psalm 82 to reflect on the nature of God and our relationship with him.

Psalm 82 is God speaking to the gods (Ps. 82:1). They have made such a mess of things. There is no justice, looking after the poor or rescuing the weak (Ps. 82:2–4). A lot of very bad shepherding, in fact. Those who are in charge are just walking about in darkness. The very foundations are at risk (Ps. 82:5). God says to them, 'I called you gods. I called you sons. But you will die like all humans do. And fall like all rulers do' (Ps. 82:6).

Who are these people? The people called 'sons of the Most High'. The people called 'gods'?

Jesus gives an answer. He says that the people who get called 'gods' are the people to whom the word of God came, and Scripture can't be broken. The NIV translates this phrase as 'set aside'. However, it is more accurately translated 'untied', or 'broken'. This is the Exodus story. When Moses is sent to confront Pharaoh, God tells him to say this: 'This is what the Lord says: Israel is my firstborn son, and I told you, "Let my son go, so that he may worship me"' (Exod. 4:22–3).

The son of God is the people of God, called out from slavery to worship God. When Israel gather to God at Sinai and worship him it is a very dramatic encounter with the living God. They step into something no one has ever experienced before. God then calls Moses up the mountain and instructs Moses in his word. God summarises everything into ten short statements and makes an artwork. He chisels his word onto a couple of stone tablets. Moses comes down the mountain with the word of God in his hands. Israel at Sinai are the people to whom the word of God comes.

But. When the word of God comes, Israel has already turned away from God. They are already breaking the top three commands. Moses is so angry that he throws God's artwork down and it breaks into pieces at the foot of the mountain (Exod. 32:19). But God's word can't be broken. God's word still stands.

There are different interpretative options for Psalm 82. Jesus majors on one of them. Those called 'sons' and 'gods' were Israel at Sinai, but they lost it. Several rabbis teach this. They call it the Fall of Israel. It's a replay of Adam and Eve in the garden. Israel were called up into the very presence of God. But then fell down.

Jesus' point to those who are about to stone him is this: if there is a new Moses, a new Exodus, a new Israel, a new covenant, then perhaps using the terminology that was used at Sinai is not so bad. Maybe even biblical.

That is the major point, but there is also a minor key. The 'gods', or *elohim*, is a term also used to describe the angels. In Judaism, angels dwell alongside God, represent the very presence of God, speak the very words of God and exert the power of God on the earth. Jesus, by stepping into that space, is declaring himself to have divine status. This is not Trinitarian Christianity. But as a way of opening up the argument, which will then head towards that conclusion and doing that while also remaining faithful to the Scriptures (which cannot be broken), this is a brilliant step. As John Ashton points out in his commentary, this is why the argument is so hostile.[1] Jesus is not using Greek philosophy to explain himself. He is using the Jewish Bible. The strict monotheism of the authorities has no place for Jesus. They can't understand him. They end up hating him.

How Does the Argument Finish? (10:39–42)

Again, they try to seize him, but he escapes from their grasp.

Death to Life

The seventh and final Contention story follows straight on from the final Provocation story. As we have seen before with these two stories, the start of the Contention is woven into the end of the Provocation. You can read it in 12:20–50.

Where Are We and What Time Is It? (12:12, 20)

We are at the Passover Festival in Jerusalem.

Who Starts the Argument? (12:20–9)

Some Greeks who want to see Jesus. Philip and Andrew try to arrange a meeting. But Jesus never speaks to them. Instead, he talks of being a seed that must die. And this is how all that follow him are to live. This is from Psalm 126. The nations will speak of the great things that God has done. But we need to sow in tears to reap with songs of joy. Jesus announces his death. This is why he came. He calls on God to glorify his name and God responds. Some in the crowd **push back** on Jesus, saying it was just thunder. Others **affirm him**, saying it was an angel who spoke (12:20–9).

How Does the Argument Develop? (12:30–3)

Jesus makes two **surprising statements** that reveal his identity, both about his impending death (12:33). The first is how his death will lead to the driving out of evil powers: 'Now is the time for judgment on this world; now the prince of this world will be driven out' (12:31). This is from Ezekiel. The evil powers will be turned around and they will fall. The nations will know that God has done this (Ezek. 38:1–6; 39:1–7).

The second **surprising statement** is how his death will also draw people to himself: 'And I, when I am lifted up from the earth, will draw all people to myself' (12:32). Being 'lifted up' is what Jesus said to Nicodemus (3:14). This is from the Exodus story. God's judgment on Jesus will be healing for those drawn to him.

How Do the Crowd Respond? (12:34–6)

They don't understand, and they **push back** on him. They don't get the references to Ezekiel or to Exodus (12:34). Jesus **challenges** them. They have him as light now; they don't have long before the darkness will overtake them. And as if to reinforce the point, he hides himself (12:35–6).

How Does the Argument Finish? (12:37–50)

John the author points out that people do not believe even though they see many signs. This is what Isaiah saw would happen. This is the paradox that we have met before, of light coming into darkness. Some do believe, even from among the authorities, who have given Jesus such a hard time. But they aren't open about it, because of the people in power who control who belongs to the community. And everyone wants to belong. Everyone wants the affirmation that comes from belonging. So they fudge it. They believe. But very, very quietly, so that hopefully the people with the power to exclude them don't notice (12:37–42).

Jesus returns and repeats his **authority** as one who has been sent (12:44–6) and his **authenticity** as one who has spoken God's word (12:47–50).

Declaration

17

The Two Witnesses

The Whole Story

There are just two stories left. It will not surprise you that they have much in common. They too are a narrative panel.

In these stories, two people speak: John the author and John who baptises. Both of them point us to Jesus and declare who he is. I called this final narrative panel Declaration. There are two stories with two witnesses who both speak twice. There is an elegant symmetry about that, because in Judaism things that are true have to be established by the mouth of two witnesses.

We will look initially at the first witness in the first story: John the author. You can read this part of the story in John 1:1–18. It is one of the most incredible pieces of writing you will ever read. In just a few sentences John covers the full sweep of Jewish history and theology. And he puts Jesus in the middle.

As we have seen, John's Gospel deliberately begins with the first line of the Jewish Bible but with some extraordinary editing. John takes what God does in the story of Genesis 1, which is to speak so that things come into being, then takes that idea of how God works back into the very nature of who God is. God speaks. But he speaks himself. 'In the beginning was the Word, and the Word was with God, and the Word was God. He was with God in the beginning' (1:1–2).

Words are fundamental to the communication of our inner self. This is why we don't know what cats are thinking, apart from basic desires like 'give me food' or 'I want to go out', which they communicate without words. When we speak words, our inside self – our thoughts, our feelings, our ideas, our reactions – comes outside in a way where others can take us inside themselves. We communicate ourselves and allow ourselves to be known.

John the author is very bold. John begins as his Bible begins, and then he puts Jesus in the middle. In the beginning was the Word. The Word was with God and was God. In the eternity before space, matter and time began – there is God. And with God is the Word. The Word is more than words. The Word is none other than God himself. According to John, it is God's very nature to make himself known.

God speaks himself to reveal himself through himself.

How can we be certain that we can know God? Because it is in his very nature to be known. In the very existence of God is the revealing of God. Having got that clear, John the author moves on to consider all the building blocks of Jewish theology, but with Jesus in the middle.

Creation

God being creator is a massive foundation stone in Israel's story and Israel's theology.

Israel stood out from all the other nations because of her belief in there being One Creator God. We struggle to relate to this because many people today are monotheistic. But for Israel, monotheism was a minority position that had to be fiercely defended. Everyone around them had many gods. Knowing God as the Creator helped them. There is only one God who made all things. The world is not in chaos brought on by ceaseless conflict between the gods. There is one God. The movement of the stars do not control our destiny. Our Creator God made the sun and moon and the stars. They are just lights in the sky so we can see and mark the passing of time. The sun is not a god. There are no other gods. There is just God.

God as Creator also helped defend Israel against idolatry. We don't make our gods. God made us. We are in his image. We don't fashion god. God fashioned us. We don't worship what we have created. We worship the one who is Creator.

God's justice and God's right to rule are founded on this truth of God as Creator. How come God decides what justice looks like?

How come God can determine what is right and what is wrong? Because God is Creator. That makes him Judge.

This is where John's Gospel goes next: creation. Having spoken himself to make himself known, God creates everything through his word: 'Through him all things were made; without him nothing was made that has been made' (1:3). This is about as good a summary of Genesis 1 that you can get.

Humanity – Made in the Likeness of God

To serve and steward his creation by his word, God makes humanity in his image (Gen. 1:26–8). Humanity is made like God. In the second creation story this idea is retold in a different way. God is very hands on. He makes a man from mud and breathes the breath of life up his nose (Gen. 2:7). The Mud-man can speak. He can conceptualise and vocalise and analyse. God gives him a course in practical zoology. The Mud-man names the animals (Gen. 2:20). The Mud-man can separate one animal from another. He can use words to name these animals and describe how they are different. He can represent reality in sounds and words and pictures and diagrams and spreadsheets. This is what marks humanity out from the rest of creation. Dogs do not name humans and represent all of reality in words. The creation of humanity by God in the image of God and with the life of God is put into one sentence in John: 'In him was life, and that life was the light of all [humanity]' (1:4).

God has life. John the author calls this life, light. All humanity has this life that is light. Light isn't something we see. Light is the means by which we see. The life that has been given to all humanity enables us to 'see'. What do we see? We see ourselves. We see other humans. We can see the difference between a pebble, a cat and a husband. We can 'see' unseen things like our identity, who we are. We can see our conscience, whether what we do is right. We can see and express our emotions, such as fear, anger and love. We can see our will and decide what we will do. We can see another 'you', another person. In Genesis 2, the Mud-man is thrilled when he sees the Wo-man. He recognises her as one with him. This ability to see others and to see myself is God-given light. We have all been made like God to know God and know each other.

Fall

The terrible Fall of humanity is described in Genesis chapters 3–11. Humanity turns from God. They are deceived by the deceptions of the talking snake in the garden and they do not hold fast to what God has said. Darkness, fear and shame enters their hearts. They hide from God and cover themselves. From now on humanity is characterised by the darkness of oppression, jealousy, murder, pain, rivalry, fear and death. The darkness doesn't understand truth and beauty and joy and forgiveness. But neither can the darkness completely defeat these good things. The conflicted nature within humanity of both darkness and light is put into one sentence in John: 'The light shines in the darkness, and the darkness has not overcome it' (1:5).

The light shines in the darkness. All humanity has light. All humanity has qualities and abilities like God. But all humanity is in darkness. The light exists within the darkness. The darkness within all of us struggles against the light within us. The darkness cannot understand the light, but neither can it overcome it. The darkness cannot completely take hold of anyone. Even the most brutal dictator has moments of truth and love. Even saintly people struggle with darkness, failure and regret. What will God do?

Israel – the Prophetic People of God

God's answer is to call a people to himself. Starting with Abraham and Sarah, God chooses a people and makes himself known to them. God speaks to them. God reveals his heart and his purpose to them. To do this, God sends them prophets who shape their life as a people. The key figures of the Old Testament – Abraham, Moses, Deborah, Samuel, Isaiah and many others – were all prophets. They were sent by God to speak for God. This gift of the prophets sent by God to speak for God is totally unique to Judaism. No other religious movement in the world has this long history of authentic people God speaks to and sends to speak his word.

The prophets shape their worship. The prophets call people to know God and to love God. The prophets reveal that God had come to his people with covenant-keeping love, that God's people belong to God.

The prophets establish their lifestyle: generosity, justice, truth-telling, faithfulness. The prophets keep calling God's people to God's ways. And the prophets see a glorious future where God comes to save his people. To be the people God speaks to like this is a precious heritage. John the author draws all that incredible history together and summarises it. After 400 years of silence, God sends a prophet to call his people to himself. It is how God has always worked. His name is John: 'There was a man sent from God whose name was John. He came as a witness to testify concerning that light, so that through him all might believe. He himself was not the light; he came only as a witness to the light' (1:6–8).

John the author has summarised the story of Israel. There came someone sent from God. They themselves were not God's light. But they came to speak of its coming. You can put every name of every prophet of the Jewish Bible into that paragraph and it sums them up. The prophets start to see that the coming of God's light into the darkness of the world will draw all the nations back to God. Isaiah is just one of many (Isa. 60:1–3).

Fulfilment and Failure

The story of Israel is the story of humanity. People fail. This is the story of the Genesis garden. This is the story of Cain. This is the story of the people among whom Noah lived. This is the story of Jacob. This is the story of Moses. This is the story of David and the kings of Israel. This is the story of Jerusalem as told by Isaiah and Jeremiah. Despite all the warnings of the prophets that God sends to his people, they refuse to listen to his Word. Eventually God's presence is taken from them because they turn so far from God. They are exiled under pagan powers. The nation is scattered and Jerusalem is destroyed. Even when they return to the land after the Babylonian exile, and rebuild the Temple, the exile doesn't really end. The promises of a righteous and glorious city of God are never realised.

But God still comes. As promised. Because his promises never fail.

Incarnation

And then we have the final mystery. The failure that sums up all the previous failures. When God does come, his people do not recognise him: 'The true light that gives light to everyone was coming into the world. He was in the world, and though the world was made through him, the world did not recognise him. He came to that which was his own, but his own did not receive him' (1:9–11).

This tragedy is unspeakable. The man who became the Apostle Paul for several years simply could not see that Jesus was Israel's promised Messiah. After he did finally realise who Jesus was, he wrote, 'I have great sorrow and unceasing anguish in my heart. For I could wish that I myself were cursed and cut off from Christ for the sake of my people, those of my own race, the people of Israel' (Rom. 9:2–4). Paul was so upset that his people had rejected their new King.

It is deeply tragic when anyone can't see who Jesus is. It is particularly tragic when it is the very people who have the prophetic heritage of Judaism. Paul goes on to write, 'Theirs is the adoption to sonship; theirs the divine glory, the covenants, the receiving of the law, the temple worship and the promises. Theirs are the patriarchs' (Rom. 9:4–5).

Has God's Word failed because the people of God who have the word of God do not recognise God? What Paul does in his writings in the New Testament, and what John the author does right now, is show that God's Word has not failed. Instead, the great prophetic truths have been fulfilled. What God promised Israel has not petered out. The very opposite has happened. It has come to completeness. John the author works through the same list as the Apostle Paul.

ADOPTION

'Yet to all who did receive him, to those who believed in his name, he gave the right to become children of God – children born not of natural descent, nor of human decision or a husband's will, but born of God' (1:12–13). We are family. We are God's family.

Israel were not born into God's family. They were adopted. God chose them and declared them to be his children. It wasn't their goodness, holiness or righteous living that made them family. It wasn't even being the genetic physical descendants of Abraham and Sarah. Some tried to make out that God was obligated to them because of his promises to Abraham. They kept forgetting that it was God's decision in every generation. God's call. God's work. God's grace.

190

As with Israel, the children are now gathered to God as our Father. But gathered by Jesus. It is not our goodness. It is not our parents. It is God's pure gift of grace of Jesus that we can say, 'We are family.' As we receive him, we receive something very precious – we become adopted children of God.

THE TEMPLE

'The Word became flesh and made his dwelling among us' (1:14). When the Word becomes flesh, everything God is, was made man. Nothing was subtracted from God. Humanity was added to God. He made his dwelling among us. As we have seen, this is Temple talk. This is the truth of the Temple as God's dwelling place, but now applied to a real man. God is no longer confined to a special space in a special building in a single city. God is on the loose. God sits by a well. God talks to a Samaritan woman with a rather dysfunctional lifestyle. Irony of ironies, God goes to the Temple in Jerusalem. God rages against the corruption. God demands that it stop. Or think of when, tragically, God arrives too late to save his friend from dying. God weeps at his tomb. God enters into the pain of the women he loves. Or think of when God has dinner, with his closest friend leaning back against his breast, God whispering in his ear.

God pitches his tent. God lives among us. The God who spoke himself to reveal himself is now with us.

DIVINE GLORY

'We have seen his glory, the glory of the one and only Son, who came from the Father, full of grace and truth' (1:14). The *shekinah* glory is the very presence of God on the earth. We have seen it, says the author of the Gospel. No longer a shimmering cloud of impenetrable power, but a man. A man who invites us round for a late lunch and spends the rest of the day with us. A man who reveals the glory. The only way we can describe this awesome reality is to use the language of how the King is described in the Psalms (Ps. 2:6–7). The Son who came from the Father.

John who baptises declares, 'He who comes after me has surpassed me because he was before me' (1:15). John who baptises understands himself from Isaiah. He is a voice calling in the wilderness, the completion of all Israel's prophets, making the way for the Lord. Good news! Here is your God (Isa. 40:9). Does John who baptises know of the eternal pre-existence of Jesus? We don't know. But he knows where he stands in relation to who is coming after him. The voice who announces the new King is surpassed by the King when he comes.

THE COVENANTS

'Out of his fullness we have all received grace in place of grace already given. For the law was given through Moses; grace and truth came through Jesus Christ' (1:16–17).

From Abraham onwards, God's people are called into covenant relationship with God. By grace they have been chosen. By grace they have been given the law to show them how to live. But God's people fail God. Because of the power of sin within they do not live to please him. What will God do? God tells Jeremiah that the covenant will be made new (Jer. 31:31). God will come with even greater grace. Even more grace will be given instead of the grace already given. In the new covenant of more grace the law will not be written on tablets of stone and carried down to God's people by Moses. The law will be written on our hearts. Living to please God will not be something we try to live up to. Living to please God will be something to live out. It's not chiselled on stone. It's engraved inside us.

Knowing God

Jeremiah promised:

> 'No longer will they teach their neighbour,
> or say to one another, "Know the Lord,"
> because they will all know me,
> from the least of them to the greatest,'
> declares the Lord.
> (Jer. 31:34)

And John the author concludes, 'No one has ever seen God, but the one and only Son, who is himself God and is in the closest relationship with the Father, has made him known' (1:18).

All of Israel's history, all of Israel's theology, all of God's great promises to save the world, now found in Jesus. You can know God. God wants you to know him. The Son has made him known.

Who Are You?

Our second witness is John who baptises. You can read his testimony in John 1:19–34.

Investigated

John is investigated by the authorities, even though he is right up north, two days' walk from Jerusalem (1:28). He has to be investigated. More and more people are seeing him as an authentic prophet of God. There had not been a prophet for 400 years so this is a big deal. And he is baptising Jews (1:26). As we have already seen with Nicodemus, baptism, or spiritual and ritual washing in water, is for pagans who have come to believe in Israel's God. Baptism is not for God's people. John's baptism does not fit in with the teachings of those in charge.

When someone effective and popular arises outside the system, it is bound to cause trouble with those in charge. They send a whole delegation (1:19). Fortunately, John who baptises has a very clear view of who he is and what God has sent him to do.

The Voice

He is not God's new King, the Messiah. He is not Elijah. In case you are wondering why the investigation wants to know whether John who baptises is Elijah, Elijah was the prophet who didn't die. Instead, God sent a chariot of fire to fetch him. You can read about that in 2 Kings 2:1–18. Quite how you get into a chariot of fire is something of a mystery. But we are in the realm of apocalyptic vision again, trying to put things into words that can't be fully described. However, the thinking was that Elijah would return. The Prophet Malachi said that Elijah would come before the Lord (Mal. 4:5–6). But John does not see himself in this way (1:21).

The other prophet person that the authorities have in mind is a prophet like Moses, who they just called 'the Prophet'. This was because when God met with his people on Sinai, they could not bear to hear God speak. They said that they were not able to receive God's word. God agreed with them, and promised this to Moses: 'I will raise up for them a prophet like you from among their fellow Israelites, and I will put my words in his mouth. He will tell them everything I command him. I myself will call to account anyone who does not listen to my words that the prophet speaks in my name' (Deut. 18:18–19).

But John who baptises is not the prophet like Moses. Because Jesus is.

So – who is John who baptises? How does he see himself? He is the Voice (1:23).

Inside Isaiah

This is an extraordinary way to describe yourself. It is brilliant in its simplicity and its power. It comes from Isaiah 40. The Voice is not on the investigators' list, because no one has thought of Isaiah in this way before. No one has seen that the Voice might be someone. That is the advantage of being a prophet. You are listening to God much more than you are listening to people.

Isaiah 40 is something of a hinge on which the book of Isaiah turns. Isaiah opens with the announcement of God's judgment on Israel because of her corruption and the stinking bad fruit that she has borne. The people of God were chosen to be like God. But they are the very opposite (Isa. 1–9). Isaiah moves on to announce God's judgment on the nations because of their violence, their immorality and their injustice (Isa. 9–24). Isaiah then returns to announce God's judgment on the corrupt leaders of Israel (Isa. 28–34).

However, in all that, Isaiah gives equal weight to declaring the great hope that God is coming to save his people. He sees it again and again:

- A new temple will be built, and all the nations will come to it (Isa. 2)
- A new people of God will be planted that will be glorious (Isa. 4)
- God himself will be with us (Isa. 7)

- A new King will come. The people walking in darkness will see a great light (Isa. 9)
- God's people will again trust in God (Isa. 10, 26)
- A new King will come. The Spirit of God will rest on him. There will be a new Exodus into a new Creation (Isa. 11)
- Water will come springing up from the well of God's salvation (Isa. 12)
- The nations will come to God's people (Isa. 14, 19)
- There will be a new leader who is a father (Isa. 22)
- God will prepare a fantastic feast for his people and he will destroy death (Isa. 25)
- Israel will be a faithful vineyard that produces good fruit (Isa. 27)
- A new righteous King will come (Isa. 32)
- There will be a new Exodus (Isa. 35)

This is a heady mix of wonderful things.

Then in Isaiah, there is an interlude, where Isaiah helps King Hezekiah (Isa. 36–39). But as we turn the page into Isaiah 40, we find the Voice. The Voice announces God is coming NOW. It is the hinge of the book. Isaiah is different from then on. The songs in Isaiah 40–66 swell up into a huge symphony of all that will happen when the Lord's servant, God's new King, comes.

John who baptises positioning himself in the hinge of Isaiah is breathtaking. He knows he has been sent by God to announce the coming of God's new King. He sees himself in the Scriptures in the very place where this happens. He finds himself in there, at that very point. It's intensely prophetic. The Scriptures are not just ancient poetry. They are actually happening.

By identifying himself inside Isaiah in this way, he is not just announcing that the King is coming. He is declaring what kind of King is going to come. The new King is also going to emerge from the very pages of Isaiah's poetry. All the signposts that point hopefully towards the King coming in the midst of judgment are going to come true (Isa. 1–35). The incredible outburst of life that will cascade into the whole world is going to be seen (Isa. 40–66). The King will come. A real ruler. But now, says John who baptises, a King with a name and a face.

No wonder John the author loves John who baptises. John who baptises took the Bible and found himself inside it. John the author does exactly the same thing for Jesus. As I am sure you have noticed, all the prophetic songs of hope that are in the build-up to Isaiah 40 are found echoing through the pages of the Gospel of John.

It is obvious that John the author is incredibly well versed in Scripture. We have seen how he uses the whole Hebrew Bible with such confidence and skill. What is more, he sees who Jesus is entirely through the lens of his Bible. He has brilliantly stitched together the story of Jesus and the story of Israel. The only question is: how did he get the idea to look at Jesus in this way? How did he get started? How did he begin to see Jesus in these rich biblical terms? It is more than possible that John who baptises showed him the way, that John the author was a disciple of John who baptises in more ways than one.

Why Baptise?

The authorities are not impressed with John as Voice. They don't engage with it at all. All they are concerned about is stopping this radical baptising. Why is he baptising if he isn't any of the recognised people? Unregulated baptising by unrecognised people has got to be stopped.

John who baptises doesn't feel that he has to explain himself to them. They don't know who he is, and they don't know why he is baptising. Not his problem. And he is just the beginning of their problems. There is someone standing listening at that very moment, standing among them. They don't know him either. They wouldn't recognise him if they met him. But he is the King that is to come. John doesn't explain himself. Instead, he needles them. 'If you think I'm trouble, just wait. There's a guy hanging around right now in this crowd. Relative to him, I'm nothing. I am not even at the level of being the one who ties his shoelaces.'

And as John who baptises points out later to his disciples, 'This is why I came baptising. I came baptising so that the King could be revealed': 'I myself did not know him, but the reason I came baptising with water was that he might be revealed to Israel' (1:31).

God's New King

Not everyone in Israel wants God to send a new King. But thousands do. And to those who are listening, John who baptises explains what the new King will be like. Out of all the richness of Isaiah, he picks three things to be the defining characteristics of the new King:

He is the Lamb of God who takes away the sin of the world (1:29)

The Spirit of God will descend and remain on him (1:32)

He will baptise with the Holy Spirit (1:33)

John the author wants us to know that these are critical to who Jesus is. If we are going to step into the space of knowing him deeply, then these are the ingredients that we will encounter.

The Lamb of God

One of Isaiah's best-known prophetic songs is when God's new King is like a lamb that is led to the slaughter (Isa. 53). Our sins are laid on him and his suffering takes them away. Isaiah sings of there being a new Exodus. God will gather his people from the nations (Isa. 43:5–13). A way will open through the sea. Water will be provided in the desert (Isa. 43:16–21; 49:9–12). And sins will be forgiven (Isa. 43:25).

The Exodus journey starts with the sacrifice of a lamb. To protect his people during the terrible judgment of Egypt, God tells them to take a lamb. One lamb per family. They are to kill it, put the blood of the lamb on the door and then go inside and enjoy roast lamb. When the angel of God sees the blood, they will not be judged; they will live. It's a lamb of God that saves them.

But how does this lamb take away the sin of the world?

To understand that, we have to put ourselves in the story. If Jesus is our Lamb of God, who are we? The bit that is easy to see is that we are Israel. God is saving us. He is protecting us from his judgment. The blood of the Lamb means we live and don't die. We were slaves to the power of sin. But now, by the death of Jesus, we have been set free from that enslaving power and are on a journey to meet with God.

But what about the Egyptians? Who are the slave masters? Who are the people who resist God? Who are the people who don't receive

God's Word? Who are the people whose hearts are hard? Who wants everything to go on just as it is thank you very much?

It's us.

When it comes to saving us from the enslaving power of sin. God has to save us from ourselves. Egypt represents the world from which God saves us. The new Passover Lamb of God saves us from the sins of the world. For the sins of the world are in us. We are not victims of a sin-filled world. We are participants in a sin-filled world. The blood of God's Lamb saves us from the power of sin that is within us. We can walk free.

On Him the Spirit Remains

The Spirit, the wind of God, is the manifest presence of God. The Spirit came upon his people to reveal God to them and empower them to work on God's behalf. The prophets spoke under the power of the Holy Spirit resting upon them.

When Joshua takes over the leadership of Israel after the death of Moses, we discover that he is filled with the Spirit like Moses: 'Now Joshua son of Nun was filled with the spirit of wisdom because Moses had laid his hands on him. So the Israelites listened to him and did what the Lord had commanded Moses' (Deut. 34:9).

Those who lead Israel to victory against their enemies are filled with the Spirit. Heroes and leaders in Israel like Gideon (Judg. 6:34), Samson (Judg. 14:6) and King Saul (1 Sam. 10:6) have powerful experiences of the Spirit of God coming upon them. David, Israel's greatest King, experiences the Holy Spirit coming upon him several years before he becomes King. David is not the one who is expected to become King. But God knows and puts his Spirit upon him: 'So Samuel took the horn of oil and anointed him in the presence of his brothers, and from that day on the Spirit of the Lord came powerfully upon David' (1 Sam. 16:13).

John who baptises knows from Isaiah that the Spirit will not just come on God's new King for a time. The Spirit will rest and remain upon him (1:32). Isaiah sings of how a descendant of David will be the new King. David's father was called Jesse. The new King will also be a 'shoot of Jesse':

A shoot will come up from the stump of Jesse;
from his roots a branch will bear fruit.
The Spirit of the Lord will rest on him.
(Isa. 11:1–2)

In the Hebrew of Isaiah there is a small pun. 'Spirit' (*ruach*) sounds like 'rest or remain' (*nuwach*). They go together well. Jesus is where the Spirit of God is comfortable to remain. The Spirit comes like a dove. It's another metaphor trying to describe a deeper reality. In my rather limited experience, doves need a high level of quietness and security in their surroundings to remain. Jesus has lots to do. He is a very busy person, with complicated meetings, many increasingly hostile conversations along with failings in his colleagues and a close friend who turns against him. And yet in relation to the Spirit he maintains throughout a posture of openness, quietness and peace. The Spirit rests and remains.

He Will Baptise with the Holy Spirit

The English word 'baptise' is from the Greek word *baptiso*. The Greek word isn't a religious word. It means to drench, dip or immerse. In our cookery age, I quite like the word 'marinade'. Jesus doesn't just receive God's Spirit himself. He pours the Spirit out on us. We get soaked with the Spirit. Using the water metaphor, Isaiah sings that when the new King comes the Spirit will be poured out and there will be great fruitfulness:

till the Spirit is poured on us from on high,
and the desert becomes a fertile field,
and the fertile field seems like a forest.
(Isa. 32:15)

Our desert will be changed to fertile field and forest. Previously barren, dry, lifeless places will flourish and grow. Think of your life with God. Imagine it flourishing like a forest. Imagine Christlike qualities springing up within you like a fertile field. Imagine faith sprouting up that God will work in your business and in your family. Or perhaps love for others growing vigorously in you. Or joy in God springing

199

up all by itself within you, filling your life with colour and vibrancy. Desert places becoming fertile fields.

The pouring out of the Spirit will lead to many people turning to God and knowing that they belong to God:

> For I will pour water on the thirsty land,
> and streams on the dry ground;
> I will pour out my Spirit on your offspring,
> and my blessing on your descendants.
> They will spring up like grass in a meadow,
> like poplar trees by flowing streams.
> Some will say, 'I belong to the Lord';
> others will call themselves by the name of Jacob;
> still others will write on their hand, 'The Lord's'.
> (Isa. 44:3–5)

John who baptises knows that as God's Spirit comes pouring out upon his people, many will turn to the Lord.

18

More to Say

Come Again

The second Declaration story also features John the author and John who baptises. As the John the author points out to us, this all happens before John who baptises is put in prison (3:24). You can read it in John 3:16–26.

As we have repeatedly seen, John writes in a single flowing style. There is no difference in tone, style or language between Jesus speaking and John writing. This makes it hard to establish for certain when Jesus stops speaking with Nicodemus and John the author starts writing. There are different views on this, but the narrative analysis helps us, because there is very significant co-relation between the first Declaration and this second one. What the author does is bring each Declaration into close relationship with the other, which helps our understanding of both.

We saw in the first Declaration John the author starts with creation, summarises all of Jewish history and theology and places Jesus right in the middle of it. In the second Declaration story we see the same approach, but with a new focus. John the author writes his second testimony in direct parallel with his first one. He begins by bringing together what God has done in creation with what God has done in salvation and new creation.

Here are the first parts of the Declaration stories side by side:

1:1–13	3:16–21
1–2 In the beginning was the Word, and the Word was with God, and the Word was God. He was with God in the beginning.	16a For God

| 3 Through him all things were made; without him nothing was made that has been made. | 16b so loved the world that he gave his one and only Son, |
| 4 In him was life, and that life was the light of all mankind. | 16c that whoever believes in him shall not perish but have eternal life. |

Creation and Salvation

John 1:1–2 connects with 3:16a. Everything starts with God. Our creation and our salvation both begin with God. So far, so obvious. But 1:3 then connects with 3:16b. God loving the world and giving his Son is brought alongside God creating the world through his Word/Son. And then 1:4 connects with 3:16c. What God did in giving us life in the existing creation sits alongside what God does in giving us the gift of eternal life in new creation. God's life in us is 'light' that makes us like God and enables us to know him. John places this uncontroversial understanding of creation alongside salvation. Through believing in Jesus we receive eternal life and know God.

Why is this bringing together of God working in creation and God working in salvation so important?

When we read, 'God so loved the world', many of us are so used to it that we aren't startled and upset by it. But when you put yourself into the mindset of a first-century Jewish person, this is not how they see things. The vast majority of Israel's prophetic history has led them to a worldview that God has chosen them as his special people, unique among the other nations. God does *not* love the world. God loves them, his people. The rest of the nations are pagans, God's enemies. Many of Israel's Scriptures speak of God's special love for his people. The other nations have no time for God and no place in God's heart. They face God's judgment. The mindset of people at the time of Jesus is that God does not love the world.

There are, yes, some Scriptures that subvert this view. Jonah is sent to speak God's judgment on the vast pagan city of Nineveh.

The rulers and the people repent, and God spares them. But this just makes Jonah angry. The reason he tried so hard not to go to Nineveh was because he knew all along that God was going to spare them and he didn't like it. It is a story that is just left hanging in the Hebrew Bible. God has saved people he shouldn't, and his prophet is rather miffed by him doing it.

We see another subversive story in the book of Ruth. The heroine, Ruth, is a Moabite woman. Moab is a notorious enemy of Israel. However, God leads her to follow him and become part of his people. She ends up in the royal line as the great-grandmother of David, Israel's greatest King. It's all a bit disturbing.

And then there is the enigma of Psalm 87:

> *Glorious things are said of you, city of God:*
> *'I will record Rahab and Babylon*
> *among those who acknowledge me.'*
> *(Ps. 87:3–4)*

The psalmist seems to be celebrating the fact that all the wrong people are being welcomed into belonging to the people of God and being 'born' into the city of God.

This mindset of Israel as God's chosen people who are loved by God, and the pagans who are neither chosen nor loved, is very dominant in first-century Israel. One reason why many Jewish people reject the message of Jesus being proclaimed after the resurrection is because they despise the idea of Gentiles joining the people of God, which is what is happening in the Church. This thinking is endemic even within the Church, and the arguments about it rage back and forth in a way that we find difficult to understand. As far as we are concerned, the fact that God so loved the world is where we begin. But it is not where most of the first-century Church begins, and they need a lot of help to even start to move in that direction.

This is what John is doing.

Changing worldview is difficult. The only way to do it is to start at the place where you know people already agree with you and try to work from that. Creation is where John begins in the first Declaration. The point he gently develops through bringing the second Declaration alongside it is that God in creation and God in salvation are God working in similar ways. God created through his Son; God saves through his Son. God made the world; God is saving the world. God loves the creation; God loves the world. Just as God created everybody, God loves everybody and is working to save them. Not everyone is going to be saved because those who are given the gift of life are those who believe in Jesus, and tragically not everybody does. But God's heart of love is to save, and that heart of love extends to the whole world.

In doing this, John is completely redrawing the first-century Jewish mind map of humanity. No longer is the world to be seen as being divided in two vertically. On the left, the pagan nations who are God's enemies. And on the right, God's people whom God loves. Instead, the world is divided horizontally, across all nations. The separation is not between nations. The separation is between those people who have stepped towards God's invitation to save them through his Son and those, from every nation including Israel, who have stepped back into the darkness of refusing God.

This is exactly what the Apostle Paul does in the first three chapters of his letter to the Romans. The reality is that everyone needs to be saved from sin (Rom. 3:1–20). The Jewish Scriptures point towards God himself coming to save. Salvation is from the Jews. But that salvation is not just for the Jews. It is for the world (Rom. 3:21–31). Conclusion: God loves the world. Application: Jews and Gentiles who believe in Jesus are to love each other and stop arguing about food.

John takes his readers to the same place. God breathed the light of life into every human (1:4). Everyone is made in the image of God. Now God is breathing new creation life into people from every nation through faith in Christ (3:16c). By connecting salvation with creation, John appeals to his readers. Let the generosity and love of God that you see in his creating of all nations help you understand the generosity and love of God in saving people from all nations. It is a theological masterclass.

Fall and Israel

Having established that, John moves to place Jesus as God's solution to the Fall and Jesus as the fulfilment of all Israel's prophetic hopes:

1:5 The light shines in the darkness, and the darkness has not overcome it.	3:17 For God did not send his Son into the world to condemn the world, but to save the world through him.
1:6–8 There was a man sent from God whose name was John. He came as a witness to testify concerning that light, so that through him all might believe. He himself was not the light; he came only as a witness to the light.	3:18 Whoever believes in him is not condemned, but whoever does not believe stands condemned already because they have not believed in the name of God's one and only Son.

John has already summarised Genesis 3 in the first Declaration. Darkness has come on everyone. Whatever light there is shines in the darkness. Those in the darkness can't see or grasp what God is doing. (1:5). John now puts Jesus into the middle of that. God did not send his Son to condemn people for being in darkness and far from God, but to save people from their darkness and bring them back to God (3:17). The Fall infected the world. The Son came to save the world.

John the author has already positioned John who baptises as the final prophet of Israel. He is the sent one who sums up the prophetic history of Israel (1:6). His message is to point people to Jesus. He calls Israel to prepare for and believe in their new King (1:7). He is not God's light that saves.

What John wants us to see from this is that none of Israel's prophets were the Light that saves. They all pointed to God. They all were a witness to God coming to save (1:8). The prophets told Israel that Israel needs to be saved just as much as anyone. God's covenant with Israel has failed because Israel is still in darkness. They cannot and do not remain faithful to God. God's Law has failed. Not because it is wrong, or so last century. It fails because Israel are not able to live in obedience because of the darkness within themselves. They are descendants of Abraham and Sarah, but they are also descendants of Adam and Eve. God's Temple presence in their midst has failed. They have lost sight of the glory and turned to idolatry. They serve gods of their own imaginations and desires. As we have seen repeatedly, all the prophets point towards the coming of God's new King as the answer to these terrible failures.

In the second Declaration, John places Jesus in the middle of all these great hopes. The world stands condemned already. The only way for the covenant to be renewed, God's people to live God's way, the glory to come and God to dwell with his people is to believe in the one that the Law and the prophets all point towards: Jesus. The Apostle Paul takes us on the same journey in Romans 4–8. Jesus is the fulfilment of Israel's hopes. Jesus does not stop and start again. He fulfils what God's word declares. And the fulfilment of Israel's Scriptures is God working to save both Jews and Gentiles. Jesus is from the Jews but not just for the Jews.

Sovereignty and Responsibility

So why isn't everybody saved? If God has come to save, why not save everyone, particularly Israel, who you would think would be most open to God? If this question never arises, then you have not been reading or teaching the Bible. The Bible's teaching raises this unanswerable question. John wisely does not attempt to resolve the question. He simply brings both parts of the dilemma together.

1:9 The true light that gives light to everyone was coming into the world.	3:19 This is the verdict: light has come into the world,
1:10 He was in the world, and though the world was made through him, the world did not recognise him.	but people loved darkness instead of light because their deeds were evil.
1:11 He came to that which was his own, but his own did not receive him.	3:20 Everyone who does evil hates the light and will not come into the light for fear that their deeds will be exposed.

1:12–13 Yet to all who did receive him, to those who believed in his name, he gave the right to become children of God – children born not of natural descent, nor of human decision or a husband's will, but born of God.	3:21 But whoever lives by the truth comes into the light, so that it may be seen plainly that what they have done has been done in the sight of God.

It is God who saves and God who adopts people to be children in his family (1:9–13). It is people who decide whether to step into God's invitation or step back into the darkness (3:19–21). Both God's gracious initiative and people's believing response are involved. John's conclusion as to why people step back when the offer is made is because they are unwilling to face the reality of who they are. They prefer the lack of self-visibility in darkness to the piercing light of receiving Jesus that reveals who we are as well. The Apostle Paul tackles the same questions in Romans 9–11.

And now the second witness, John who baptises, reappears to testify to Jesus for the second time.

The Bridegroom

This second part of the second Declaration begins with Jesus in Judea, baptising (3:22), although we learn at the end of the story that it was his disciples who did the baptising (4:2). John is also baptising, at Aenon near Salim. Aenon is the Greek way of writing the Aramaic word for 'springs', and we are told that John was baptising there because 'there was plenty of water', which is the one thing you need if you are one who baptises by calling. One possible location has been identified as the Wadi al-Far'a, about four miles north east of Jerusalem. It seems likely that in the overlap between Jesus and John, this moment occurs when both are baptising quite near to each other.

As in the first Declaration, baptising causes controversy. However, this time it is not a delegation from Jerusalem who are investigating John who baptises (1:19–23), it is a 'certain Jew' who argues with John's disciples (3:25). This looks like a literary device which allows the author to place himself into the story without drawing attention to himself.

We don't know what the argument is about. It could be about why John is baptising. It is much more likely to be about why Jesus' disciples are baptising. When new people turn up and start doing what you have been doing for several years, it can cause tensions. John baptises so that Israel will be ready for God's new King to be revealed. It makes sense that those gathering round Jesus and seeing him as Messiah would continue the practice of baptism. This is not Christian baptism because they have no idea about the crucifixion for sins and the resurrection into new covenant life. This is entirely Jewish at this point, although it does carry forward into Christian baptism. The Jews use washing to enact stepping from one reality into another. In this case people are stepping into the reality of being disciples of Jesus. It is not difficult to imagine that John's disciples are a bit annoyed about this.

What we do know is what happens after the argument. They go back and report to John, 'Jesus has started baptising and everyone is going over to him', which is a good indication of what they have been arguing about (3:26).

John's reply mirrors what he said to the Pharisees:

1:24–27 Now the Pharisees who had been sent questioned him, 'Why then do you baptise if you are not the Messiah, nor Elijah, nor the Prophet?' 'I baptise with water,' John replied, 'but among you stands one you do not know. He is the one who comes after me, the straps of whose sandals I am not worthy to untie.'	3:26–8 They came to John and said to him, 'Rabbi, that man who was with you on the other side of the Jordan – the one you testified about – look, he is baptising, and everyone is going to him.' To this John replied, 'A person can receive only what is given them from heaven. You yourselves can testify that I said, "I am not the Messiah but am sent ahead of him."'

John embodies so beautifully the prophetic history of Israel. He points away from himself to Jesus and he is comfortable in his calling and role. He strongly affirms that the followers of Jesus will baptise those who also choose to become disciples of Jesus.

The second Declaration continues to follow the narrative shape of the first:

1:29–34	3:29–35
29 The next day John saw Jesus coming towards him and said, 'Look, the Lamb of God, who takes away the sin of the world!	29 The bride belongs to the bridegroom. The friend who attends the bridegroom waits and listens for him, and is full of joy when he hears the bridegroom's voice. That joy is mine, and it is now complete.
30 This is the one I meant when I said, "A man who comes after me has surpassed me because he was before me."	30–1 He must become greater; I must become less.' The one who comes from above is above all; the one who is from the earth belongs to the earth and speaks as one from the earth. The one who comes from heaven is above all.
31 I myself did not know him, but the reason I came baptising with water was that he might be revealed to Israel.' 32–3 Then John gave this testimony: 'I saw the Spirit come down from heaven as a dove and remain on him. And I myself did not know him, but the one who sent me to baptise with water told me, "The man on whom you see the Spirit come down and remain is the one who will baptise with the Holy Spirit."	32–3 He testifies to what he has seen and heard, but no one accepts his testimony. Whoever has accepted it has certified that God is truthful. 34 For the one whom God has sent speaks the words of God, for God gives the Spirit without limit.

34 I have seen and I testify that this is God's Chosen One.'	35–6 The Father loves the Son and has placed everything in his hands. Whoever believes in the Son has eternal life, but whoever rejects the Son will not see life, for God's wrath remains on them.

We have the same problem of not being entirely sure when John who baptises stops speaking and John the author starts writing. The most obvious break point is 3:32. John the author starts to speak or write alongside John who baptises who is still speaking in the first Declaration. The two witnesses agree with each other and speak the same testimony.

An Authentic Voice

John claims his authenticity comes from Isaiah. He is the Voice announcing the coming King. He comes baptising so that Jesus might be revealed (1:31). Jesus speaks with an authentic testimony of what he has seen and heard (3:32). He is the King who has come down from heaven. But as we have seen, knowing who is authentic happens within a mutually defined group. Those who are baptised by John do recognise Jesus. Those who do accept Jesus do know that he is speaking the truth (3:33). But many stand outside and dispute the authenticity of both John and Jesus.

The Giving of the Spirit

The Spirit came down and remained on Jesus (1:32). He is the one who will drench or baptise God's people with the Holy Spirit (1:33). John the author emphasises in the second Declaration that this is not a single event but a way to live. Because Jesus gives the Spirit 'without limit'. There is a never-ending immeasurable flow of the Spirit of God into the people of God from the Son of God (3:34).

The Chosen Son

Jesus is God's chosen one (1:34). He is the Son raised up to rule, whom the Father loves and who has come to give eternal life, which is to know God and to be saved from God's judgment and wrath (3:35–6).

The Bridegroom

John who baptises does make one new declaration of Jesus which in effect summaries all of Israel's history and theology. Jesus is the Bridegroom who has come for his Bride (3:29). This is Isaiah:

> for the Lord will take delight in you,
> and your land will be married.
> As a young man marries a young woman,
> so will your Builder marry you;
> as a bridegroom rejoices over his bride,
> so will your God rejoice over you.
> (Isa. 62:4–5)

It is difficult to take on board the full depth of meaning in those few words. God is wooing us. God is calling us to become one with him. God is inviting us to step into faithful covenant love, with joy, delight and happiness in each other.

This is Hosea:

> I will betroth you to me for ever;
> I will betroth you in righteousness and justice,
> in love and compassion.
> I will betroth you in faithfulness,
> and you will acknowledge the Lord.
> (Hos. 2:19–20)

Hosea has a remarkable calling. He is sent by God to marry a woman who is unfaithful to him. This is a painful struggle. Hosea is called to live out how God feels about his people (Hos. 1). It is in the experience of the pain of loss and the anger of rejection that God

211

makes this incredible declaration. Despite his people's unfaithfulness and turning away from him and squandering of all he has given them, God is going to draw them back to himself with tender, faithful love. That is the story of Israel, which is what Hosea tells. It is the story of humanity. It is our story. But God has come to save us. And John declares to us that such is the depth of God's heart towards us that we are the Bride of a faithful, pure lover and are to be joined forever to our Husband.

Admission

19

The Way In

No Condemnation

We have now looked at all the stories in this section of the Gospel. Except one. No Condemnation is a stand-alone story. You can read it in John 8:2–11. It may be in italics in your Bible. As often explained in a footnote, this story does not appear in many of the early versions that we have of the Gospel.

Before printing was invented, copies of the Bible were made by hand. Although copying was done with great care and diligence, very small differences did occur. Once a small difference happens in a copy it gets carefully reproduced in the copies made from that one. So perhaps at some point a copyist missed this story out by mistake, and it is missing from all subsequent copies. Or the Gospel was revised after copies had started to be made, and the story was either added in or taken out. We will never know. This book is not a historical–critical study but takes a narrative approach. We are taking the text as it is, and this story is in the text that we have. However, it is helpful that both the textual analysis and the narrative analysis place this story as being in some sense separate from the others.

From our point of view as readers, the story accomplishes two purposes. It gives us a bit of a break from having to read three Contention arguments in a row, and it gives us a profound insight into the basis on which we might meet with Jesus.

The story has echoes of all the panels. It has an element of the Contention stories: Jesus is interacting with the authorities who are trying to undermine him. But Jesus does not speak of his authority, identity or authenticity as he does in the Contention stories. It has something of the Provocation stories: Jesus does something that challenges the authorities' interpretation and application of the Law. But there is nothing here that proclaims him as the new King, as there is in the Provocation stories. There is a strong resonance with the Invitation stories: yet again we find Jesus in one-to-one conversation with a woman, treating her with dignity, respect and empowerment. But while he calls her to a new life, he does not invite her into a discipleship relationship, as he does in the Invitation stories.

The panel that connects most with this story are the Demonstration stories. A significant person comes to Jesus – the teachers of the Law and the Pharisees (8:3). They ask Jesus to 'help' someone else – a woman caught in adultery (8:3–5). Jesus is reluctant in his response. He doodles in the sand with his finger (8:6). But this causes them to step forward. They keep questioning him (8:7). Jesus then gives instructions: 'Let any one of you who is without sin be the first to throw a stone at her' (8:7). The miracle occurs in the hands and feet of others. They drop their stones to the ground and walk away. And only a few know what has really happened. The only person who knows what Jesus says next is the woman (8:8–11). But this is not an Elisha sign.

This short story is a summary of the Gospel.

First, Jesus is not saying that the Law doesn't matter. He is not saying that Moses was wrong and we live in more enlightened times. At the end of this story, adultery is still very destructive and wrong and needs to be stopped. But we discover that with Jesus' word it can be stopped – without putting to death those who are caught in it. There is something particularly horrible in that it takes two to commit adultery and yet only the woman is brought for humiliation, condemnation and judgment. According to the Law, both deserve death (Lev. 20:10). But where is the man? We can only guess at the murky reasons lying behind that detail. Thankfully, Jesus does not insist on the Law having the last word. He reserves that for himself and speaks it personally and privately to the woman.

Second, Jesus highlights the problem we all have with the Law. Knowing what is right does not make us live right. We need more than that. Both the authorities and the woman have a problem. The authorities are using the Law self-righteously. They are using the Law against the woman to condemn her. But they are blind to their own sin – until Jesus helps them. The woman is condemned by the

Law, but she is trapped and stuck in her condemnation – until Jesus saves her.

Third, Jesus saves everyone in the story from themselves. He saves those whose instincts are to judge and condemn others. He saves them from that. We hear the sound of stones falling from their hands into the sand and their feet walking away. He also saves the woman, stuck in shame and condemnation. He brings her into a safe place, just her and him. The voices of accusation, condemnation and shame are silenced. The only word she will hear now is from him. He then helps her to face her sin and to walk free. All by his word. If you want to read this story in a longer, more theological form, read Romans 7–8.

The Old Testament story sitting underneath this one is about a man. Israel's greatest King – David – committed adultery and then tried to cover it up by arranging for her loving and faithful husband to be killed in battle (2 Sam. 11). No one knew, although the commander of the army must have suspected. Then God sent Nathan the prophet to confront David. He too was forgiven and did not die (2 Sam. 12:13). There were terrible consequences to his adultery: the child died. But we catch a glimpse of how God's word of mercy can save us from our sins. David was so affected by this he wrote a song from the depths of his heart of how God cleanses us from everything that has gone wrong deep within us (Ps. 51).

This is the way in. This is the way in to meet with Jesus. All the voices of shame and guilt are silenced and you stand face to face with Jesus, hearing his word alone. That which prevents us from drawing close to God is torn apart and we can go in, which is where we will go very soon, when we have had a look at what it is that we are going into.

The Narrative Panels

Demonstration

We have looked at the first and the second signs: The Wedding at Cana and The Healing of the Royal Official's Son. We have seen how they fit together. They have the same storyboard, an identical narrative shape.

We have found two more stories with the same shape: The Feeding of the Five Thousand and The Raising of Lazarus. Four stories that all come together and create a space. With Jesus in the middle. So that you can know him.

Invitation

We have looked at the stories *before* the first and the second signs: The First Disciples and The Woman at the Well. We have discovered how these stories fit together. They have the same storyboard, an identical narrative shape. We have found two more stories with the same storyboard: The Anointing for Burial and The Last Meal. Four stories that all come together and create a holy space. Where you can see Jesus. Where you can know him and find friendship with him.

Provocation

We have looked at the stories *after* the first sign and the second sign: Closing Down the Temple and The Healing at the Pool. They have the same storyboard, an identical narrative shape. We have found two more stories with the same shape: The Healing of the Man Born Blind and The New King Comes. Four stories that all come together and create a beautiful space. Where Jesus stands before you. Speaking to you. So that you can know him as he really is.

Contention

We have looked at the two stories *after that*: A Night Visit and No Interruptions. They have the same storyboard, an identical narrative shape. Within the stories are six categories of spoken word. This time we found five more stories with the same shape: The Bread of Life, Water Within, You Will Die in Your Sin, The Shepherd and the Gate and Death to Life. Seven stories that all come together and create a challenging space. Where Jesus is there. Speaking so clearly of his identity. So that you can know him.

*

As we immerse ourselves in these stories, our friendship with Jesus grows. We see such depth to him. He is a real person whom we can know. A real person we can meet. A friend we can know. Someone we can love and who we know loves us.

We have seen how the story of Jesus is the story of the Old Testament being relived in him. He is the Word made flesh.

Jesus is our Elisha. He comes to pull down our need to control others which we find so deep within ourselves. The desire to control kills friendship, which is why Jesus came to get rid of it in us.

We are his Jacob. Despite all our shortcomings, he invites us close to him where we can sit with him and truly be ourselves with him. We don't have to hide or pretend. There is no need to deceive. We can be freed from our desires to grasp for the things that God has promised to give us. Grasping for things ourselves undermines friendship, which is why Jesus is transforming us.

He is Isaiah's new King. He performs provocative signs to the corrupt powers. He is unlike any person of power that we have ever seen before. He is a true King who lays down his life, so that others can be fruitful. He calls us to follow him to the place of surrender to God. In doing this we discover that we can give ourselves for others. We too can be a seed that falls into the ground and dies so that fruitfulness can come from our lives.

He is Ezekiel in our Exile. And he is our Exodus from slavery to sin. Both Exile and Exodus are happening together. We are in Exile. This is not our true home. Corruption, deception and darkness are still all around us and also within us. We long for something better. But the Exile is ending because the new Exodus has begun. We are on a journey to a new life and a new land where we will dwell with God.

The Timeline

Twenty-two stories are brought together to create a space for friendship, all set out in an elegant sequence that draws us into relationship with Jesus.

As we have already seen, in contrast to the other Gospels, John the author is very precise about the locations of his stories. This adds to our understanding of how the stories from each narrative panel fit together. John the author also includes some very detailed references to time and is very particular about how each story connects with the story that follows. By being alert to how he identifies the passing of time, we can see the timeline. There are seven literary devices that he uses:

1. THE FESTIVALS CREATE A TIMELINE

In contrast to the other Gospels, there are three Passover Festivals recorded in John. The first Passover is when the first Provocation story happens, Closing Down the Temple (2:13), and the first Contention story follows with Nicodemus (3:1). The second Passover Festival in the Gospel is 'near' at the third Demonstration story, The Feeding of the Five Thousand (6:4), and the third Contention story follows with the arguments about flesh and blood. The third Passover in the Gospel is 'near' when we read the third Invitation story, The Anointing for Burial (11:55), which sets the context for the final Provocation story, The New King Comes (12:1), the Contention story that follows, Death to Life, and the final Invitation story, The Last Meal (13:1).

There are three other festivals in the Gospel. The second Provocation story, The Healing at the Pool, which continues straight into the Contention story that follows, is during a festival (5:1). It makes sense for this festival to be Shavuot, the Festival of Weeks, which occurs seven weeks after Passover.

When the Festival of Tabernacles happens, Jesus goes, secretly at first, to Jerusalem (7:2, 10) and then teaches in the Temple courts. This is the Contention story, Water Within (7:14, 37), which leads straight into the Admission story that follows, No Condemnation.

The Contention story, The Shepherd and the Gate, occurs during the Festival of Dedication or the Festival of Lights (10:22).

The Festivals create a timeline of something over two years in duration, starting before the first Passover and leading up to the third Passover.

2. DIRECT TIME JOINS BETWEEN STORIES

Some stories are linked with direct connections showing that one immediately follows another. The first Declaration story concludes with John who baptises giving testimony about Jesus. He gives this testimony 'the next day', which is the day following the investigation by the Pharisees (1:29). The following story, the first Invitation story, starts with the same expression, 'The next day' (1:35). Following another 'next day' within this story, where Jesus decides to go to Galilee (1:43), the first Demonstration, starts 'on the third day' (2:1). These three stories are all directly joined in time and are set within the space of a single week.

This direct join in time is repeated between the second Invitation and the second Demonstration stories. After his unlikely encounter with The Woman at the Well, Jesus stays in the village of Sychar two more days (4:40). The following story, The Healing of the Royal Official's Son, starts with a recap of this: 'After the two days he left for Galilee' (4:43).

The same direct joins in time are seen between the third Invitation story and the fourth Provocation story (12:1, 12).

3. NARRATIVE JOINS BETWEEN STORIES

In these connections between stories there are no time references. But neither is there any pause between the stories nor passing of time in the narrative. Instead, the stories are joined by shared content which shows that one story naturally follows the other.

All the Provocation stories are followed by Contention stories. In each case there is a narrative join. In Closing Down the Temple, Jesus is in Jerusalem for the festival. He does many healing signs but does not entrust himself to anyone because he knows what is in their hearts (2:23–5). Then Nicodemus comes to see him at night (3:1–2). There is no time gap in the narrative between the stories. And Nicodemus is portrayed as a specific example of the people just described at the end of the previous story.

This is repeated between The Healing at the Pool and the Contention story that follows. In fact, the stories overlap. The end of the Provocation story is the beginning of the Contention story. Content is shared because Jesus healing on the Sabbath in the Provocation is the reason for the Contention that follows.

This overlap and shared content between Provocation and Contention stories is repeated with The Healing of the Man Born Blind and The New King Comes. In both cases, the end of the Provocation story is the start of the Contention story that follows.

The Admission story is Jesus freeing a woman from sin and the condemnation of others. The Contention story that follows is about how only Jesus can free people from sin. The Contention opens with Jesus saying that he is the Light of World (8:12). In the following Provocation story of The Healing of the Man Born Blind, the same statement is repeated (9:5). The following Contention story of The Shepherd and the Gate occurs, at least in part, during the Festival of Dedication, or the Festival of Lights (10:22). There is no narrative break or noting of the passing of time between these three stories and it would appear that John the author is writing them to be read together.

4. NARRATIVE PAUSE BETWEEN STORIES
These occur at the end of the first two Demonstration stories which both lead to Provocation stories. The Demonstration stories have a clear endpoint. After The Wedding at Cana, Jesus goes down to Capernaum with his mother, brothers and disciples and stays there a few days (2:12). The Provocation story that follows, Closing Down the Temple, begins with a deliberate time reference: 'When it was almost time for the Jewish Passover, Jesus went up to Jerusalem' (2:13). The stories are joined with a deliberate pause. The same device connects The Healing of the Royal Official's Son with the Contention story that follows.

5. NARRATIVE LINKS BETWEEN STORIES
There are two points where John the author deliberately connects stories by using a short narrative link to explain the passing of time. They are both because Jesus withdraws for his own safety. After the Contention story of The Shepherd and the Gate, Jesus withdraws north to Bethany across the Jordan (10:40). From there he walks back

to Bethany near Jerusalem for The Raising of Lazarus. He has not been up north long, because the disciples' objection to returning to Judea is because 'a short while ago the Jews there tried to stone you, and yet you are going back?' (11:8).

After The Raising of Lazarus he withdraws again, this time to Ephraim (11:54). For the next story he is back in Bethany, where he is anointed with perfume. This occurs six days before the Passover (12:1). Therefore, The Raising of Lazarus is located somewhere between the Festival of Lights (November/December) and Passover (March/April), with deliberate narrative links both before and after the story.

6. A WOVEN NARRATIVE JOIN

This occurs just once. The end of the Contention story with Nicodemus is woven into the start of the second Declaration. It is hard to see the join where Jesus stops talking and John the author starts narrating.

7. TIME GAPS BETWEEN STORIES

There are two substantial time gaps that John the author makes clear by using the festivals. The second Provocation story, The Healing at the Pool, and the second Contention story that follows are both set at a 'Festival' (5:1), most likely the Festival of Weeks. This occurs in the Jewish month of Sivan, which is May in our calendar. The next stories are the Feeding of the Five Thousand and the Contention that follows. These are both set near Passover (6:4). This occurs in the Jewish month of Nisan, which is March/April in our calendar. Fully ten months separate these stories.

The Feeding of the Five Thousand and the Contention that follows both occur in Galilee, and John the author tells us that Jesus then went around in Galilee as he did not want to go about in Judea because of the threat to his life (7:1). The next two stories happen in Jerusalem at the Festival of Tabernacles (7:2). This occurs in the Jewish month of Tishri, which is September/October in our calendar, five months later.

This gives the timeline shown on page 224.

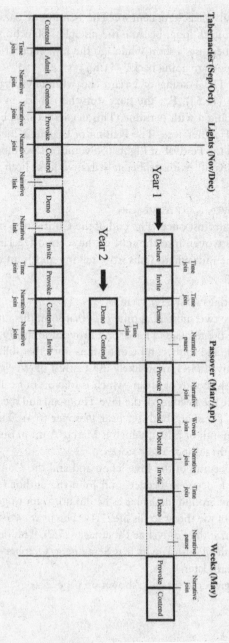

Timeline of the Stories of the Life of Jesus

Tabernacles (Sep/Oct)

| Contend |
| Time join |
| Admit |
| Narrative join |
| Contend |
| Narrative join |
| Provoke |
| Narrative join |
| Contend |
| Narrative link |
| Demo |
| Narrative link |
| Invite |
| Time join |
| Provoke |
| Narrative join |
| Contend |
| Narrative join |
| Invite |

Lights (Nov/Dec)

Year 1

Year 2

Declare
Time join
Invite
Time join
Demo

Demo
Time join
Contend

Passover (Mar/Apr)

Narrative pause

Provoke
Narrative join
Contend
Woven join
Declare
Narrative join
Invite
Time join
Demo

Weeks (May)

Narrative pause

Provoke
Narrative join
Contend

You will have to imagine
June, July, and August

224

Elegance

This is an extraordinarily elegant structure. There are three sets of stories: two sets of ten stories and one set of two stories. To add to the symmetry, the two sets of ten stories can each be viewed as two sets of five stories.

The first set of five stories is made up of one story from each of the five narrative panels. The second five stories repeat this pattern, in exactly the same order. A woven join in the middle brings the two sets of five stories together. John the author points to this structure by using the literary device of first sign and second sign. By this means, the building blocks of the five narrative panels are revealed and the other stories of the same narrative shape can be discovered.

In this set of ten stories, because of the two narrative pauses and the woven join, a third set of five stories appears in the middle. This set also contains one story from each of the five narrative panels.

Then there are two stories that stand apart, separated from the two sets of ten stories by long time gaps. John the author draws our attention to this by locating the stories in relation to the festivals. The third Demonstration story in this set of two, The Feeding of the Five Thousand, is one of the places where John's Gospel lines up very directly with the Synoptic Gospels. By everyone's account, it was a major turning point in Jesus' ministry. John communicates the significance of what happened partly by these two stories being very much on their own and partly by the fact that The Feeding of the Five Thousand is the only Contention story that happens outside Jerusalem. It is also the only Contention story that does not involve the authorities but is the place where lots of ordinary people find what Jesus says too difficult and stop following him. Even though five loaves fed five thousand, many people do not want to eat with him.

In the second set of ten stories, the geographic focus shifts significantly south. All the stories occur either in or very near Jerusalem. While the antipathy of the authorities is signposted in the first set of ten stories, it is in the second set that their anger and their rejection build to breaking point. John the author conveys this in the first five stories by using a series of alternating Contention stories. But it is The Raising of Lazarus that triggers the decision by the authorities to arrest Jesus and persuade Pilate to crucify him. This story is high-lighted and slightly set apart by the use of the narrative links on either side of the story.

This Demonstration story starts the final five stories, which also include one story from all the narrative panels, except Declaration. There cannot be another Declaration story here, as we know from the other Gospels that John who baptises has been murdered by Herod. Instead, there are two Invitation stories. This creates another elegant symmetry. The first thing that Jesus does in the Gospel is to invite some people to his house to make friends. The final thing that Jesus does before we enter the timeless time is to declare his followers to be his friends and invite them to his Father's house, where he will go to get things ready.

The Most Holy Place

The pathway is elegant and has been beautifully crafted by the author. But I kept thinking about how the Gospel is a set of stories that create a space where we can meet a person. What we have been doing, as we have journeyed through the Gospel, is looking *through* the stories to see the person behind the stories. It slowly dawned on me that maybe there was another correspondence between the Gospel and the Temple. Maybe there is a deeper way of looking at how these stories all fit together.

The Tabernacle in the desert was built to a design revealed by God to Moses on the mountain. It was made of ten finely woven curtains joined together in two groups of five: 'Make the tabernacle with ten curtains of finely twisted linen and blue, purple and scarlet yarn, with cherubim woven into them by a skilled worker. All the curtains are to be the same size – twenty-eight cubits long and four cubits wide. Join five of the curtains together, and do the same with the other five (Exod. 26:1–2).

The Temple in Jerusalem was built to the same specification as the original tent. God's space was called the most holy place. It was an open-ended cube built of five sides exactly twenty cubits in each dimension. 'He prepared the inner sanctuary within the temple to set the ark of the covenant of the Lord there. The inner sanctuary was twenty cubits long, twenty wide and twenty high. He overlaid the inside with pure gold, and he also overlaid the altar of cedar' (1 Kgs 6:19–20).

A tent in the desert made of two sets of five curtains, and a five-sided, open-ended, gold-covered cube in Jerusalem, within which God dwells. Inside this most holy place, where the very presence of the Living God is found, is placed the ark, or box, containing the covenant Law that is a sign of the covenant God has made with his people. And there are two room-sized angelic figures that are a sign of God's living presence with them. Each of these figures is ten cubits high and has a wingspan of ten cubits, made up of two wings each five cubits long (1 Kgs 6:23–8).

On the sixth side, the human entrance to God's space on earth, is a full-height decorative curtain of beautifully woven material. Only the High Priest is able to enter behind the curtain into God's space, and that once a year, bearing blood sacrifice for the forgiveness of sins.

These are all human constructions done by highly skilled people who are filled with God's Spirit (Exod. 31:1–11). However, they make what Moses has been shown by God. As the writer of the letter to the Hebrews reminds us, the earthly construction of the Tabernacle in the desert is built to a spiritual specification that has been revealed by God and points to spiritual realities much greater than itself (Heb. 8:1–5).

Maybe John the author has adopted this approach in his deliberate construction of the Gospel. Not a skilled weaver, but a skilled writer, working with words to create a space in which we can go to meet with God; working with the Spirit of God to produce something of human scale, but which gives access to spiritual reality so much greater than itself.

We have seen how the stories come together to form the narrative panels. As we look through each panel, we see a different side of Jesus. They are views from different perspectives. That is what we do when we really get to know someone. There is a complexity and depth to people which we only appreciate when we get to see them from many sides. A way to see the structure of the Gospel is to see it in the same way as the Temple. The sets of stories come together to form a five-sided cube of pure gold. A five-sided cube of stories that we can hold in our hands, but which we can look through and see Jesus.

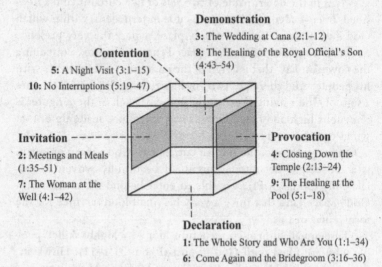

Demonstration

3: The Wedding at Cana (2:1–12)

8: The Healing of the Royal Official's Son (4:43–54)

Contention

5: A Night Visit (3:1–15)

10: No Interruptions (5:19–47)

Invitation

2: Meetings and Meals (1:35–51)

7: The Woman at the Well (4:1–42)

Provocation

4: Closing Down the Temple (2:13–24)

9: The Healing at the Pool (5:1–18)

Declaration

1: The Whole Story and Who Are You (1:1–34)

6: Come Again and the Bridegroom (3:16–36)

First Set of Ten Stories as Holy Place

This isn't just a space where we can come and see Jesus. The invitation is to come and *be in* Jesus. To be so close that we are one. Where we can go inside with him.

But what is the way in?

This might be the place for the story that stands apart in the Gospel: No Condemnation. This is the sixth side: the way in, the woven curtain through which we can now go. Here are the second set of ten stories and the space that they form for us to meet Jesus.

We have access not just to see Jesus, not just to know him, but to be in him. The condemning stones of guilt and shame fall from our hands and the curtain parts for us to go in and encounter Jesus in the fullest way possible. To be one with him.

That is where we will go now.

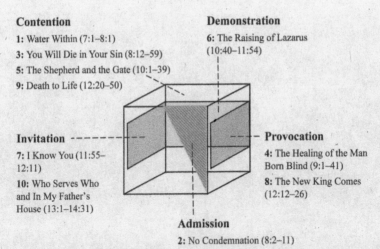

Contention

1: Water Within (7:1–8:1)

3: You Will Die in Your Sin (8:12–59)

5: The Shepherd and the Gate (10:1–39)

9: Death to Life (12:20–50)

Demonstration

6: The Raising of Lazarus (10:40–11:54)

Invitation

7: I Know You (11:55–12:11)

10: Who Serves Who and In My Father's House (13:1–14:31)

Provocation

4: The Healing of the Man Born Blind (9:1–41)

8: The New King Comes (12:12–26)

Admission

2: No Condemnation (8:2–11)

Second Set of Ten Stories as Holy Place

PART THREE

Come Inside

Timeless Time

20

In Christ

Introduction

At the very end of chapter 14, time stops. Time does not start again until the beginning of chapter 18.

This is what Jesus says at the very end of the story of The Last Meal: 'Come now; let us leave' (14:31).

But no one moves. What follows is like a scene from the film *Inception* where they have found a way to mess with time and space in a world created by imagination. Except this is real. Jesus speaks for three whole chapters, but time does not pass. The clock has stopped. There is virtually no physical movement. Only once does Jesus move, when he looks up to heaven to pray (17:1). Everyone else is stationary. There is very little dialogue. Only once do the disciples speak. And only to say, 'What does he mean . . .? We don't understand what he is saying.' (16:18). That's what my wife says when we watch *Inception*.

Then after Jesus' prayer, which is the whole of chapter 17, the clock starts again, the action unfreezes and everyone starts moving: 'When he had finished praying, Jesus left with his disciples and crossed the Kidron Valley' (18:1).

If you were a teacher marking the Gospel as an essay, you would point out that this is poor writing. The main character says, 'Let's leave,' but then talks for three chapters. That in itself is fine. Main characters do tend to go on about things. But the author does not acknowledge that in the narrative. It looks like he has written as if just a short prayer of blessing lies between the end of 14 and the beginning of 18. And that, for many scholars, is simply strange.

I hope that I have convinced you of John's skill and attention to detail. He has written this very deliberately. First-century people did not have cinema, but they did have the same powerful imagination and intellect as we do. Only they had to communicate all their profound thoughts in words. This is one of John the author's deep ideas. We are meant to see that the clock has stopped. Because it has.

Everything we are about to read is being spoken in a time frame where the time is always now. It was in the disciples 'now' when they first heard it. But it is not in our past. John is inviting us into a place where it is *always* now. Jesus is speaking these words to us now. I call it the timeless time.

Eternity has this quality. We tend to think of the eternal as being unendingly long. It is. But the eternal is also unendingly present. Eternal is as unceasingly *now* just as much as it is unceasingly continuous. That is why, when you are immersed in something that you enjoy, it can seem like time stands still. For that period of time, you are in a 'now' moment.

We know that God is able to move up and down the timeline of the Universe because he exists outside space and time. He can turn the pages of time just as we can turn the pages of a book. But he is also very present at each point in time. He is not absent at one point to be present at another. He alone moves so fast that he is truly stationary. God is able to hold everything in our world in his present without distorting the timeline, which is the sort of ability that comes with the territory of being God.

This is a moment in the Gospel where we step into something of that. For these chapters, it is always now.

There is, of course, an Old Testament story where time stands still. It is where Joshua is fighting the King of Jerusalem. This is long before Jerusalem is captured and becomes the city of David. The King of Jerusalem, and several other kings, have attacked a tribe who are friendly with Israel and the tribe pleads for help from Israel. In the middle of the battle, Joshua calls out for the sun to stand still and the moon to stop. With God's help they win a famous victory against the odds (Josh. 10:9–14). It is a very strange story, and it is difficult to know what to make of it. But if you find that story a bit strange, and the implications it has for time and space, you should try studying quantum physics.

John is blissfully unaware of physics. But he does see that it is possible for Jesus to speak to everyone from a place where it is always now. This is what is happening in chapters 15–17. In chapter 18 the clock will start again, and Jesus will be crucified. But for now, he is sitting right beside you, talking to you.

We will discover that the Jesus who speaks in the 'now' is the same Jesus we have been getting to know. The narrative panels all repeat in the 'now'. There are some limitations because of this context of Jesus being in this 'now' moment. There is almost no dialogue. There is no action. There are no representative people interacting with Jesus because Jesus wants this moment to be just between you and him. But everything we have seen of Jesus in the narrative panels is brought into this moment. This part of the Gospel is not a story; it is one continuous speech by Jesus. However, the narrative panels form the structure of the speech. As in the first section of the Gospel, the speech starts and finishes with an Invitation panel. In between those two quite long sections, the speech is made up of three parts, each of which repeats. The Provocation, Demonstration and Contention panels have been woven together into a continuous narrative with each story appearing twice in a double repeating pattern.

It's all very elegant.

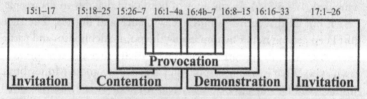

The Timeless Time Unwrapped

In the Vine

The first section of the timeless time is an Invitation segment. It is in two parts, opening with the teaching of Jesus as the true vine. You can read this in 15:1–8. There are five ingredients: (1) Jesus who is God's planting; (2) The Father who is working; (3) Our living union;

235

(4) The call to abiding; (5) God who is answering. John the author has written this part in a spiral. It is a way of writing that draws us up and in. The first time round the spiral it is ingredients 1–2–3–4. Then we go round them again, but the second time round it is a bit quicker: it goes 1–3–4. And the third time around is quickest of all: just 2–4. And then we get to number 5. We get to the heart of what Jesus has invited us into.

Jesus Who Is God's Planting

Jesus identifies himself as the vine: 'I am the true vine' (15:1); 'I am the vine' (15:5).

Jesus is the vine. It is an organic, living image. To understand that, of course, we need to look into the Old Testament. The vine is the people of God. After the crossing of the Red Sea, Moses sings of how Israel is planted by God as his people, his inheritance and his dwelling place (Exod. 15:17). Unfortunately, in the Old Testament the vine is often not growing well. Isaiah sings of the failure of the vine (5:1–25). The song starts happily with the vineyard owner working hard to create the vineyard. But the grapes aren't good; the vine yields only bad fruit (Isa. 5:1–2). God says to his people, 'What more can I do?' In the end, God decides that the only option is to dismantle the vineyard (Isa. 5:3–6). Isaiah sings of how God delights in his people Israel, but all that grows is injustice, violence and distress. The rich just keep getting richer by oppressing the poor. Alcoholism and party culture are rife. People are deceitful with each other and wise in their own eyes. What is wrong is spoken of as if it were good. Money buys justice. And no one pays God any real attention (Isa. 5:7–25).

God judges his people. They are uprooted and sent into exile. Even when they return to the land, they are still, in reality, in exile. Their great prophetic hopes have not been realised. Psalm 80 picks up on this, pleading with God to restore his people and make his face shine upon them again (Ps. 80:1–3). The psalmist retells the story of the vine, how God brought his people out of Egypt and planted them in good ground, but the vine has been ravaged and abandoned. However, the psalmist sees a future where God will again tend his vine:

Return to us, God Almighty!
Look down from heaven and see!
Watch over this vine,
the root your right hand has planted,
the son you have raised up for yourself
(Ps. 80:14–15)

The psalmist sees that God will plant a new root from the existing stock. The metaphor suddenly changes. The new root will be a son God has raised up for himself.

Other prophets see the same thing, that God will take a shoot from the vine of Israel to create a new planting and a renewed people. Jeremiah prophesies that God will raise up a new righteous branch, or shoot. He will be a King and will reign wisely (Jer. 23:5; 33:15). Zechariah sees a man whose name is Branch. He will build a new temple (Zech. 6:12). Isaiah sings that 'the branch of the Lord will be beautiful and glorious'. Everyone will be holy. All sins will be washed away, and the branch will be a living temple, continuously overshadowed by the presence of God (Isa. 4:2–6). Ezekiel prophesies twice that God's vine has become useless. God's people have become unfaithful. God is going uproot his vine and judge his vine with fire (Ezek. 15:1–8; 19:10–14). But in the middle of these warnings, Ezekiel prophesies that God himself will take a shoot from the vine that has gone so wrong and plant it on his mountain. This vine will be splendid and fruitful (Ezek. 17:22–4).

Jesus places himself in the middle of all these prophetic hopes and proclaims *himself* as the new people of God. He is the new shoot from the old stock who is being freshly planted by God. By this means, the people of God are going to move from failure to fruitfulness. God is going to tend his vine and the fruit will be good.

The Father Who Is Working

The Father will tend him as the new vine: 'My Father is the vinedresser. Every branch in Me that does not bear fruit, He takes away; and every *branch* that bears fruit, He prunes it so that it may bear more fruit . . . *and they gather* them, and cast them into the fire and they are burned' (15:1–2, 6).

Jesus as the vine is cared for by God. The branches that are pruned are *'in me'*. He doesn't say, 'My Father is going to deal with you lot and cut you all into the little pieces you deserve.' He says, 'If there is no fruit *in me* the Father will cut, and it will be gone.' Or, if there is fruit, the Father will prune the branch and it will grow more fruitful. The branches are an integral part of the vine, and Jesus identifies the vine as being him.

The cutting off and the pruning back are both done with the same goal: further fruitfulness in the vine. It is not going to be a story of endless failure and regret. The Father is going to look after the vine and make sure it is fruitful. For our fruitfulness we have to face that cutting is a permanent feature. It is either cut out or cut back. The presence or absence of fruit determines which kind of cut occurs. This is not about eternal destiny or final judgment. The metaphor is strong (cutting, withering, burning), but this teaching is given where the time is always now. The vine is the people of God now, being lovingly tended by God now. Some things in us get cut right out. Attitudes and behaviour that do not reveal the beautiful fruit of Jesus have to go. Other times we experience God cutting into us where we have been fruitful. Fear not. Trust God. You will grow to be even more fruitful.

Our Living Union

'You are already clean because of the word I have spoken to you . . . you are the branches' (15:3, 5). This talk of the Father cutting, pruning and burning creates some anxiety. Jesus speaks some reassurance: 'You are already clean'. This is a witty word play. 'Cut', 'prune' and 'clean' are all very similar sounding words in Greek. The word 'prune' is very close indeed to 'make clean' – there are just two letters different. Jesus is reassuring us, his friends and followers, that we are already in the vine because we have already been cleaned/pruned by his Word. We know that we are in the vine because we can see where Jesus' Word has left its mark on us.

Being the branches of the vine is an extraordinary thing. We are joined to Jesus and have become part of him. We are not just members of a club or names on a list. Friendship with Jesus so connects us to him that we become one with him and become part of him. To be a friend and follower of Jesus is to step into this extraordinary place of living union with Jesus. Our friendship is now so close that we are in effect one. The Apostle Paul uses the same language when he writes of us being 'in Christ' (Rom. 6:1–11; Eph. 1:3–10). God's people are no longer separate from God but are found in Christ. Paul urges us to look back at the crucifixion and resurrection of Jesus and teaches us that we share in it. Because we are in Christ we were crucified with Christ. Because we are in Christ we have been raised with Christ. John invites us to understand the same truth but approaches it from the other direction. He invites us to understand our oneness with Jesus *before* we read the Crucifixion and Resurrection stories and to read those stories with this perspective of being deeply joined to Jesus and one with him.

The Call to Abiding

Having given us this extraordinary gift of being one with him, Jesus invites us to do all we can to remain in that good place: 'Abide in Me, and I in you. As the branch cannot bear fruit of itself unless it abides in the vine, so neither can you unless you abide in Me . . . he who abides in Me and I in him, he bears much fruit, for apart from Me you can do nothing . . . If you abide in Me, and My words remain in you' (15:4, 5, 7, NASB).

Remaining or abiding in Jesus is where we are called to live. Jesus comes back to this three times in this story as we go up the spiral staircase. It is the same word that is used for spending time with Jesus and hanging out with him. We have seen it before: '"Come," he replied, "and you will see." So they went and saw where he was staying, and they spent that day with him' (1:39).

In the first Invitation story the two disciples abide with Jesus. And now, says Jesus, that is going to become permanent. Just think what would happen to you if you spent a couple of days with Jesus. Well, you are. You are in him. You are round his house and he is at yours. His life is flowing into you. His word is being spoken to you. His heart is being expressed to you. You are part of him now.

Jesus gives us personal responsibility to abide with him. God's sovereignty will not override your responsibility. We understand that with things like driving on right side of the road, having proper meals and brushing our teeth every day. God is gracious. He helps us in our weakness, but God's grace will not override us. Like all friendships, abiding in Christ can be allowed to wither if you wish. To be deeply connected to Jesus is to be fruitful in life. To neglect your friendship puts that at risk.

God Who Is Answering

All of this gives rise to the outcome of answered prayer: 'ask whatever you wish, and it will be done for you' (15:7). As we go up the spiral, we get drawn into the place where God answers our prayers. All the ingredients – the Father working on us, our living union with Jesus where his life flows into us, and our abiding with Jesus – all work together to this end. They enable us to join in with what God is doing through bringing everything to him in prayer. Fortunately, this is not a blank cheque! It flows from our going up into ever deepening union with Jesus.

There are some prayers I have prayed that I am glad God did not answer as they would have borne very bad fruit. And there is perplexity that we can never explain when some of our better prayers remain unanswered. But the invitation that Jesus gives us is to be deeply one with him and to be completely part of all he is doing in the world through prayer.

This incredible invitation to be in living union with Jesus, being worked on by the Father and to join him in all he is doing through prayer brings God glory. As we bear fruit, which is making visible to others the life of Jesus that flows within us, it becomes obvious that we are friends and followers of Jesus (15:8).

An Invitation

This is an Invitation story. There are many features that connect:
1. In the Invitation stories, Jesus (and in one story Mary) start what become open-hearted, deep conversations. This is another one of those. It doesn't get much deeper than Jesus inviting us to become one with him. This the same as Jesus talking to

Nathanael about heaven opening and heaven and earth connecting. This is the same as Jesus talking to the woman at the well about God seeking those who will come to him and worship in Spirit and truth. This is the same as Jesus washing the feet of his disciples and calling them to be priests in God's house and assuring them that the Father will come and make his home with them.

2. In the Invitation stories, social conventions are set aside and people end up connecting very closely with Jesus. Social conventions are a way of protecting people in their own space and regulating how people interact so that people know what to expect and feel safe in a public setting. In this story all such barriers are radically set aside. Jesus invites you to become one with him. He invites you to have nothing at all between you and him, for him to be in you and you to be in him. Your friendship with Jesus can't get any closer than this. There are no barriers at all.

3. In the Invitation stories, Jesus shows that he knows. In this story, because Jesus is speaking personally to everyone, there is no specific 'knowing' moment with someone, as that would cut across his conversation with you. But I hope that you know by now that he knows. He knows you and he is inviting you to be one with him.

4. In the Invitation stories, following the meals and conversations, people become friends and followers of Jesus and immediately begin to participate in what Jesus is doing, often by inviting others to come to him too. In this story we join in through our prayers that God answers. Prayer is a priestly role: bringing the needs of our broken world before God. We have seen in the Invitation stories how the friends and followers of Jesus are called to be priests in God's house.

As we have seen in Chapter Ten, underneath the Invitation stories are the Old Testament stories from the very beginning. The vine is God's people, God's planting. The people of God begin with Abraham and Sarah, Isaac and Rebekah, Jacob and Rachel. They are the family that God chooses to be the beginning of his people. God makes a covenant that from them his people will grow and all nations on earth will be blessed. This is why Psalm 80, which describes God's people as a vine, opens with a plea to God as the Shepherd of Israel, who is Jacob. Two sons and two grandsons of Jacob are mentioned (Ps. 80:1–2). John is taking that whole story of God choosing his people and he is both retelling it with Jesus in the middle and including you. There is a new people of God, a new vine. You are now one of the branches. You are now one of God's chosen people. You are part of the new planting from the old stock.

So far, we have looked at the first part of this Invitation story. We will now look at the second part. It is no surprise that this too is full of what it means to be invited to be friends and followers of Jesus. The focus on this second part of the Invitation story is covenant. Because, as we have seen, to be a friend of Jesus and part of the people of God is to be in covenant relationship with God.

21

Covenant Love

The second part of this Invitation segment in the timeless time is found in 15:9–17.

Dynamic Relationship

When we understand ourselves as being part of the vine, the people of God, there is a danger that we think of that in a static way. Vines don't move very much. But the Invitation stories are very dynamic. The first Invitation story starts with Andrew talking to John who baptises. Jesus walks by and John points him out. Andrew and the other disciple start following Jesus. He ends up inviting them both to his house, where they eat together and talk at length. Andrew immediately goes and finds his brother Simon and brings him to Jesus. Jesus sees him and says that he is going to be so changed as a person that he may as well have a new name.

To be invited to be a friend and follower of Jesus is to experience

dynamic powerful change in your life. John the author creates that sense of dynamic pulsating life by the way he goes on to describe how our living union with Jesus in the vine works. He uses another literary technique that creates a sense of vibrant, swirling movement. He doesn't write the words and thoughts in a straight line; he doubles back on himself and jumps across what he has just said. The best way to illustrate this is to put the words in a diagram. One thing you might do is trace the path of the words as you go round the diagram. It starts in the middle.

What you can see immediately by drawing it in this way is that the way Jesus relates to us is modelled entirely and completely on the relationship he has with his Father. We are not being made part of the Trinity by being brought into living union with Jesus. But by having oneness with Jesus as branches in the vine, we are being drawn into experiencing everything in our relationship with Jesus that Jesus has with the Father. The bottom half of the diagram, which is describing our relationship with Jesus, reflects entirely the top half, which is Jesus describing his relationship with the Father.

There are three powerful conclusions from this:

1. Jesus loves us in exactly the same way and to the same extent that the Father loves him. Wow.

2. Out of our love for Jesus, it is now possible for us to live a life of obedience to Jesus in exactly the same way that Jesus lived a life of love and obedience to the Father. Wow again.

3. Receiving Jesus' love and then responding with our love and obedience to him is how we stay close to him. We are in this living union, abiding with Jesus just as he lives in living union, abiding with his Father.

To live in the vine is to keep moving round this dynamic relationship with Jesus. We start by remembering that the Father deeply loves the Son. We then recognise that Jesus loves us in exactly the same way as he is loved by the Father. We then receive his love and drink deeply of his love. This enables us to step forward in obedience to Jesus, out of our love for him. And so our lives continuously change from the inside out as our friendship with Jesus deepens.

New Covenant Love

This is classical new covenant teaching as prophesied by Jeremiah and Ezekiel. Jeremiah sees that God is not going to abandon his plan to have a people who live in covenant love with him. God is going to have a new people living in a new covenant (Jer. 31:31–4). The new covenant relationship with God will be characterised by:

1. Unconditional love and commitment from God to his people
2. All God's people knowing God and living as God's friends
3. The complete and total forgiveness of sins
4. God's people living a life of obedience to God because God will write his ways deep within their hearts

Ezekiel sees the same thing from a different angle, that God will gather his people from all the nations, renew their hearts and put his Spirit within them so they can live a life of love and obedience to God (Ezek. 36:24–38).

God's new people, his new planting, live in new covenant relationship with him. To live like this is to live with joy (15:11). There is no deeper joy than knowing that you are loved by God and in return living a life of love for him and living in a way that you know pleases him.

The problem with the word 'obedience' is that we immediately imagine an endless multiplication of difficult rules. There is no life and there is no joy living under a system of complex rules. For Jesus, this is not what obedience means. He wants us to live a life of simplicity. Obedience can be summarised in just one word.

Love

This is the only instruction on how to live in the Gospel of John. Jesus says it twice at the beginning and end of this part: 'My command is this: love each other as I have loved you' (15:12, 17).

As Jesus does in the other Gospels, he summarises obedience to God in one word: love. Love God and love each other. Now that needs some definition, and Jesus gives a simple one: to love is to lay down your life.

As soon as we read this, we immediately have a problem, particularly if we are from the United Kingdom. As soon as we hear these words, 'Greater love has no one than this: to lay down one's life for one's friends', we immediately think of another story: the story of the First World War. Very unfortunately, Jesus' definition of love has been used to describe the sacrifice of those who died fighting the First World War. But when Jesus said to love is to lay down your life, he did not mean the First World War as an example. It is like having the wrong tune in your head when you are trying to sing a different song. To lay down your life for your friends is not to go to war. It is to come to the cross.

War may be necessary sometimes to stop the rise of oppressive regimes, although history shows us that its effectiveness in achieving this is rather limited. War does include bravery, sacrifice and willingness to die for a greater good. But war, particularly the First World War, also includes foolishness, the abuse of power, and unnecessary suffering inflicted on whole populations. War is not the cross. No matter how grateful we are for those who fought for our freedoms, we must not allow the story of war and the story of the cross to mingle in our minds. We must turn off the persistent melody of war in order to understand rightly what Jesus means when he says that we are to love as he loved us.

To love is not to take up power and get your own way. To love is to empower others. To love is not to grab territory for yourself and to accumulate possessions and power for yourself. To love is to give: to give time, to give money, to give attention, to give affection, to give affirmation, to give forgiveness. To love is not to demand justice for yourself. To love is to absorb the sin of others even if it is unjust for you. To love is not to return sin for sin, but to respond to sin with grace, forgiveness, mercy and a desire to bless. No wonder we need to be in living union with Jesus and new covenant relationship with God, empowered by his Spirit to deliver on this.

Called to Be Friends

We have been called to be friends with God. We have been called to become like God. We have been invited to walk free from the wreckage and pain of our lives and join in with what God is doing. We have been given living union with Jesus. We are in a new covenant relationship of love with God. Everything that Jesus knows of God he is making known to us. We are not servants. We are friends (15:14–15).

As with all the Invitation stories, the stories from the very beginning are sitting underneath what Jesus says here. In the Old Testament, both Abraham and Moses are described as being friends with God. It is through the two of them that God establishes his covenant relationship with his people Israel. With Abraham he initiates it and with Moses he explains it. It is no surprise that friendship with God is a key part of this section of the Invitation story on the new people of

God and the new covenant with God in Jesus. God is drawing us into what he did with Moses and with Abraham.

Moses has a tent which he pitches outside the camp. He goes there to meet with God. The *shekinah* glory of the presence of God comes down and Moses speaks to God 'face to face, as one speaks to a friend' (Exod. 33:7–11). Moses is concerned about resources. Who is going to go with him and help him? God assures him: 'I will go with you.' Moses asks God, 'Teach me your ways so I may know you' (Exod. 33:13). This is covenant love. Receiving God's loving friendship and then responding to him. When Moses teaches on the covenant relationship, he says repeatedly that love for God leads to obedience to God (Deut. 10:12; 11:1).

Abraham too is called God's friend (2 Chr. 20:7–8; Isa. 41:8). There is a story where God visits Abraham and has dinner with him and Sarah. God then speaks with Abraham and discusses his plan to judge the cities of Sodom and Gomorrah because so many people have been crying out to God for justice; they have been treated so badly in these places. Abraham does a beautiful piece of Middle Eastern style negotiation with God until God makes it clear he has haggled enough (Gen. 18:1–33). Jesus picks up on this story. Friendship with God is being brought into a place of knowing what God is doing and being involved in what God is doing (15:15).

Every friendship starts somewhere. All those who end up in covenant friendship with God know that it was God who started it. By some mystery it was God who took the initiative. One of the roots of the Hebrew word for 'covenant' is 'to cut' or 'to choose'. There is an image of a meal here. Do you want chicken or beef? You have to make a cut. You have to choose something from a larger set. Moses knows that God has chosen his people (Deut. 10:15). Abraham knows that God has chosen him and called him. Jesus picks up on this idea that our friendship with God was initiated by God. He has chosen us. It is his doing that we have been brought into the vine, the people of God. It is because Jesus reached out to us that we know him. He chose us to be in living union with him. Jesus has given all this to us, so that we can bear fruit for him in our broken world (15:16).

This section of the Invitation story finishes as the first section does, with an invitation to join in with all that God is doing by lifting our voice in prayer to him. Friends of Jesus are priests of God, called to bring the needs of God's world before him (15:16).

22

In the World

Not of This World

In the timeless time there are two Contention segments. You can read them in 15:18–25 and 16:1–4a.

In the Contention stories we have seen many arguments, most of which remain unresolved. They start with people questioning Jesus, like Nicodemus, who ends up just going quiet. Some people do respond positively and express faith in Jesus. But many do not, and as the arguments go on, people start to turn against him. Their rejection of Jesus builds up to the extent that they threaten him with violence.

When people question you, hate you and become violent towards you, it is very hard to handle.

In the Contention stories we see Jesus handling all this brilliantly. We see him speaking to others, but also to himself, of his identity in God. He knows that he is an authentic person sent by God. He is not dependent on other people's responses to him. He doesn't need them to affirm him. He is robust. He knows where he belongs. He knows where he is going. We see him drawing on the Prophet Ezekiel to say surprising things which, when we dig a bit deeper, help us to understand who Jesus is and how he sees himself. But when he says these things, they work to reveal the hearts of the people listening. They either step closer or they start to step away.

In the two Contention segments of the timeless time, Jesus warns us that we will face the same situation. We need to be ready to face it like him.

Not of the World

We don't belong to the world. The world around us is not going to love us. We have been chosen out of the world (15:19). As in the Contention stories, this is the Exodus story being applied to us. As Israel were taken out of Egypt by God's power, so we have been taken out of the world. We don't belong here. We are on a journey to a new life in a new land.

The way people respond to us is not personal to us (15:18). The same is true of Jesus. He knows that when people hate him, what is really going on is that they hate God (15:23). It is like this for us too. If people reject us it is because they are rejecting God. If they listen to us it is because they are listening to God. Neither our failures to convince people of the truth of Jesus nor our successes in doing so say anything about us. They both simply reveal where people stand with God. If the church is just us and a few friends, it is not a lesser church than if thousands have gathered. How people respond to our Invitation to know Jesus is out of our hands. This is so liberating. We are a prophetic people. How people respond to us is not about us. It is about God.

Speaking God's Word

But we must speak up, just as Jesus spoke up. We must do the works of God, just as Jesus did (15:22–4). We are an apostolic people, sent by God, just as Jesus was sent by God to announce good news in both what he said and what he did. God has sent us to reveal hearts. As people hear the gospel and see the gospel in action it reveals where they stand in relation to God. The gospel either saves them or it shows them to be in a place of rejecting God's love. As in the Contention stories, this is Ezekiel being applied to us (Ezek. 33:1–9). Like him, we have been sent to speak God's Word. What happens next is not up to us. It isn't rational to reject God's love. I have never been able to understand why people refuse God. But as we know, many things that people do are not actually that rational (15:25).

In the second Contention segment in the timeless time, Jesus speaks to us to make sure that we are ready for this (16:1). Rejection by others, particularly those we are close to, can be very tough. But this is all part of being friends and followers of Jesus. We go through what he went through. We are in living union with him.

Knowing that this is coming helps us to be ready. Our identity is not in this world. Our identity is not in our family or our gender or our work or our reputation or our relationships, important though all these things are to us. Jesus handles the Contention arguments so well because he knows who he is. We know who we are. Our identity is rooted in Jesus. We are branches in God's vine. Jesus knows that his authority comes from his relationship with his Father. Our authority does not come from our position or role in work, in society or in the church. Our authority comes from our friendship with Jesus. We don't need job titles or other people's permission to have authority in him. Jesus knows he is an authentic person who can be trusted. His authenticity comes from a combination of the Scriptures and his own experience. Our authenticity comes from these sources too – the Scriptures and our changed life in Jesus. It is they who show that we can be trusted.

We too can handle the unresolved arguments that come our way with grace and dignity. We too can draw on the Exodus stories and the Exile prophecies to know who we are and where we are going so that we can stand firm in our calling.

A Sign to the World

In the timeless time there are two Provocation segments. You can read them in 15:26–7 and 16:8–15.

We have seen in the Provocation stories that Jesus takes the initiative and does prophetic signs. He makes a whip and closes part of the Temple down. He sends a man who has been healed into the city, carrying the mat he has lain on for thirty-eight years. He sends a blind man groping through the city with his eyes covered in mud to wash in the Pool of Siloam who comes home seeing. He rides into Jerusalem on a donkey with everyone shouting his praise as King. The disciples don't understand until later. The authorities reject the sign and demand proof of authority to do these things. What Jesus says in response is highly provocative.

Taken together, these stories all reveal that God's judgment is coming on the corruption of the nation and particularly on the deadness and empty formality of their religious life and on the abuse of power by those in charge. The prophetic signs all speak of the same thing: God's new King has come. He will build a new Temple, a new dwelling place of God on the earth.

All these aspects are seen in the Provocation segments of the timeless time.

Taking the Initiative

Jesus takes the initiative. He sends us the Advocate, the one called alongside us, the Spirit of truth who comes from the Father, just as Jesus came from the Father (15:26). Before we look into this, we need to pause and recognise how the narrative panels greatly help us to understand what Jesus is saying here. We have seen in the Invitation stories that Jesus invites his friends and followers round for meals and draws very close to them. We have also seen in the Provocation stories that the same Jesus makes a whip, turns over tables and challenges the Temple authorities. We find the same richness and diversity in the work of the Holy Spirit.

In the Invitation story of chapter 14, the Spirit is promised to Jesus' friends and followers. Jesus is going to the Father, but he will come back to them, not in the body but by the Spirit. The Holy Spirit is Jesus with us. He enables our friendship with Jesus to be real and life-giving. But there is more to the coming of the Holy Spirit than the Invitation to friendship with Jesus, vital though that is. We discover in these Provocation segments that the coming of the Holy Spirit on the Church also acts as a Provocation to the world. The Holy Spirit being sent to the Church is a sign and a challenge to those who are resisting God.

Spirit-Filled Church That Speaks to the World

The Spirit-filled church is the dwelling place of God. We are the visible sign of God's living presence on the earth. As Jesus tells us, 'the Spirit . . . will testify about me. And you also must testify (15:26–7).

The coming of the Spirit of God on the people of God is the sign that speaks to the world. The presence of the Spirit on God's people announces that Jesus is God's new King. It is a strange sign. We are like the man born blind who has washed in the pool called 'Sent' (which is what *Siloam* means) and can now see. We are like the lame man who has been freed from his paralysis. And the Spirit-filled Church has the same vulnerability as Jesus. We don't have all the trappings of power. We are riding on a donkey, gentle and humble. And yet, as we know from the massive persecutions of the Church around the world and throughout history, that the Spirit-filled Church is a sign that greatly provokes the powers.

We are what Jesus announced he would do when he shut the Temple down for an hour, whip in hand. The Spirit-filled Church is the sign that Jesus is King, and he is building the dwelling of God on the earth. The Apostle Paul says the same thing in his letters to the churches he serves (Eph. 2:17–22). The Council of Jerusalem, called to work out what to do with all these Gentiles who were joining the Church, saw the same thing (Acts 15:16–18). The Holy Spirit coming is not just for our good. The Spirit-filled Church is a proclamation to the world.

In the second Provocation segment in the timeless time, Jesus reveals how the Spirit sent to the Church will speak to the world (16:8–11). He will convict the world, or he will prove the world to be in the wrong. The Greek word used here (*elegcho*) is difficult to translate because it carries a range of meanings, all of which are probably meant in this context. It means to convict or help someone to see that they are wrong so that they might change. It means to refute or argue against. It means to find fault with. It means to rebuke severely. All of these Jesus did in the Provocation stories through the signs he did. The Holy Spirit filling the Church continues this work. The world may repent, or it may plot to take the life of the Church. But the sign of the Spirit-filled Church in their midst can't be ignored. The sign is announcing that Jesus rules and the world is in the wrong.

WRONG ABOUT SIN

The world is wrong about sin because they don't believe in Jesus (16:9). This isn't God being cross because people doubt the existence of God or don't attend church. It is much deeper than that. To believe in Jesus is to entrust yourself completely to him. Because you know that only he can save you from your sin. The world doesn't trust Jesus because they are wrong about sin.

The world is wrong about sin in a number of ways. Some say that there isn't a problem with sin at all. Others say that there is a problem, but it isn't my problem; I'm essentially a good person. Others say that the problem is so bad that nothing can be done about it. The Spirit-filled Church announces the crucifixion of Jesus which stands against all of these positions. There is a problem with sin that Jesus as the Lamb of God died to deal with. The problem of sin affects everyone. Each person is called to personally recognise sin within and come to Jesus to be saved from themselves. There is a powerful solution to the problem of sin: the cross. Forgiveness for sin and freedom from sin are both freely given to those who believe. The Spirit-filled Church calls people to believe in Jesus and therefore calls out these other positions on sin as being wrong. Not believing in Jesus is the critical sin in John's Gospel. No other sin is addressed. Not believing is the sin that blocks the solution to all sin. John the author knows that if we can unblock unbelief, all other sin will get sorted out.

WRONG ABOUT RIGHTEOUSNESS

The world is wrong about righteousness because Jesus is going to the Father. The Greek word for righteousness here (*dikaiosyne*) doesn't just mean behaving in the right way. It also means who is in the right, who is approved. The world is wrong about the righteousness of Jesus. The world declares Jesus guilty and condemns him to death. But they do not have the final word. God vindicates him and declares him to be in the right. He raises him to life. He raises him to rule for ever as God's new King. The ascension of Jesus, his going to the Father, is the sign that speaks that Jesus is the one approved by God and that the world is wrong. The world says that there is no need to pay attention to Jesus. He is not someone that you need to listen to.

He is certainly not someone to whom you must surrender and bow the knee of obedience. The Spirit–filled Church declares that the world is wrong about this. Jesus has ascended to the Father. He rules. He, above all, is the one we listen to, the one we follow.

The world is also wrong about righteousness in the sense of how we are approved of by God, how we are declared to be 'in the right' with him. The world looks to itself. Surely, I am good enough, on balance, for God to approve of me. But – only one person has gone to the Father. Only one person has been able to ascend to him. Our righteousness does not qualify us. Righteousness cannot come to us by our works. We are called to a righteousness that comes from faith. We can only be declared to be 'in the right' with God because we believe in the person and work of Jesus who died and ascended on our behalf. We, in living union with him, can make the same journey. But only because we are found in him. The Spirit-filled Church is the sign that announces that the only way to the Father is Christ.

WRONG ABOUT JUDGMENT

The world is wrong about judgment because the ruler of this world has been condemned. Corrupt rulers, and even tinpot dictators in small settings, always think they are going to get away with it. Deep down they know they are acting corruptly. But none of them will stop and admit it, because they know that will lead to the end of their rule. And ruling, whether that be a nation, a company or just a few poor people, is what they want to hold on to. Corrupt rulers love power, and they fight hard to keep hold of it. They are wrong. They are not going to get away with it. Judgment on everyone is coming. Judgment is coming that brings to the light everything that is happening, brings justice to bear and puts everything right. That judgment has already begun. In the coming of Jesus, the dark powers that stand behind the evil in the world are facing justice. That process will roll out to include everyone. The Spirit-filled Church is the sign that speaks of God's restorative justice. In the resurrection of Jesus, God has announced that he will have the final word over everybody and everything. The Spirit-filled Church speaks to corrupt power. You will be judged, and your evil work will be put right.

The Songs of Isaiah

We know from the Provocation stories that the Prophet Isaiah sits underneath. In Isaiah, the many promises that are made of the Spirit coming all include God's justice coming too. The Spirit coming is accompanied by the just rule of God. In Isaiah 11, God's new King comes. The Spirit is upon him. He will judge the earth and destroy the wicked. This will be to such an extent that even violence in the animal world will be put right. In Isaiah 32, God's new King comes. The Spirit is poured out and God's justice and righteousness come. In Isaiah 42, God's servant comes. The Spirit is on him. He, in a quiet and gentle way, brings justice to the nations. In Isaiah 44 God's people come. The Spirit is poured out upon them. But those around them are blind and cannot see. They are stuck in their idolatry. The two exist side by side. This is where we live – announcing something that some tragically cannot see.

We Need More Time

We saw in the Provocation stories that at the time of Jesus doing the sign, the disciples don't understand it. They need time to grapple with what Jesus is doing, to reflect on it and to study the Scriptures to work out what Jesus means by what he is doing. This Provocation segment ends with us being in the same position. Jesus says to us, 'I have lots more to say but you can't bear it. Don't worry. The Spirit will lead you into everything that is true and show you everything that is me' (16:12–15).

You can take your time. You are in the timeless time.

23

Living in the Last Days

Going Away

To be a friend and follower of Jesus is to live in a testing but creative tension. One the one hand, we see God working, and that gives us great joy. On the other hand, we see so much that still needs to be done. We witness so much evil, sickness, sorrow and pain. This gives us great grief. In our own friendship with Jesus we experience the same tension. We have times of closeness to Jesus. We have such intimacy. We hear his voice. We know so deeply that he is with us. This brings us great joy. And on the other hand, we have times when we wonder where on earth he is. We feel his absence; we sense his silence. That gives us grief.

In the timeless time there are two segments where Jesus speaks of this. What he is doing is drawing in the Demonstration stories. But that doesn't become clear until near the end of the second segment. What is reassuring is that these contrasts of joy and grief that we experience are a demonstration to us that we are truly friends and followers of Jesus. And Jesus explains why grief and joy are both needed in following him.

The first segment you can read in 16:4–7. Jesus says it is for everyone's good that he goes away. Unless he goes to the Father, the Advocate, the one called alongside, the Spirit, cannot come. He says something that at first sight appears strange and puzzles many scholars: 'None of you asks me, "Where are you going?"' (16:5). But only back in chapters 13 and 14 there was a lot of asking about this. We are in the timeless time. The author doesn't want us to look back to previous chapters. This is a moment that stands apart. We are all here together. Jesus is speaking to everyone. And most of us don't need to ask because we already know.

But imagine that you are Mary Magdalene, or Jesus' mother, or the disciple whom Jesus loved. Imagine the grief and the pain that will fill your life at the death of Jesus. Him going away is not a happy prospect. Now, resurrection into new creation and the sending of the Spirit upon the Church is good. But how is that better than having Jesus in the flesh? How is that better than holding him, walking with him, eating meals with him, speaking with him?

It is better. But it is not better in the sense of ignoring the grief and pretending it isn't real. It is better because going through the grief will give rise to something good. This is where we get our first taste of the Demonstration stories that are sitting underneath this segment. This is Jesus and Mary standing together at Lazarus' tomb, weeping. The grief is going to give rise to something good. But the grief is real. The grief is not set aside or marginalised. Jesus steps right into the middle of the grief. It is not an act. He experiences the full pain of it all. The grief is entered into fully. It's just not the end of the story. In the timeless time, John the author is drawing us into the grief that Jesus' close friends are going to experience at his death. That grief is going somewhere good. But the grief is real. John wants us to see that their experience is our experience. We are going to experience grief and loss because we are friends and followers of Jesus. But our grief will go somewhere good.

Absence and Presence

The second segment you can read is 16:16–33. This is a long section where the same thing is laboriously repeated three times. Jesus says it. Then the disciples repeat it and say, 'We don't understand it.' Then Jesus says it again and tells them that he knows that they don't understand it. This is a literary device that creates emphasis. If we were going to write this in an email, we would write it in CAPITALS and underline it. And possibly we would change the colour of the text as well.

This is what is said so many times: 'A little while, and you will no longer see me, and again a little while, and you will see me.'

The reason this is repeated and underlined is that this is the tension in which we all live. We all experience both parts of this. We all

257

experience the terrible absence of Jesus and the pain of things going so wrong. And we experience the glorious presence of Jesus and the joy of him working in our lives. We are back to realised eschatology. Into all the brokenness of the world, into all the sickness, death and corruption that we experience, the presence of Jesus enters and we see him at work. We can sense the Demonstration stories here too. On the one hand we see Jesus' abrupt reluctance over the wine. His push-back against the royal official. His complete absence at the death of Lazarus. His gentle teasing of the disciples at the feeding of five thousand, forcing them to confront their complete powerlessness to provide food for the people. On the other hand, we see Jesus stepping into those situations of pain and loss and grief, and drawing others to participate in the miracle.

Grief gives rise to good. Grief isn't good, but it ultimately gives rise to good. Jesus uses the analogy of childbirth (16:21–2). The only way for a baby to be born is through the process of pain and grief. Joy comes through the experience of grief. The cross reveals this. The only way for a new creation to happen is for Jesus to suffer and die a humiliating and painful death. The Apostle Paul uses the same imagery when he talks of creation groaning, us groaning and the Spirit groaning – all for the new creation to come (Rom. 8:22–7).

And it is here that Jesus challenges us. In this reality of grief that can break through to joy he is asking us to live out the Demonstration stories ourselves.

In each of the Demonstration stories, a significant person comes to Jesus and asks him to help. Jesus is reluctant, but that causes the person to step further forward in faith. Jesus gives instructions, and the miracle occurs in the obedience of others. Jesus then goes on a journey that separates him. Well, the crucifixion and the ascension are one way of him going on a journey that separates. But what of the other parts of the story? This is what Jesus says to us: 'Very truly, I tell you, my Father will give you whatever you ask in my name. Until now you have not asked for anything in my name. Ask and you will receive, and your joy will be complete' (16:23–4).

This is a very deliberate act of empowering delegation. Jesus is calling us to step into his shoes. He is not asking us to be him. He is asking us to take hold of what it means to be in him. We are not asking in our name. We are to ask in his name; we are to ask on the basis of who he is. But he is asking us to do what he did – to ask the Father to work so that grief can turn to joy. This means that we will step into the space where we experience both the grief and the joy of others. We will weep at Lazarus' tomb. We will have joy at the party where God answers our prayers for the wine and the credit for it goes to someone else. We too will have the challenge of hearing what God is doing and walking by faith into that. We too will invite others to participate in the miracle and to take part in all that God is doing.

No wonder we need close friendship with Jesus and the empowering of the Spirit on us to step into this.

24

Priests of God

Jacob's Ladder

The final section of the timeless time is the second Invitation story. You can read it in John 17:1–26. It is a prayer. Jesus is inviting us not just to listen to him as he prays, but to be in him as he prays, and to come with him as he connects very deeply with the Father.

We have seen what happens in the Invitation stories: Jesus invites people close. They go to his house and have a meal together. They talk. They feel deeply connected to Jesus. The normal social barriers that keep people apart are gently set aside. And now, in the timeless time, we have come so close to Jesus that we have become one with him. When I described this to my wife, she said, 'That sounds like a good date night.' This is what the Invitation stories are all about: friendship, love and union.

Sitting underneath the Invitation stories are the stories right at the beginning of the Bible, particularly the story of Jacob. Jesus promises Nathanael that what Jacob saw in his dream is going to become real: 'Very truly I tell you, you will see heaven open, and the angels of God ascending and descending on the Son of Man' (1:51).

This prayer is that. This prayer is Jacob's ladder, heaven and earth coming together in Christ.

When he awakes from his dream of the heavenly ladder, Jacob realises that the heavens have opened. He has ascended to hear God speak the promises of covenant love over him. And God's presence and power have descended to bless him. He realises that he has been sleeping in a temple space, the house of God. He sets up his stone pillow as a pillar to show that this place, in the middle of nowhere, is the house of God and the gateway to heaven. Like Mary, he pours out oil as an offering of worship because he has been caught up into the very presence of the living God (Gen. 28:1–21).

The prayer is written like a ladder. Everything that Jesus says contains movement. Some of the prayers are Jesus going up to be face to face with God. Some of the prayers are for God to come down to bless us. Some of the prayers are for God to come down in order to lift us up. Some of the prayers are Jesus going down into crucifixion, which is the route for him to be lifted up in glory.

It is the same for us. When we pray these prayers, we are either going up into the heavenly realms to meet with God or praying for God to come down in order to lift us up.

To help us, John the author has arranged the prayer in a beautiful cascade, or chiastic structure. The chiasm increases the sense of movement as the prayers move out towards the middle point and then back again. And the pairing of the prayers in the chiasm deepens our understanding of what they mean. Prayers are brought together which then interpret each other. For example, in the section that we are about to pray, 'the hour has come. Glorify your Son' (17:1) is paired with 'by finishing the work you gave me to do' (17:4). We know that Jesus' hour is his crucifixion. By pairing the prayers together we can see that the work of Jesus is finished at crucifixion, and that is how he is glorified. The deepest move down leads to the greatest step up. To lay down your life is to rise up in glory.

This prayer is difficult to understand when read in a static way. It can just seem jumbled, repetitive and confused. When we introduce Jacob's ladder as the story underneath the prayer and we see that the prayer is full of movement, bringing earth up to heaven and heaven down to earth, it becomes much easier to understand.

Every aspect of the prayer draws in what we have discovered from the Invitation stories.

Jesus is inviting us to go up with him into the Father's house (17:1, 5, 24). The Apostle Paul uses the same language when he describes that God has 'raised us up with Christ and seated us with him in the heavenly realms in Christ Jesus' (Eph. 2:6). Jesus is inviting us to ascend into the very presence of God. To go into the Temple was to go into the presence of God while standing on earth. In Christ we do the same. We are not removed from the earth. But in Christ we are welcome in his home as those who are one with God (17:11).

Jesus is inviting us up to be friends of God, in covenant relationship with God. We are loved by God. We are one with God. That is what covenant means – to bring together as one. Jesus prays for that covenant love to characterise our friendships, that we would be one with each other even as God is one with himself (17:20–3). Jesus prays that we would have the joy, the glory and the love that come from being one with God, that all this would flow down the ladder to us. The love the Father has for Jesus is in us (17:13, 22, 23, 26).

Jesus is praying for God to come down and protect us as his covenant people who belong to him. He is praying over us the promises God spoke to Abraham, Isaac and Jacob to care for them (17:11, 15).

Jesus is praying for his Word to come down to us (17:8). Just as Philip, Nathanael, Simon and Mary received him and believed his Word. Just as Abraham and Jacob believed God's Word. And that lifts us up. We too are raised up and set apart for God because we receive his Word (17:17). God is revealed to us (17:6). He is made known to us (17:26). We have eternal life, which is to know God (17:2–3).

Jesus is praying for his own obedience in going down into death (17:1, 4). He sets himself apart in this (17:19). He is praying for us to live obediently to God as we too are sent into the world (17:18).

We have become priests. And by 'priest' I don't mean having a recognised leadership role within a church organisation. All friends of Jesus are priests of God. We are the people who belong to God. We come into God's very presence. We declare the greatness and the glory of God. We speak the covenant blessings of God over the earth. We give ourselves fully to God and, like Mary, let our hair down in love for Jesus and pour out the perfume of our love on his feet. That is what priests are. We live deeply and intimately connected to God through Christ. You can do that as a cleaner and as a managing director. Heaven is open.

Let's pray (17:1–5).

A1   After Jesus said this, he looked towards heaven

  B1   and prayed: 'Father,

    C1   the hour has come. Glorify your Son,

      D1   that your Son may glorify you.

        E1   For you granted him authority over all people

          F1   that he might give eternal life

            G1   to all those you have given him.

          F2   Now this is eternal life: that they know you, the only true God,

        E2   and Jesus Christ, whom you have sent.

      D2   I have brought you glory on earth

    C2   by finishing the work you gave me to do.

  B2   And now, Father,

A2   glorify me in your presence with the glory I had with you before the world began.

A: God we are looking to you. We may feel that we are in a nowhere place, like Jacob in the desert. But we are standing in the gateway to your glory. We are in your very presence. The way to you is open.

B: Father, we are your children. We are called to be your friends. We open our hearts to know you more and we receive your loving embrace. We come boldly before you.

C: Thank you, Jesus, for being glorified on the cross. You finished the work that you were given to do. You stepped down obediently into death. And we are saved. We ask that you give us the same willingness to be obedient and loyal to you. Help us to lay our lives down to complete the work that you have given us to do.

D: God, we live to bring you glory. We offer our bodies as living sacrifices – which is our true worship (Rom. 12:1). As we give ourselves to you, let this rise like a song of worship to you. May you be honoured by our obedience.

E: Father, we are so glad that Jesus was sent from you. That he revealed you. That he spoke your Word and acted under your authority. Here we are, Lord. Send us. May your rule come on earth through our lives and our words. Help us to step out today, following you and trusting in you to work through us.

F: Father, you have given us eternal life. You have given us life that can never die. That life is knowing you. We draw close to you. We have become one. We love you Father, Son and Spirit.

G: Father, you have given us to Jesus. We belong to him. May he be the focus of our day.

Amen.

*

We can see how the image of Jacob's ladder works in the prayer. Jesus looks **up** into heaven. He looks **up** to the Father. He prays to go **down** into crucifixion and finish his work. He prays that his obedience will rise **up** and bring glory to God. He knows that he has come **down** as one sent from heaven and that he has brought **down** to us the gift of eternal life that lifts us **up** to the Father. God has come **down** to raise us **up** and has given us to him. These movements up and down flow in with the chiastic structure and have a beautiful symmetry. The whole prayer works in this way.

We are priests of God. We are people of prayer. God has us in his grip and we hold on to him alone.

Now we go with Jesus into his death so that heaven can be opened for all.

Crucifixion

25

On the Mount of Olives

Introduction

It will hopefully not surprise you that in John each of the stories of the crucifixion is one of the narrative panels. Everything that we have discovered about Jesus is seen in the story of his death.

One of the perplexities of John's Gospel is how different it is from the other three, and yet so connected. This book is not the place to look into all the detail of that. However, in the stories of the cross this complex relationship between John and the other Gospels really stands out. John's account of the crucifixion is so different from the others. And yet it is also so the same.

This is a moment where it helps us to read John side by side with the other Gospels. That contrast helps us to identify exactly what John is doing. In some places John deliberately focuses his account by leaving things out. In other places John deliberately amplifies his account with unique material. We will look at both these aspects. We will then be able to see how each of the stories of the crucifixion connects with each of the panels. John tells us the crucifixion in this way because he wants us to see that the death of Jesus has complete coherence with the life of Jesus.

On the Mount of Olives

The arrest of Jesus is such a short story in John. You can read it in John 18:1–11. To read the contrasting story from another Gospel, I suggest Matthew 26:31–56. Let the stories dwell in your mind. Look at where they are different and where they are the same.

What Does John Leave Out?

There is nothing about Jesus telling the disciples that they will all run away. There is nothing about the prediction of Peter's denials, as John has already covered that in the story of The Last Meal. There is no desperate prayer in Gethsemane and the sweating of blood. There are no disciples falling asleep instead of praying. There is no kiss from Judas. Although Judas led the arrest party there, he is just in the crowd. Jesus doesn't challenge the crowd saying, 'Am I leading a rebellion?' And at the end there are no disciples running away.

It is important to note that there isn't a right story and a wrong story. If you put the Gospel stories together, they dovetail perfectly. John the author is focusing our attention on an aspect of the story that he wants us to see. In seeing it, our friendship with Jesus will deepen.

What Is Unique to John?

In John's story, Jesus is in charge throughout. As those sent from the High Priest come towards the garden to arrest him, Jesus goes out to meet them. He challenges them: 'Jesus, knowing all that was going to happen to him, went out and asked them, "Who is it you want?"' (18:4).

You can imagine it. 'Excuse me, can I help you? I'm trying to have a prayer meeting here. Are you looking for anyone in particular?' All the while knowing exactly what is going on. They tell him they are looking for Jesus of Nazareth (18:5). So Jesus replies. And as he speaks, it has a very powerful impact on them: 'When Jesus said, "I am he," they drew back and fell to the ground' (18:6).

They pick themselves up. And when they have got their lanterns and their dignity back, he asks them again who they are looking for. They tell him again: Jesus of Nazareth. Jesus admits that is who he is. But he has got something he wants them to do. So – he tells them: 'I told you that I am he. If you are looking for me, then let these men go' (18:8).

Jesus is completely in charge. But he does not resist arrest. Simon Peter does a bit of resisting. But sword-fighting is not Simon's strong suit. All he manages to achieve is to cut the ear off the High Priest's servant. Luke tells us that Jesus heals the ear, which is a nice touch (Luke 22:51). John's story is the same as Matthew's, with Jesus telling Peter to put that sword away. What is different in John is Jesus' explanation as to why: 'Put your sword away! Shall I not drink the cup the Father has given me?' (18:11).

And that is it. They arrest him.

Why Does John Focus His Story Like This?

This is the Provocation panel. This is how the new King speaks to power.

Jesus is completely in charge. He has more authority than all of them put together. When he speaks, they fall over. When he wants something done, he tells them to do it. But he has no weapon. He stops his followers from using their weapons. He has no organisational position. He makes no appeal to those in charge. He doesn't try to lean on anyone or bully someone to change their mind. He speaks to power. But he does not take up power to try to defeat power.

John leaves everything out of the arrest story except the parts that communicate this.

This is what it means to follow the new King. This is what it means to be in him. This is what it means to live a cross-shaped life. You can speak to power. But you cannot take up the dark tools of corrupt power to protect yourself from power. You can speak to power. And you speak from the place of having more authority than any of them. But you cannot use power to save yourself. You cannot take up power to defeat power.

This decision to not respond to power with power is always made at the first encounter. This is why the Provocation panel is the first story of the cross. If you respond with power to power there is no going back. Jesus makes this decision as he goes out of the garden to meet those who have come to arrest him.

Jesus explains why this is the way the new King will reign. As in all the Provocation stories, he quotes Isaiah. He has a cup to drink that the Father has given to him. This is the song of Isaiah in chapter 51. As the song starts, God sings over his people: those of you who seek the Lord, remember that you are children of God, you are people in covenant with God (Isa. 51:2). Everything that has gone wrong will be put right by God. All injustices will be judged. God will have the final word over everything (Isa. 51:3–6). Don't worry about what people do. Only what God does will last. Be strong in God. There will be a new Exodus and everlasting joy. Don't be afraid of people, even the very worst of them. Even of the ones who make ready to destroy you (Isa. 51:7–14). I will put my words in your mouth. I will cover you with my hand (Isa. 51:16–17).

And just as you thought there was going to be a happy ending, there is a cup to be drunk:

> *Awake, awake!*
> *Rise up, Jerusalem,*
> *you who have drunk from the hand of the Lord*
> *the cup of his wrath,*
> *you who have drained to its dregs*
> *the goblet that makes people stagger.*
> *(Isa. 51:17)*

Jerusalem isn't going to drink the cup. At least, not yet. Jesus is going to drink it. Jesus is going to the cross in our place. He is going to drink the cup of God's wrath right down to the dregs. To defeat corrupt power, it is no good taking up more power. To defeat corrupt power the darkness has to be digested. The darkness has to be drunk. Jesus drinks the righteous anger of God against all violence, against all brutal killing, against all bullying, against all ethnic cleansing, against every nasty, cruel, belittling, dehumanising, money-grabbing action. God is angry with all these things. God is angry with every way that people destroy others and take advantage of others and exploit them. Why do people in power do these things? To get what they want – which is more power. Powerful people oppress others in order that no one else can be powerful.

But corrupt power can be stopped. God drinks it. And dies for it. And gives none of it back. Corrupt power stops at the cross.

26

At the House of the High Priest

The story of the trial at the House of the High Priest is also a short story in John. You can read it in John 18:12–27. To read the contrasting story from another Gospel, I suggest Matthew 26:57–75. Do the same as we did for the first story. Let the stories live in your mind. Look at where they are different and where they are the same.

What Does John Leave Out?

In the three Synoptic Gospels Jesus is taken to one house for one trial. Matthew tells us that it is the house of Caiaphas. The whole Sanhedrin assemble and there is a lengthy process of investigation with furious debate. There is nothing of this in John. There are no false witnesses that repeatedly come forward, only for their cases to fall to pieces. There is no mention of the attempt to remember what Jesus had once said about destroying the Temple and rebuilding in three days. There is nothing about the attempts to bully Jesus and pressurise him into speaking, but that he remains silent. There is nothing about the High Priest committing an act illegal in Jewish Law, putting the defendant under oath and asking him a direct question. There is nothing about Jesus' reply, directly quoting from the Prophet Daniel: 'From now on you will see the Son of Man sitting at the right hand of the Mighty One and coming on the clouds of heaven.' There is nothing about the High Priest tearing his clothes and shouting 'Blasphemy'. There is no spitting on Jesus, or mocking him, or blindfolding him and beating him up.

What Is Unique to John?

John reports Jesus' trial being conducted in two houses in two parts. He is taken first to Annas, who is the father-in-law of Caiaphas, the

High Priest that year (18:13). At his house, Annas tries to conduct a theological enquiry into Jesus' teaching and find out more about his disciples. Jesus does reply to this, but only to a limited degree: 'I have spoken openly to the world . . . I always taught in synagogues or at the temple, where all the Jews come together. I said nothing in secret. Why question me? Ask those who heard me. Surely they know what I said' (18:20–1).

One of the officials slaps Jesus for saying this. Apparently, it is not the way to talk to the High Priest when he is asking theological questions (18:22). Jesus graciously but relentlessly skewers the man. 'If I have done wrong tell me what it is. If I haven't done wrong, why did you slap me?' Good point.

After his fairly fruitless theological enquiry, Annas sends Jesus to Caiaphas. Annas knows that he isn't going to get anywhere with Jesus. He also knows that Caiaphas will put the boot in, even if he has to do something illegal. Caiaphas has already said as much (18:14). Annas sends Jesus to Caiaphas and lets him get on with it.

John reports in his account that Peter follows the arrest party who take Jesus, bound, to Annas' house. 'Another disciple' is with him, as they cautiously go with the soldiers to Annas' house. This disciple who is with Peter goes straight into the courtyard with Jesus and the arrest party, because he is 'known to the high priest'. He then goes back to the security at the door and arranges for Peter to be allowed in. Not only is this unnamed disciple 'known', but he also has considerable authority.

Then Peter is in difficulties. The girl who was doing security on the door goes over to the fire-pit and challenges him: '"You aren't one of this man's disciples too, are you?" she asked Peter. He replied, "I am not"' (18:17).

Matthew and Mark both tell the story of Peter's denials. But they put them altogether at the end of their story of the trial. Luke also tells the story of Peter's denials as one unit. But he places them altogether at the start of his account. All three Gospel writers make clear that the three denials happened over a period of time. John separates the first denial from the other two in his story, with the enquiry by Annas between them.

Apart from Jesus being unsuccessfully grilled on his teaching by Annas, John leaves everything else out. He focuses entirely on Peter. How Peter gets access to a secure area in the private accommodation of a very senior figure at a highly sensitive moment. None of the other Gospels cover this. And how he is repeatedly challenged, denying any connection with Jesus on every occasion.

Compared to the accounts in the Synoptics with the repeated questionings and beatings of Jesus, John's account is short. It isn't the story of Jesus' trial. It is the story of Peter's denial.

Why Does John Focus His Story Like This?

This is the Invitation panel. This is a story of discipleship.

Jesus isn't just going through a personal trial. He also has to endure the trial of one of his disciples failing badly under pressure. Jesus knows that Peter is weak in this way. He knows that Peter has further to go on his discipleship journey. He knows that Peter's courage and passion will get him into this situation, and that his weakness will then get the better of him. He knows that 'other disciple' and Peter will probably act together. He knows that the 'other disciple' will have access to the house but will not experience any challenge. He knows all this is going to happen.

Inviting people into your life to be discipled isn't just about them seeing you over a nice meal. It's them seeing you under pressure and sharing in your pressure. Jesus gets a slap, but he plays a straight bat. Peter gets a dig. But fear gets the better of him and he retreats to deception.

Discipling people is not just seeing them grow and change. It's seeing them falter and fail as well.

The stories of Jacob sit under this story. Jacob is always trying to wriggle out of difficult situations using deceptive means. Peter has still got some Simon in him, just as Israel has the odd Jacob moment. Even though he has the new name, he still hasn't completely become the new person.

27

Before Pilate

The story of Jesus before Pilate is very much longer in John. You can read it in John 18:28–19:16. To read the contrasting story from another Gospel, I suggest Matthew 27:11–31. Get yourself right into the story. Look at where they are different and where they are the same. Look at where they connect and where they diverge.

What Does John Leave Out?

As in the trial before the High Priest, John leaves out the forceful and bullying behaviour of the chief priests and elders (Matt. 27:12). In John, what the Jewish authorities have to say to Pilate is more measured and dignified. He draws something of a veil over their other behaviour.

Another detail that Matthew includes, which John does not, is that Pilate's wife awakes having had a vivid dream of Jesus. She sends an urgent message to her husband, cautioning him not to 'have anything to do with that innocent man' (Matt. 27:19). However, in John's account, Pilate repeatedly states that there is no basis for the charges. The absence of that story does not create any substantive change in the narrative.

Matthew has Pilate washing his hands and protesting his innocence. With this strange gesture he attempts to give moral responsibility for Jesus' death to the crowd, which they accept (Matt. 27:24–5). John leaves that part of the story out. It isn't as simple as washing your hands. In John it is Jesus who talks to Pilate about exactly who has authority and who has responsibility (19:11).

All the Gospels have the crown of thorns being placed on Jesus' head, which would cause terrible pain and profuse bleeding. They have Jesus being dressed in a royal robe and mocked by the soldiers as 'King of the Jews'. They tell us that Jesus is savagely beaten around the head. Luke places this midway through the proceedings and records how Pilate sends Jesus to Herod, it being Herod's soldiers who mock and abuse Jesus. Like Luke, John places this event in the middle of his story, where it adds hugely to the meaning of what is happening. But John, like Matthew and Mark, does not include any reference to Herod, or any mention of which soldiers do the abusive mocking of Jesus. Matthew and Mark simply place it at the end of their story, where it is just another terrible thing that happens to Jesus.

What is Unique to John?

A lot. There are a number of unique features of John's story that together make this a complex and deep narrative.

1. PILATE'S JOURNEYS INSIDE AND OUTSIDE THE PALACE

There are seven scenes, all of which portray Pilate having to shuttle between the inside and the outside of his Palace. He goes inside to where Jesus is being held. He comes outside where the Jewish authorities are standing, and the crowd is gathering. The reason they stand outside is that Jewish Law prevents them from going inside a Gentile residence. They would become unclean and would not be able to enjoy the Passover feast. Pilate repeatedly walking inside and then outside again, which the other Gospels do not have, reveals the utter hypocrisy of the authorities. It is deeply ironic. While the authorities are fastidiously obeying the Law to celebrate the Passover, they are completely breaking the Law by condemning an innocent man to death using deceptive and manipulative means. Irony has huge power to reveal things that otherwise might be missed. We are brought up short by the clash of seeing these things side by side, like two shocking colours that don't match.

Scene 1 – Outside

Pilate comes outside to meet the authorities and hear the charges. It seems that the authorities have been in touch with Pilate overnight and have a done a deal, because now Pilate starts to go back on it. It sounds like he wants to start the trial all over again. Then he tries to give the whole thing back to them. They are shocked and angry in their response (18:29–32).

Scene 2 – Inside

Pilate goes inside to question Jesus about his identity, authority and authenticity (18:33–8).

Scene 3 – Outside

Pilate goes outside to say he finds no basis for the charges and perhaps he should release Jesus as the customary political gesture to honour the Passover (18:38–9).

Scene 4 – Inside

This is not well received (18:40), and Pilate goes back inside. He has Jesus flogged (19:1). It's likely that his tactics here are to try to save Jesus' life. By beating him up he can argue that enough has been done. Jesus is beaten, ridiculed and dressed as a Mock King, probably during the time that Pilate sends him to Herod. But John either doesn't know about that aspect or more likely sees it as an unnecessary detail in his story (19:2–3).

Scene 5 – Outside

Pilate comes back outside and says again that he finds no basis in the charges (19:4). In a very calculating move, he then brings out Jesus as Mock King. This is no pantomime. Everybody sees how brutally Jesus has been treated. Pilate's plan is to make them back down. A brutalised king doesn't need to be killed. It doesn't work (19:6). He tells the Jewish authorities to crucify Jesus themselves, knowing full well that it is against their Law to do so. They tell him, 'We have a law.' This is very compressed. They have a law prohibiting crucifixion, but they also have a law commanding death for those who blaspheme. They want Pilate to do this for them. They know that if they kill Jesus themselves by stoning there will be massive repercussions, possibly a full-on riot because Jesus is so popular, and people's expectations are so raised. This is why they negotiated a deal with Pilate for him to order Jesus' death. That way the likelihood of public disorder and military action is much reduced. And now Pilate is going back on the deal. They have to pressurise him. They use scare tactics: 'he must die, because he claimed to be the Son of God' (19:7).

Scene 6 – Inside

It works (19:8). Pilate isn't just afraid of the whole situation getting out of hand. He is now afraid of who Jesus might be. Pilate is politically in a precarious position. He has been Governor for more than five years, but his political support in Rome has gone. Riots and disorder would not go down well with his bosses. But this is something else. With all his Romans superstitions in mind, is he dealing with a god-like man? Back inside, the effect that Jesus has already had on him is eating away at him (19:9). But Jesus doesn't talk to fear. He says nothing. Pilate tries to play the power game with Jesus (19:10–11). But he gets nowhere.

Scene 7 – Outside

He goes back outside. And now another deep irony. The Governor, a loyal Roman ruler, is accused of not being Caesar's friend by the Jewish authorities, well known for their, sometimes violent, antipathy to Roman occupation. Nobody in charge is speaking the truth. They are piling the political pressure on each other (19:12).

The outside to inside movement finally stops. It's now nearly midday. Pilate moves from his palace to the judge's seat. He has nearly given in. But he has one more go at releasing Jesus. He brings Jesus out again as Mock King on the raised platform known as the Stone Pavement. Several scholars take the view that Pilate may even seat Jesus on the judge's seat, or near to it, his aim being a gross mockery of Jesus sufficient to get the crowd to feel that enough has been done. Why would you kill such a weakened, powerless, beaten-up man being mocked as 'King' and now 'Judge' when he clearly is neither King nor Judge but possibly in danger of death from his injuries. He tries one more time: 'Shall I crucify your king?' (19:15).

This leads to possibly the saddest, most shocking reply in the Bible: '"We have no king but Caesar," the chief priests answered' (19:15).

There is such a maelstrom of thoughts and emotions going on in the minds of the Jewish authorities. It is likely that there is jealousy at Jesus' popularity. There is anger at what they perceive to be his false teaching and the undermining of their authority. There is also urgent need for political leadership. If the Jesus movement is allowed to grow unchecked, it is probable that there would be some kind of uprising that Rome would put down with violence. Everything might be lost – a fear that Caiaphas has voiced (11:50). But now John wants us to see something deeper.

This is a denial of their faith.

They are the people whose theology teaches that God alone is King. But they are occupied by the biggest Empire in the world with rulers who like to think of themselves in god-like terms. Tricky for them to negotiate that potential conflict between theology and politics while also retaining their power and position. This is made even more difficult when there is a rising view among the people that God's new King is coming. But this terrible statement to Pilate is not them negotiating the fragile complexities of the tensions between their theology and their politics. This is a complete denial of their Scriptures. This is the abandonment of everything the prophets have ever said.

It is simply so sad.

Pilate gives up trying to save Jesus. He knows they have won. He cannot be seen to align himself with someone opposed to the Emperor. Theirs has not been a battle for truth, but a battle for power. He gives the command for Jesus' crucifixion.

2. THE PROCLAMATION OF JESUS AS KING AND JUDGE

Reading Matthew, you will see that the question of Jesus being King is briefly covered at the beginning of the story in two sentences. 'Are you King?' asks Pilate. 'So you say,' answers Jesus. Then the narrative moves on to the release of Barabbas and the crowd's demands to crucify Jesus.

In John, the question of Jesus' identity as King dominates the story. On the inside of his palace, Pilate and Jesus have a debate about Jesus as King and the nature of his kingdom (18:34–8). Then Jesus is beaten and abused and ironically presented as Mock King. This is placed right at the heart of the story. It is not something that happens off to one side. Presenting Jesus as King forms the centre-piece of Pilate's repeated attempts to save Jesus' life (19:1–6). And then comes the final scene on the raised stone pavement where the judge sits in judgment. Jesus is presented there, possibly seated on the judgment seat itself (19:13–15). He doesn't look like a judge. He doesn't look like a king. But at the very moment when Pilate gives the order for crucifixion, Jesus is sitting where the judge sits, and the Roman Governor of the Province proclaims him King: 'Here is your king' (19:14).

Jesus knows he will become King by this means (18:32). He knows that the route to authority is sacrifice and obedience. He knows that to become Judge he is going to be judged. He knows that to become King he is going to be condemned. He knows that there is a cup to drink so that corrupt power can finally be defeated and the rule of God can come.

The lifting up of the Son of Man as King comes in this deeply ironic form. The moment of his greatest weakness and vulnerability is the moment he steps into the fullness of his authority. God's new King ascends to power on the cross. The giving of his life is the beginning of his reign.

3. THE APPROACH OF THE PASSOVER

In John, this whole story with Pilate is set within the imminent reality of the Passover about to begin. The Passover about to begin looms over everything. The story opens with this: 'By now it was early morning, and to avoid ceremonial uncleanness they did not enter the palace, because they wanted to be able to eat the Passover. So Pilate came out to them' (18:28–9).

Then we get the repeated journey of Pilate, inside, outside, inside, outside. Every time Pilate moves, we are reminded. Why is he doing this strange inside–outside movement? Because the Passover is about to begin. In effect, the opening statement is repeated seven times without having to be written. The clock is ticking, counting down to the Passover.

And then the story climaxes. As Pilate goes the judge's seat, the Passover is beginning: 'When Pilate heard this, he brought Jesus out and sat down on the judge's seat at a place known as the Stone Pavement (which in Aramaic is Gabbatha). It was the day of Preparation of the Passover; it was about noon' (19:13–14).

This is the moment. This is the time. The Jewish nation ceases work. The yeast is taken from their houses and burned. The slaughtering of the Passover lambs begins. The great celebration of the Exodus is upon them.

Why Does John Focus His Story Like This?

I am hoping you have seen this one. This is an awesome Contention story. As we have mentioned before, John is not inventing material. He is deliberately choosing the elements of the story that help him fulfil his narrative purpose and fit with his narrative structure.

It is a double Contention. There are two arguments going on simultaneously. Pilate is in both. On the outside he argues with the Jewish authorities. On the inside he argues with Jesus.

THE INSIDE CONTENTION

Even though Jesus is under arrest and speaking to the senior Roman official of the country, as with other Contentions, the arguments cover the familiar territory of identity, authority and authenticity.

Pilate appears to be interested in Jesus' identity, because he asks him, 'Are you the king of the Jews?' (18:33). But Jesus forces him to admit that it is not a question that he himself is asking or even particularly interested in. What Pilate can't understand is why the chief priests are so angry that they want Jesus dead (18:35). Jesus tries to explain how his authority as God's new King clashes so badly with the Jewish authorities. But he does so in a way that Pilate will understand: 'My kingdom is not of this world. If it were, my servants would fight to prevent my arrest by the Jewish leaders. But now my kingdom is from another place' (18:36).

Jesus makes clear that his authority is not in direct competition with the chief priests or even with Pilate. It's greater than both of them. But this is why those with him don't fight for him. His authority is from 'another place'. His authority is above and beyond human authority. When Jesus was arguing with the Jewish authorities, he used Father–Son language to communicate that his authority came from God and not from human institutions. Knowing that this will be meaningless to Pilate, Jesus uses language that connects to Pilate's view of the world. As a believer in the gods, Pilate would understand the existence of other powers that dwell in 'other places'.

But it would seem that Pilate is not persuaded. No one is persuaded in the Contentions. He uses sarcasm to try to trap Jesus: 'You are a king, then!' (18:37).

Jesus manoeuvres around this by keeping that statement in Pilate's mouth. 'You say that I am a king.' He then makes an authenticity statement: 'In fact, the reason I was born and came into the world is to testify to the truth. Everyone on the side of truth listens to me' (18:37).

Jesus is a messenger of truth. He has existence and purpose before he was born. His birth was a 'coming into the world' to achieve that purpose, to tell the world the truth. And here we are back in the self-validating circle of authenticity and credibility. 'Pilate, I have come to tell the truth. If you are interested in truth, then you will listen to me.' But Pilate isn't listening. It would appear that Pilate has doubts about whether anyone tells the truth, whether anyone is credible, and whether such a thing as truth even exists. To him, such lofty ideals have been corrupted. Truth is not a currency that he deals in. Life is no longer about what is true but about what is possible. His world is one of political expediency in order to retain power.

He dismisses talk of truth and goes outside.

When he comes back inside, Pilate uses language he does understand. A crown of thorns thrust brutally upon the head, followed by beatings and humiliation. Jesus replies in a language he understands. Calmly taking the pain and the beating without any bitterness, any rage, any fear or any loathing.

It scares Pilate. He has not met this before. In anyone.

Then his fears concerning the identity of Jesus are heightened by the chief priests referring to Jesus' claim to be God's Son. The question

281

arises in his mind: where is this man from? This is not about Galilee and Bethlehem and the birthplace of prophets. This is a Roman fear of accidentally getting on the wrong side of the gods. Jesus' kingdom is from another place. Where is he from? But Jesus won't tell him.

Possibly to assuage his own growing fears, Pilate tries to threaten Jesus with his power. 'Your life is in my hands,' he says. But Jesus is unmoved. He has no fear of human power. He reminds Pilate that his power is simply derived and is not his own. He can only do what his bosses have given him to do. This is the problem at the heart of human power: it is inherently insecure. It can disappear in a moment. Jesus does help Pilate at this point by reminding him that Pilate has to do what governors do. He has to make a judgment on the case and follow it through. In terms of responsibility and blame, it is not Pilate who is in the frame. It is the one who has created the case and handed it to Pilate to judge who will bear the final responsibility and take the blame.

From then on, Pilate ups his game. He tries to set Jesus free. It is extraordinary that right at the point of facing his own death, Jesus brings on board the most senior Roman official in the country to act as his defence lawyer while the man is really meant to be there as his judge.

THE OUTSIDE CONTENTION

All that Pilate does in his arguments with the Jewish authorities is attempt to save Jesus' life. From the very beginning of the story he is pushing back. Again and again, Pilate tries to save Jesus' life.

But he loses the argument.

28

The Place of the Skull

We have now reached the heart of the story: the death of Jesus. The pinnacle of his mission to love the world. Crucifixion was a brutal way of killing a person. But yet again, John has carefully and prayerfully chosen what to record for us. You can read his account in John 19:16–42. To read the story from another Gospel, I suggest either Matthew 27:32–65 or Luke 23:26–56.

What Does John Leave Out?

A lot. There is no Simon of Cyrene being forced to carry the cross. There are no distraught women following him to Golgotha. There is no drugged drink offered to Jesus to kill the pain before they lift him up. There are no crowds or authorities standing around, shouting abuse and mocking him. There is no darkness. There is no calling out of Psalm 22, '*Eloi, Eloi*', and the misunderstanding that he is calling Elijah. The two others crucified on either side of him are mentioned, but that is all. There is no thief on the cross asking Jesus to remember him. There is no centurion. There is no mention of the curtain in the Temple being torn in two. There is no earthquake and there are no resurrections.

Where Do the Stories Connect?

The place where it happened is remembered in all the Gospels: the Place of the Skull. Grisly. The number of those crucified is in all the Gospels: three, with Jesus in the middle. The sign provided by Pilate is in all the Gospels: 'The King of the Jews'. The dividing up of his clothes and casting lots is in them all. His mother and other women standing watching him die is in them all, although the number and the names recorded differs a bit. Wine vinegar being offered as a drink, quite near to the moment of his death, is in all the accounts. Breathing his last and giving up his spirit is in them all. Joseph of Arimathea requesting the body from Pilate and burying Jesus in a tomb nearby is in every Gospel. And all this happening on the Day of Preparation for the Sabbath is in all the Gospels.

What Is Unique to John?

A lot. This is detailed story. John knows why the soldiers cast lots when dividing the clothes: because Jesus owns a rather nice woven undergarment that they decide not to tear into pieces. John knows there are four soldiers who share the clothes. He knows the full text of the sign that Pilate has made and that it is written in three languages: Hebrew, Latin and Greek. He knows that the disciple whom Jesus loved is also at the cross. He includes the very touching scene of Jesus bringing together the two people closest to him: his mother and his much-loved friend. He knows that Jesus requests his final drink. He knows Jesus' final prayer: 'It is finished.' He knows that the soldiers are ordered to break the legs of all those crucified, which would kill them because they could no longer breathe. When you are hanging by your wrists on a cross, the only way to breathe is to push up against the nails through the feet. He knows that when the soldiers come to do it, Jesus is already dead. But just to make sure, Jesus' side is pierced with a spear and 'blood and water' flow out. He knows that Nicodemus comes to help Joseph with the burial and that he brings the spices, possibly worth more than £100,000. He knows that the tomb is in a nearby garden.

Why Does John Focus His Story Like This?

We have seen how John the author uses many literary devices to help us read his Gospel well. In this story there is another literary structure that was commonly used. In this structure, each subsection of the story starts and finishes with the same statement or a highly related statement. When we see this, it can seem to a Western reader just rather clumsy writing. The author seems to repeat himself. A lot. To the Eastern reader, what this does is signpost that there is a highly developed underlying structure to the story. So it makes the reader stop and think.

It is very noticeable that, in his account, John makes very little mention of the violence and brutality of the crucifixion. He draws a veil across all physical and verbal violence and abuse. The first section of the story begins and ends simply with the fact of Jesus being crucified:

- 'Finally Pilate handed him over to them to be crucified' (19:16).
- 'There they crucified him, and with him two others – one on each side and Jesus in the middle' (19:18).

The next section of the story begins and ends with Pilate having the disputed sign written:

- 'Pilate had a notice prepared and fastened to the cross' (19:19).
- 'Pilate answered, "What I have written, I have written"' (19:22).

The third section of the story begins and ends with the soldiers dividing the clothing:

- 'When the soldiers crucified Jesus, they took his clothes' (19:23).
- 'So this is what the soldiers did' (19:25).

The fourth section of the story begins and end with Jesus bringing together his mother and the disciple he loved into a new family:

- 'Near the cross of Jesus stood his mother' (19:25).
- 'From that time on, this disciple took her into his home' (19:27).

The next section of the story is of Jesus' death, and it begins and ends with everything now being finished:

- 'Later, knowing that everything had now been finished' (19:28).
- 'Jesus said, "It is finished." With that, he bowed his head and gave up his spirit' (19:30).

The final section of the story is of his burial, and it begins and ends with a reference to it being the Day of Preparation:

- 'Now it was the day of Preparation' (19:31).

- 'Because of the Jewish day of Preparation and since the tomb was near by, they laid Jesus there' (19:42).

What is going on? This is the Declaration Panel of the Crucifixion story. It is John the author taking his summary of the entire story and theology of Israel that we read in John 1 and focusing it upon the cross of Christ. Not for nothing is the cross at the centre of the story of Jesus. 'For God so loved the world that he gave his Son' is a beautiful summary of the Gospel. John the author now shows us how every part of Israel's story finds fulfilment at the cross.

1. 'The light shines in the darkness, and the darkness has not overcome it' (1:5).

Or as John the author writes: 'Carrying his own cross, he went out to the place of the Skull' (19:17). The death of Jesus is a very dark moment in human history. Not just an innocent man, but the Creator of the world is brutally killed. Those who have pushed for this to happen are largely in the dark. They didn't know what they were doing. Those in the darkness did not see or understand the light that was shining in their midst. They didn't comprehend that Jesus is the light, which is the other meaning of that word, but neither have they overcome Jesus as the light.

The death of Jesus is also the brightest moment in human history. The cross isn't defeat. It is victory. Jesus dies. But the light multiplies. It is in the deepest darkness that the brightest light shines. That is what the crucifixion of Jesus is. A light shining in the darkness, which darkness doesn't understand and cannot overcome.

2. 'There was a man sent from God . . . He himself was not the light; he came only as a witness to the light' (1:6, 8).

Or, as Pilate belligerently replies to the Chief Priests, 'What I have written, I have written' (19:22). Whatever you make of Pilate, he announces repeatedly and clearly that Jesus is God's new King. He announces it to the nations. He has it written in three languages. God's

King has come. At the very point that Jesus ascends to rule as King by his death on the cross, Pilate has it written out three times for all to see.

Pilate is not in the light himself. His decision to have Jesus crucified is not based on discovering the truth. He makes a political decision based on his desire to hold on to power. It is so deeply ironic that such a flawed and vulnerable man makes such a clear statement about Jesus. But John the author wants us to see that the prophetic tradition of Israel which culminates in John who baptises is not the only voice proclaiming Jesus as God's new King. In a mysterious and yet compelling way, God arranges for the Roman Empire to declare it too. Pilate is not the light. But he is a witness to the light.

3. 'He was in the world, and though the world was made through him, the world did not recognise him' (1:10).

Four soldiers gather around the cross and gamble for Jesus' underwear. As far as they are concerned, it is just another day at work. They have no idea that the Lamb of God is taking away the sins of the world, even as they are taking off his clothes. They have no idea that they have the Creator in their hands. It never dawns on them as they smack in the nails to execute a man, that God is in Christ reconciling the world to himself, not counting their sins against them (2 Cor. 5:19).

Four is the biblical number that represents completeness. In this moment, it represents complete ignorance. The world as represented in the four soldiers do not know him. The cross is, to this day, something that reveals where people stand. Whether they know or don't know. See or can't see. The cross separates. It is either the fragrance of life or the stench of death (2 Cor. 2:15). It is either foolishness to those who are perishing or the power of God to those who are being saved (1 Cor. 1:18). At the cross, Creator God is in the world. But the world does not recognise him.

4. 'Yet to all who did receive him . . . he gave the right to become children of God' (1:12).

In the next section of the Crucifixion story the action moves from four soldiers to four women standing by the cross. Four men who do not recognise him. Four women who do receive him. Jesus sees them. And he sees the disciple whom he loved standing nearby (19:26). His mother and this man are the two people who are closest to him, who understand him the best and love him the most. He gives them to each other and makes them into a new family.

Quite apart from anything else, Jesus is dying so well – thinking of others and full of amazing grace. But, as with the soldiers, there is a deeper meaning to this part of the story that John the author wants us to see. Jesus' death on the cross recreates the family of God. Those who receive Jesus do not just have their sins forgiven. They enter into a whole new family gathered around Jesus. The terms most used in the New Testament to describe Christians are all taken from the family: sisters, brothers, mothers, fathers. The Church is the family of God, made so by God.

It all starts here. It is a picture of what the Church is and what the Church does.

5. 'The Word became flesh and made his dwelling among us. We have seen his glory' (1:14).

This is Temple talk. This is Israel's theology of Temple being restated with Jesus in the middle. Jesus is the pitching of God's tent. Jesus is the glory of God being revealed among the people of God.

Temple building is something that gets 'finished'. Moses and Solomon both finish their work of creating God's dwelling: 'And so Moses finished the work' (Exod. 40:33).

And now this finishing moment has come for Jesus. He is dying. As he prophesied in John 2, the Temple that is his body is being destroyed. His work of being the Temple dwelling of God and his work of revealing God's presence is finished. He's finished, which is what John the author makes clear in this section of the Crucifixion story. Jesus knows everything is finished. He has one final drink, and speaks his final words: 'It is finished' (19:30).

Then he gives up his spirit. The earthly Temple is done. His ascension to rule has begun. A new Temple is going to be built. But first, he has a day off. A Sabbath's rest. No new Temple building for him tomorrow.

6. 'For the law was given through Moses; grace and truth came through Jesus Christ' (1:17).

The authorities did not want the crucified bodies left on the crosses during Passover. The way to deal with that was pretty brutal – break the legs. That makes it impossible to breathe and the crucified person suffocates to death. Pilate agrees, and the soldiers get their orders. But when they come to Jesus, they find him already dead. They don't bother to break his legs. Instead, they shove a spear into the chest cavity. Blood and water flow out. The heavier red blood cells have settled, leaving clear plasma and fluids, and both the heavier blood cells and the clear plasma flow out together. A man sees it. A man standing near the cross. A man who tells the truth.

Joseph of Arimathea, a wealthy and influential man and a secret disciple of Jesus, asks Pilate for the body. Pilate agrees. Joseph is helped by his friend and fellow leader Nicodemus. One of them either owns or quickly obtains an unused burial cave in a nearby garden. Nicodemus brings spices, possibly worth in excess of £100,000. They wrap the body and bury Jesus in the tomb.

It is the Day of Preparation. The special Sabbath is about to begin. The Passover is in full swing.

All this points to this moment being the one where Jesus starts the new Exodus and brings in the new Covenant of Grace with the forgiveness of sins and the knowing of God. The Covenant of Law was given through Moses. The Covenant of Grace has come through Jesus. The cross is the place where the transition occurs.

There are a number of features that John the author has included to show this is happening:

1. IT IS THE DAY OF PREPARATION
This whole sub-section starts and finishes with that statement. It is the Day of Preparation for both the Sabbath and the Passover. Tomorrow is a very special day indeed. This day of getting everything ready is the day and the time when the Passover lambs start to be sacrificed. All yeast is taken from the houses and burned. Everyone stops work. Everything is gearing up for a week-long celebration. It isn't just their most important

annual holiday. It is the celebration of the story that is the foundation of their whole identity as a people. They were slaves and God set them free. God came to rescue them. God provided a lamb. By the blood of the lamb they were 'passed over'. God's judgment did not fall on them. It fell on the lamb. And by the blood that was shed and the power of God at work, their new life of freedom began.

2. JESUS' LEGS WERE NOT BROKEN

One of the regulations for preparing the Passover lamb was as follows: 'It must be eaten inside the house; take none of the meat outside the house. Do not break any of the bones' (Exod. 12:46). By including this unique insight, John the author is emphasising the death of Jesus as being God's provision of his Passover Lamb.

3. HIS SIDE WAS PIERCED BY A SPEAR

Instead of breaking the legs to cause death, they check the death by piercing the chest cavity.

The Prophet Zechariah sees this moment. You can read about it in chapter 12 of his book. He sees that God will come. He sees that God will defeat all his enemies and save his people. When that happens, grace will be poured out upon God's people and they will see God pierced: 'And I will pour out on the house of David and the inhabitants of Jerusalem a spirit of grace and supplication. They will look on me, the one they have pierced, and they will mourn for him as one mourns for an only child, and grieve bitterly for him as one grieves for a firstborn son' (Zech. 12:10).

John the author is taking this prophetic scripture and adding it into the story of Jesus' death. Jesus is God's Passover Lamb who takes away the sin of the world and who has started the new Exodus from slavery to sin. The Exodus journey led them to Sinai, where the Covenant of Law was made through Moses. John the author wants us to see that it is in the crucifixion of Jesus that the new Covenant of Grace is established.

4. BLOOD AND WATER FLOW OUT FROM JESUS

This is a hugely symbolic moment. It is not just reporting the biological fact that Jesus' blood has settled into cells and plasma after death. It has massive meaning for the man who sees it.

The Prophet Zechariah goes on to say that when God is pierced, 'On that day a fountain will be opened to the house of David and the inhabitants of Jerusalem, to cleanse them from sin and impurity' (Zech. 13:1).

In seeing this, the prophet is bringing together a number of other scriptures and is adding in more detail. The one they have pierced comes from the Prophet Isaiah. The suffering servant was punished by God and pierced for our sin:

> *But he was pierced for our transgressions,*
> *he was crushed for our iniquities;*
> *the punishment that brought us peace was on him,*
> *and by his wounds we are healed.*
> *(Isa. 53:5)*

The fountain that makes God's people clean from sin comes from the Prophet Ezekiel: 'I will sprinkle clean water on you, and you will be clean; I will cleanse you from all your impurities and from all your idols. I will give you a new heart and put a new spirit in you' (Ezek. 36:25–6).

Zechariah brings these two together. The piercing of God leads to the fountain from God. Blood and water flow together. The suffering servant is pierced for sins. The fountain of cleansing flows.

This idea of blood and water working together is also found in the first Exodus story. God saves his people by two mighty acts of power. In the first one that leads to Israel being set free from slavery, blood is shed. It is by the blood of the lamb that God's people are set free. But then the power of Egypt pursues them and threatens to take them back into slavery. God's people need another work of power from God. This is the crossing of the Red Sea and the drowning of the Egyptian army in the waters. God's people are saved by blood and saved through water. John the author wants us to see that Jesus' death is not just one aspect of the Exodus story, but the whole story being fulfilled. Jesus comes down from heaven as Moses comes down from Mount Sinai. He comes not with the gracious gift of the Law written on tablets of stone. He comes with the gracious gift of Grace, and the ability to write God's ways into our hearts and lives.

No wonder John the author concludes his summary of how Jesus is found in the middle of the entire story of Israel with these words: 'No one has ever seen God, but the one and only Son, who is himself God and is in the closest relationship with the Father, has made him known' (1:18).

The death of Jesus on the cross reveals the heart and purpose of the Father like nothing else.

29

Inside the Empty Tomb

This leaves us with one more panel: the Demonstration story, with the stories of Elijah and Elisha underneath. This is the next story. You can read it in John 20:1–9. To read the story from another Gospel, I suggest either Matthew 28:1–8 or Luke 24:1–12. Or both. Jump into the stories. Feel the early morning sun rising on your back. Imagine the combination of grief and shock that happens to Mary. What would you make of the empty tomb?

It is slightly unfortunate that a great big number 20 has been added to the front of this story. Sometimes chapter divisions come at strange places. This story is not strictly a story of resurrection. In the Resurrection stories Jesus is physically present, even though there is also the mystery of him being there and not being there, which happens in all the stories. But physicality is what he has, even when it is hard to recognise him and he appears and disappears at will. In all the stories there is talking, seeing, touching and eating. Jesus speaks. He gives instructions. 'Go and tell the disciples.' 'Receive the Holy Spirit.' 'Believe.' 'Come and have breakfast.'

In this story there is no physicality. The very opposite – there is no body at all. This is an Ascension story rather than a Resurrection story. The body of Jesus has gone to the Father. So the story sits and looks both ways. It is connected to what has just happened: the death and burial of Jesus. The tomb, the stone, the linen cloths and the women are in both the burial story and this story. But it also connects to the Resurrection stories, largely, as we shall see, through Mary Magdalene.

What Does John Leave Out?

John focuses on just one woman: Mary Magdalene. He leaves out all the others. This is not because John is down on women. Quite the opposite. But in typical Johannine fashion he focuses our attention. There is no conversation about who will move the stone, which only occurs in Mark. There are no guards at the tomb, just the stone rolled away. There are no angels, or instructions from them to tell the disciples that Jesus is raised from the dead. The message Mary brings is that the body must have been moved. And we aren't told any detail in John as to how she establishes or discovers that there is no body.

Where Do the Stories Connect?

The day and the time are the same across all the Gospels. It is after the Sabbath, the first day of the week. It is very early, around dawn. It is women who come to the tomb – or at least one woman – in all the Gospels. The discovery that the stone has been rolled back and there is no body in the tomb is in all the Gospels. The disciples are told, although it is a little unclear between the Gospel accounts as to who does that and when. Both Luke and John have Peter running to the tomb and then returning to where he is staying.

What Is Unique to John?

As in other stories in John, because the author has pared back several details, that which he has added in truly stands out. Three people are in the story: Mary Magdalene, Peter and the disciple whom Jesus loved. We discover that this disciple can run faster than Peter. But he is more cautious, certainly around death. He gets there first, but he waits outside and peers into the tomb. Peter arrives, panting, and plunges straight in. The linen used to wrap the body is still in place, but without a body inside it. The body has been taken but without disturbing the linen wrapping, which must have simply collapsed gently upon itself. We are not sure, because nobody tries unwrapping it, whether the spices have gone as well. The cloth that was used to wrap Jesus' head is also still in its place, slightly separate from the linen used to wrap the body.

294

It's an extraordinary discovery, one that has never been seen before. When Jesus called Lazarus out of the tomb, they had to unwrap him. This is something else.

John the author tells us that when the disciple whom Jesus loved sees all this, he believes. But it is not the resurrection that he is believing. They still do not understand from the Scriptures that Jesus had to rise from the dead (20:8–9). What he is believing is that Jesus has been glorified. He has gone to the Father.

They go back to where they are staying.

Why Does John Focus His Story Like This?

This is an Ascension story. This is someone going with their body to God. There are two of these in the Hebrew Bible: Enoch and Elijah. We don't know much about Enoch, except that he walked so far with God that one day God told him not to bother going back (Gen. 5:24). It is the Elijah/Elisha story that we are interested in. You can read about this in 2 Kings 2:1–18.

In the Demonstration stories, a significant person comes to Jesus to ask for his help for someone else. However, in this story, as with the Elijah/Elisha story, the initiative is entirely with God himself, to take Jesus up into heavenly reality, leaving only some linen behind.

In the Demonstration stories, Jesus appears reluctant to start with. There is delay. In this story, we don't have any dialogue. But we do have delay. The ascension of Jesus to the Father does not happen directly from the cross. No chariot of fire descends and takes him from his sufferings. Unlike Elijah, he goes right through into death. And then waits. He experiences his own delay.

In the Demonstration stories, Jesus gives instructions and others are caught up into the miracle. It is in the hands of the servants that the wine is brought forth. It is in the hands of the disciples that the bread is multiplied. In this story, God puts his hands to it. God moves the stone. God removes the body. God takes all the roles. He is the need. He is the answer to the need. He is the delay to the need being met. He is the means by which the need is met. In the hands of God, death turns to eternal life.

Narrative Structure

All five panels feature in the Crucifixion story, as follows:

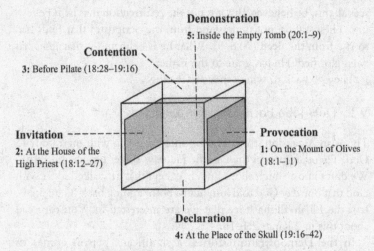

Demonstration

5: Inside the Empty Tomb (20:1–9)

Contention

3: Before Pilate (18:28–19:16)

Invitation

2: At the House of the
High Priest (18:12–27)

Provocation

1: On the Mount of Olives
(18:1–11)

Declaration

4: At the Place of the Skull (19:16–42)

The Crucifixion Stories as Holy Place

Resurrection

30

New Creation

We have seen that crucifixion is not defeat. Death is not the ignominious end of Jesus. Crucifixion is his glorification. Through death, Jesus rises to the Father. This raises the question: why the resurrection? Why does he come into a newly embodied state? What is the purpose of some people encountering Jesus for relatively short periods of time over just a few weeks?

The answer is four-fold. First, the resurrection of Jesus is the start of the new creation. It is an event of enormous significance for everyone and everything. Second, the resurrection enables Jesus to care for his friends and help them to work through the deeply emotional transition they are experiencing. Third, John the author is helping us to see that the risen Jesus is the same person as the incarnate Jesus. Our friendship with Jesus goes safely through his death, ascension and resurrection and we encounter him again, albeit in his new-creation body. Our friend now lives and will never die. Finally, the Resurrection stories give us a framework for our lives and show us what really matters in this overlap of the ages in which we live. The resurrection shows us who we are and how to live.

The Start of the New Creation

The resurrection of Jesus is the start of the new creation. The resurrection is not simply a flag-waving exercise to prove that the crucifixion worked properly. It is the key move in God's strategy to eliminate evil, put everything right that has gone wrong and bring everything together under his new King (Isa. 11).

Jesus is the first person to go through death and into the new creation. He is not Lazarus, who came back into the body he had before and would die again. Jesus' body has been moved, but not into another tomb. Jesus' body has been raised into a new reality and a new physicality. The seed of Jesus' incarnate body has been sown into the ground of death. And just as when the plant appears from the seed there is no seed left, there is no incarnate body left behind. The seed has all been taken forward into the plant. The mortal body has been transformed into an immortal body. The perishable transformed into imperishability. As with the ascent of Elijah into the heavenly reality, only his clothes have been left behind. The new creation is more real and more physical than the existing creation. Our time, space and matter are no longer physical boundaries and limiting factors. Jesus can choose the time, space and means of his appearing into our reality. Our reality, as we know, is made by electronic charges moving in a probability pattern. The new-creation reality that Jesus now inhabits is far more substantial than that.

In Jewish theology there is resurrection from the dead, but it will happen at the end of the age. Strangely, and unexpectedly, the resurrection comes forward from the end of the age and happens first of all in Jesus. Jesus as Messiah represents and embodies Israel and is the fulfilment of all her covenant promises. In him and through him the covenant is renewed (Jer. 31), sins are forgiven (Zech. 13), the Exile is ended (Dan. 9), the Spirit is given (Joel 2; Ezek. 36), the resurrection begins (Ezek. 37), and the new creation comes (Isa. 11). The way things are going to be has already begun. The future has invaded history. The renewal of all creation is underway in Christ.

There is a symmetry to the beginning and end of John's Gospel. The Gospel begins at the beginning, with the self-revealing God who makes himself known through his Word and creates all things through his Word (1:1–3). The Gospel ends at the new beginning. It is the first day of the week (20:1). God's new creation of God begins in Jesus' body. And with the launch of the new covenant, God invites us into even deeper friendship through him so that we can all know God.

Pastoring Through Change

As a disciple-making pastor, Jesus is only too aware that his friends, and to some extent us too, will need his help to process the incredible transition that has happened. He has talked about it before. But he knows that they did not understand. They need him to help them. All change is difficult. This change especially so. He is both going away and coming back. His going away was deeply painful. Their loss palpable. Their close friend and teacher was suddenly and brutally executed by the government. His body appeared to have been stolen or moved, which hugely disrupted their grief. They are confused, deeply sad and afraid. But then at least one of them begins to realise that Jesus is not dead but has ascended to the Father. Then they all discover that he has also been resurrected into the new creation and can only for a short time appear bodily in the existing creation.

All these aspects of his 'going' are challenging to process well. What is more, Jesus needs to move them rapidly forward in their understanding not just of what has happened, but why it happened and, more particularly, what they are now stepping into. He does it so beautifully.

Jesus Is Still Jesus

The Resurrection stories each fit with a different narrative panel. John the author wants us to know that the Jesus we encounter raised to new-creation life is the same Jesus that we have seen and become friends with through his incarnate life. The narrative panels repeat to reveal that the incarnate Jesus and the new-creation Jesus are one and the same person. He has not been eradicated in death or replaced in resurrection. He has passed through them as himself into his new-creation body.

Jesus isn't just going away. He is coming back to them and to us. The brief appearances in the body will give way to permanent presence by the Spirit. But Jesus is still Jesus. As we saw in the timeless time, Jesus in the Spirit is the same as Jesus in the body. In the new creation, he is no longer bound by our time, our space and our physicality. His person has entered into a reality that transcends all these. Because of this, he is now available and accessible through time and across the world. The means by which he, in the new-creation body, will now personally interact with us in the existing creation is by the Spirit. Friendship with Jesus will be mediated not by body but by his life-giving Spirit.

Who We Are and How to Live

All of this also creates the framework for our lives as friends of Jesus. Because the resurrection of Jesus is the bringing forward into time of the way things will be at the end of time, we live in the middle of a very creative tension. First, there is something much greater to come. But second, it has already begun. Holding both these dimensions of reality together is how to live as a follower of Jesus. And John, like all New Testament writers, holds to both.

There is a glorious future coming. All dead will be raised. Everything will be judged. Everything good will be preserved and brought into the new age. Everything evil will be destroyed (5:28–9). Whoever eats of the bread of life will live for ever (6:51). The bride-groom will come, and God will be joined to his people with such depth that marriage is the only metaphor that can describe it (3:29).

But what is to come in fullness has already begun. Those who were dead to God have already come to life (5:24). The difference between good and evil is now clear to see (3:21). Those who were far from God have been brought close (4:29–30).

These are the two dynamic sides of the eschatological coin: the end of the age is dynamically connected to and being made real in the present. Our lives are characterised by God working now. But we live with anticipation that there will be more to come.

Because John's purpose is to write a Gospel that enables us to develop deep friendship with Jesus now, his emphasis is naturally on the current activity of God rather than the future activity of God. The other Gospel writers have more to say about the future activity of God in things like the return of Christ, the resurrection of the dead and the judgment of the nations. John does not have a different eschatology from the other Gospel writers. It is because of his purpose that he naturally writes more about the realised aspect.

John the author shows us that it is the Spirit who brings the power of the age to come into the present. The work of the Spirit is to take what Jesus has done and make it real to us now (16:12–14). The water of the Spirit flows out from the side of the crucified and risen Jesus (19:34). The river of the Spirit will flow from within those who come to Jesus (7:37–9). The Spirit brings us the power of the age to come, the power of all that has been accomplished in the death and resurrection of Christ. The Spirit is Jesus walking with us, talking to us, encouraging and directing us. But our friendship is full of life. He is God's empowering presence.

In the resurrection narrative not only do we meet Jesus. We also see what truly matters now in the overlap of the ages and we receive power to enable us to follow Jesus into the new creation.

31
Mary

The Start of the New Creation

What would you do if you had conquered death, had entered into a new physicality that was so self-organising that it was no longer subject to decay, and you could move freely through time and space? March on Rome? Deal with the evil empire? Expose the wicked corruption of the wealthy who have become rich by exploiting the poor?

Jesus does none of those things. He leaves them for others to work on. Jesus goes for a personal meeting with a close friend. Everything else can wait for now. You can read it in 20:11–18. Jesus is real, tangible and embodied. He speaks. He listens. He can be held, although more on that in a moment. However, he is not immediately recognisable – mostly because Mary is not looking for a living Jesus but for a dead body. We do tend to only see what we are looking for.

Pastoring Through Change

Mary is not expecting the resurrection. She is a good Jewish girl. Resurrection comes at the end. She has come to anoint the body of Jesus in death and to cry the deep, painful sobs of the bereaved. The absence of the body, the presence of angels and even of Jesus himself cannot dislodge her from this view. She fits everything she sees into a single narrative. Someone has taken the body.

Until Jesus speaks her name.

There is instant recognition and mutual knowing. She calls him 'Teacher'. She holds him, as indeed you would. Their relationship is unchanged. What a moment. From deep sorrow and loss to deep joy and life.

But not everything is unchanged. Jesus gently helps her with that. Although their friendship is as solid and close as ever, much has changed, and there is no going back. She cannot hold him. There is nothing in the word 'hold' to suggest that she is clinging to him inappropriately, or that Jesus is in a frail condition and she might somehow break his new body. What Jesus gently challenges is the underlying hope she has in hugging him. Mary wants what everyone wants after a very close friend tragically dies but then comes back alive. She wants everything to return to the way it was before. Meals together, walks with other close friends, long afternoons talking about God and life and hopes and dreams. Everything that friends who love each other want.

But neither of them can go back to the way things were. Mary in the existing creation cannot hold on to the new-creation Jesus and keep him bodily in the old. The new creation begun in Jesus will not be limited to Jesus being present in the old way as a single body in a single place at a single time. New-creation Jesus has much bigger plans than that. Holding on to the new-creation body of Jesus and trying to keep him in the same space is not the way forward. Although there will be no change in their friendship, the way their friendship is going to be mediated is changing. A few brief meetings with the new-creation embodied Jesus will soon give way to relationship with Jesus by the Spirit. The Spirit is going to become her teacher. Mary can hold fast to Jesus but not by his body. Jesus gently tells her: 'Do not hold on to me, for I have not yet ascended to the Father' (20:17).

She mustn't hold his body. She must let him ascend to the Father and send his Spirit.

Instead of holding on to him, she is to go for him. Jesus gives her a new role: to go and announce his ascension into new creation life to rule with God. She is to go and invite others to step into this experience of deep friendship with a living man who has conquered death and has a new-creation body. So off she goes. She embodies his wishes for him.

Jesus Is Still Jesus

This is not the Lazarus story. This is not Mary and Martha weeping by the tomb and sending to Jesus for help. This Mary has no expectation of anyone helping her, apart from possibly the man she thinks is the gardener. Perhaps he knows where the body might be found. She makes no request for a sign. There is no, 'Had you been here things would have been different.'

This is the Invitation story. All the Invitation stories are in view. Jesus does not give Mary a new name, but he does speak her name, as he did to Peter. And as we shall see in a moment, her identity and her very nature are going to be made new, just as Simon was to become a new man called Peter. Mary is being like Nathanael, who came sceptical to Jesus, not expecting anything good to come from Nazareth, but suddenly it dawns on him that he is unexpectedly talking with someone very special. The same thing happens to Mary, talking to who she thinks is the gardener and discovering that it is Jesus. Mary is like the woman at the well, questioning in her initial conversation with Jesus because she is yet to discover who he really is. The woman at the well rebuffs Jesus' request for a drink because she is processing the shock of a Jewish man talking to a Samaritan woman. Mary rebuffs Jesus' question as to why she is crying and who she is looking for, because all she can think about is who has moved the body. Both women experience an utterly surprising, life-changing encounter with Jesus. Both of them immediately go off to tell others about him. This is Mary being like Mary who anointed Jesus for burial before his death, which this Mary never gets to do, but is what she came to do. Both of them stand so close to Jesus in his death, one just before and one just after. In the way they respond, Mary to his impending death and this Mary to his recent death, both of them reveal their great love and deep affection for Jesus.

In terms of the Old Testament sitting underneath, Mary is being Jacob all alone in the desert, not realising that she is standing in the presence of God with angels ascending and descending, until God shows her what is going on. Jesus has used the ladder that Jacob saw in his dream. He has ascended to the heavenly reality in death and he has now popped down to meet Mary in new-creation life.

The specific Old Testament story sitting under Mary's story is one from Genesis. As with the story of Jacob and his ladder, it is a Temple scene. The story takes place in a special space where humanity meets with God and walks with God. But we have gone right back, further than Jacob, to the original family. You can read it in Genesis 2:4–25. As with the Gospel story, this is a story of a man talking to a woman in a garden. It is a love scene. One of complete purity and with beautiful depth of intimacy. In the story, the first person that the newly created man talks to is a woman who meets him in the garden. In the Gospel story, the first person that the new-creation man Jesus talks to is a woman who meets him in the garden. The priority for new-creation Jesus is not the exercise of power but the pursuit of love.

However, the Genesis story ends badly. The man's and the woman's friendship is distorted by the abuse of power in their relationship. They are thrown out of the garden and exiled from God's presence, and their fate is death. But in the Gospel story with Jesus, the new-creation man in the garden, the end of the story dramatically changes. In the Genesis garden, the man and wo-man had life but they chose death. In the Gospel garden, the man and wo-man have death but are given life. All that was lost has been restored at the cross.

All the echoes of the Genesis stories of meeting women at wells are brought in. Like the story of Hagar, Mary knows that Jesus sees her, knows her and cares for her. Like the story of Rebekah, the new bride has been found. Isaiah too is singing his song (Isa. 54). The barren woman, deserted and distressed in spirit, abandoned for a brief moment, is brought back with deep compassion.

Who We Are and How to Live

We live in what the Scriptures call the end times or the last days (Acts 2:17; 2 Tim. 3:1–5). We live in the overlap of the ages. The new creation has begun but the existing creation is still going. By the work of the Spirit, the new creation is stepping into the old. What does that mean?

We know that to understand John we need to read the Old Testament story at the same time as the Gospel story. As we hold them together, the meaning comes into view. We see in the Genesis story that the wo-man is made from the man. She is made out of his side. However, what we discover from the Gospel story is that the new creation is not yet coming into the existing creation in bodily form. Mary cannot hold on to the new body of Jesus and keep the new-creation body in the old creation. The new creation is coming into the existing creation at a much deeper level than bodily physicality.

Mary's bodily existence will remain for many years in the existing creation. It is everything else about her that will made new, made from Jesus. She will be a new-creation person, made new in the image of Jesus, but remaining in an existing-creation body. But her identity, her priorities, her hopes, her self will be made from the new creation.

When we are called to be friends of Jesus, we too become new-creation people bearing the likeness of Jesus while remaining in our existing-creation body. Like Peter, we have been given a new name and a new identity. Having made us into new-creation people, Jesus works by his Spirit in us to reshape everything about us to become like him. This reshaping occurs naturally through the process of being called to be his friends. My close friends have all changed me for the better. If you were to ask them, they will probably tell you that there has been a good start, but more progress is required. With Jesus the relationship is even deeper, the changes even greater. The whole New Testament is built on this understanding as to who we are in Christ (2 Cor. 5:17; Gal. 6:14–15; Gal. 4:19).

The final step in this life-changing process will occur after our death, when, at the end of the age, the dead will be raised and we too will enter into the fullness of new-creation life with a new body suited to our new nature (John 5:25).

The priority for the risen Jesus is close friendship with those who love him. That is where his work of making all things new begins.

32

Risen in Their Midst

The next story of the resurrected Jesus is a tightly connected sequence of two stories, each with two parts. A Provocation story and a Contention story have been woven together. It is one of John the author's favourite approaches: a repeating pattern of stories. You can read them in 20:19–29.

- Story A/Part 1: Jesus rises in the midst of the disciples (20:19–23)
- Story B/Part 1: The disciples tell Thomas, who refuses to believe (20:24–5)
- Story A/Part 2: Jesus rises in the midst of the disciples (20:26)
- Story B/Part 2: Jesus helps Thomas, who believes (20:27–9)

By bringing two narrative panels into such close, interwoven relationship, John the author is highlighting something important about people. We show ourselves to be present through the consistency of our beliefs, values, words and actions. But people don't have a single application of their inner selves in certain fixed directions. We integrate the various aspects of our person. We overlap one aspect of ourselves with another. John has created the dynamic, biblically rich space for us to meet with Jesus by his use of the narrative panels. But he does not allow us to imagine that his methodology is the sum of Jesus' mind. People are much more complex and interesting than that. The narrative panels serve us, but they do not master Jesus.

The Start of the New Creation

The evening of the first day, the disciples gather together. They have the empty tomb just down the road, the disciple whom Jesus loved probably sitting with them and expressing his belief in the ascension of Jesus, and

Mary telling them of her meeting with Jesus. But you can imagine their persistent sense of loss, their abiding pain in Jesus' death, and their confusion and fear. They lock the doors. One of them may be next.

Jesus rises in their midst.

As a new-creation person standing within an existing creation, his body has physicality. His appearance has continuity with himself, particularly with recent events. He shows them his hands and his side. Whatever the new-creation appearance of that is, it has evident meaning to them and communicates to them that he is a crucified but now living person. In his aliveness we also see his crucifiedness.

Even as a new-creation person, Jesus is an embodied living soul. A person is a unity of all that constitutes a 'me' – thoughts, emotions, memories, values, sequencing and analytic abilities, communication abilities – interacting with and perceived through the physicality of body. The body is thus a symbol of the person. A symbol makes real what cannot be seen. When a person dies and the body begins the process of decay, it is sadly so evidently not an embodied person. It is a corpse, a symbol of the absence of the person, just as the living body was a symbol of the presence of the person. A symbol is different from a sign. A sign is not that to which it points. Think Fire Exit. Nobody tries to climb out through the Fire Exit sign. The body is a symbol. It is that which it is making perceptible.

Unlike us, who can only move slowly through space and are fixed in our body and bound to our time, new-creation Jesus can choose the bodily means, time and place of his becoming visible in the existing creation. The new creation is not less real or less tangible than our existing creation. It is more so.

Pastoring Through Change

In this sequence of two connected stories, Jesus has two purposes: (1) To show the disciples that his new-creation living presence with them is now permanent and this is what constitutes the Church. A Church is the gathered followers of Jesus with the living Jesus in their midst; (2) To show that the permanent presence of his person is not to be verified through visible means. I can't see the electricity that powers my computer, but I know it is there.

STORY A/PART 1: JESUS RISES IN THE MIDST OF THE DISCIPLES
(20:19–23)

The first story begins with the disciples gathering, having scattered during the events of the trial and crucifixion. This is positive. However, it is a gathering of fear. What will the authorities do?

Jesus comes and stands in their midst. A man they thought was dead appears among them. The sense in the story is not that of Jesus waiting outside for the door to be unlocked, or even that he comes through the wall. The sense is that Jesus chooses to become visible in his being with them, much as if he were to suddenly stand up in the middle of a seated group. The reality that Jesus is with them and standing among them as a permanent presence is reinforced by the fact that Jesus doesn't leave. He doesn't wave goodbye and go outside. By the time they are telling Thomas, he is simply no longer visible to them, which isn't the same as not being there.

Underneath the Greek phrase 'stand in their midst' is an Aramaic verb (*quwm*), which means 'to set up, rise up and establish'. This is closely associated with building the Temple. After the Exile, the leader Zerubbabel rises up and begins to rebuild the house of God (Ezra 5:2).

Jesus speaks, 'Peace be with you!' This is much more than, 'Calm down, everyone,' although I am sure some reassurance was included. This brings in Psalm 122, which is a psalm of ascent, a song celebrating God's people going up into God's Temple. The imagery is identical to this story. God's people have gone up to God's house. Their feet are standing there. They are in the place of God's presence and rule. They are all there together. In that place, the great blessing of 'peace be' is spoken twice. This is what Jesus does. Standing and speaking this blessing is Jesus showing them that he is standing in God's house. As Jesus promised, the new Temple is being built (2:19–21). The authorities previously demanded that Jesus show them a sign that he has authority over their Temple. The building of the new Temple is the sign that he declares and now does. This is what the Church is. The Church is the gathered people of God with Jesus standing in their midst. The people of God are the dwelling place of God.

Jesus shows them his hands and his side. The new-creation Jesus is eternally marked as the crucified man, the Lamb of God who takes away the sins of the world. His identity is now visible in his body.

It isn't just some scars from nails and the spear that the disciples are invited to 'see'. It is the purpose of the scars and the meaning of the crucifixion that Jesus reveals. Sins are forgiven.

Jesus speaks the second blessing of Peace and sends them into the world. John the author uses two different Greek words here for 'send', because sending has two different aspects. A sent one is sent *to* others, to accomplish or convey something to them. A sent one is also sent *from* someone, to represent the sender. Jesus is sent by the Father (Greek: *apostello*). This word emphasises that Jesus has been sent to accomplish something for others. The disciples are sent by Jesus (Greek: *pempo*). This word emphasises that the disciples represent Jesus and are from him. For the world to know what Jesus has accomplished for them, the disciples are to be like him and represent him. They are in effect his existing-creation body.

In order for the church to fulfil the calling to be Jesus to the world, Jesus breathes on them the Holy Spirit. This expression in Greek only occurs here in the whole Testament. It is drawing in the story of the creation of the first human where God makes man from mud and breathes life up his nose (Gen. 2:7). It is also drawing in the vision of Ezekiel where, as Ezekiel prophesies, the dead bones of God's people are brought to life and breath enters them (Ezek. 37:9–10). This is a moment of new-creation resurrection happening to existing-creation people. This is what the followers of Jesus become. Disciples of Jesus are those who have been given new-creation resurrection life within themselves by the breath of God upon them. And empowered by this new nature and Spirit-breathed life, the Church embarks on the mission to announce the saving work of Jesus to the world.

Forgiveness of sins is not something that the Church simply announces as available. Jesus gives his disciples the authority to **pronounce** forgiveness and declare that it has happened. Or not. The Church is given authority, not to save people, because that is the work of Jesus, but to tell those who have been saved that they are saved. Disciples are empowered to recognise other disciples and declare to future disciples that they have been brought into the new covenant where sins are forgiven and people know God.

So what exactly do the disciples tell Thomas?

Do they tell him that the new Temple of the living God is being built? Do they tell him that the dwelling of God is no longer a building but a people where Jesus forever dwells in their midst? Do they tell him that fear has given way to joy because Jesus is now permanently present with them? Do they explain that his visibility is temporary because he lives in a new-creation reality, but that his presence is continuous because the new creation is not limited by time and space? Do they explain that in crucifixion, the new covenant with God has been established and all sins are forgiven? Do they talk about the continuous outflow of new-creation life from the open side of God's Messiah? Do they explain to him that Genesis and Ezekiel have now been outworked together and that the new people of God have become a new creation within by the breath of God upon them? Do they engage him in the mission of God to reach the world? Do they recognise him and include him as one whose sins are forgiven?

Do they heck.

STORY B/PART 1: THE DISCIPLES TELL THOMAS, WHO REFUSES TO BELIEVE (20:24–5)

They say the one thing that Thomas missed. They fixate on the one thing that is temporary. And in doing so they exclude him from themselves. 'We have seen the Lord!' they say. Thanks. John the author has signposted the likelihood of this happening because he describes the disciples as being 'overjoyed when they saw the Lord'. They are not overjoyed because they understand the enormity of all that is happening. Because they don't. Now before we point too many of our fingers, let's remember we are the same. The first time, or even the first ten times that we hear about Jesus, we don't understand very much. The first time we receive the Holy Spirit, we haven't got the first clue what is happening to us. When we first begin to be part of church, we have no idea of the enormity of what we are getting connected with. And let's not forget, their teacher has just died. They are not sitting in the study poring over books and reading up about the Exile and the Exodus. They are in the shock of grief.

Thomas is not one to take this lying down. They have seen something that he has missed out on. So naturally, being a man, he raises the stakes on them. 'Right then,' he says, 'if you have seen the Lord, I want to see him *and touch him*.' This isn't doubt. Doubt is the honest inability to conclude something for certain because of insufficient evidence. Thomas isn't doubting what they have said or even what they have experienced. He is demanding that Jesus give him the same experience and a bit more. He takes a strong stand. He wilfully withholds belief in the ascension and resurrection of Jesus until he has seen and touched the body himself. Deliberately withholding faith until personal conditions are met is not the same as properly questioning the testimony of others and weighing the evidence with a clear mind.

Thomas, like Mary, is wanting things to return to the way they were before, when Jesus was incarnate in an existing-creation body. If Thomas wants to verify the presence of the incarnate Jesus in the flesh, he could simply see him and touch him. He insists that the same conditions apply. But – you can't have forgiveness of sins and friendship with God without crucifixion. You can't have crucifixion without that being the end of Jesus in the flesh. As with Elijah, you can't have ascension without the body being removed. And you can't have resurrection into new-creation life without Jesus being embodied in a new and dynamic way that cannot simply hang around the existing creation for people to look at and touch on demand. Things, as they say, have most definitely moved on.

Thomas gets a bad press and a reputation he probably doesn't deserve, but I doubt that he cares. Jesus the disciple-making pastor takes us back round this again to make sure that everybody, us included, gets the point.

We wait a week.

STORY A/PART 2: JESUS RISES IN THE MIDST OF THE DISCIPLES (20:26)
Thomas could be the first person to believe in Jesus because of the testimony of the Spirit-filled Church. But the disciples botch it and Thomas reacts strongly against them. He demands what they cannot provide. So now no one can do anything – apart from Jesus. And being the kind pastor that he is, we go back to the start and have another go at this. Although I enjoy that Jesus lets a week go by before he sorts out the mess. What is significant about that delay is that it is now the first day of the week again. The Church gathers with Jesus risen in their midst. The Peace blessing is spoken. We are standing in a temple space. We are meeting with the living God among us.

STORY B/PART 2: JESUS HELPS THOMAS, WHO BELIEVES (20:27–9)
Jesus provides what Thomas requires. Thomas sees the new-creation body of Jesus. He is invited to touch the new-creation embodiment of

the crucified man. But Jesus' gentle approach to Thomas is the same as his approach to Mary. Mary was allowed to hold Jesus but was asked not to hold on to his body. Holding on to Jesus is now going to be by receiving the Spirit, not holding the body. Thomas too is allowed to see and touch Jesus, but he is asked to do that in a way that shows that seeing and touching the new-creation body of Jesus is not the way forward.

What Jesus says to Thomas doesn't come out as clearly in some of the English translations as it does in the original. Jesus invites Thomas, 'Put your finger here; see my hands. Reach out your hand and put it into my side' (20:27).

Last time I checked, the finger doesn't see. Jesus invites Thomas to see without seeing. Jesus asks Thomas to take hold of all that has been accomplished in his death, ascension and resurrection. Getting hold of Jesus is moving from a process involving sight and touch to one that is through heart and mind. This does not make it a lesser process, but a better one. It is better that Jesus 'goes away', because getting hold of the enormity of all that Jesus has done for us is much, much deeper than simply seeing the body of a man who has had some painful wounds.

Jesus calls Thomas to faith: 'Do not be unbelieving, but believing' (20:27, NASB).

Give up your deliberate and conscious refusal to believe. Give up your demand that somehow everything goes back to the way it was before. This is an impossible demand. Be believing, not because you have seen something with your eyes, but because you have got hold of the truth with your hands and your heart. Not being able to see Jesus does not mean that the resurrection is not true. Not seeing Jesus does not mean that he is not there, because the way to access the truth and see the truth is by the Spirit of God, speaking through the Word of God, brought to you through the voices, feet and hands of the Church of God.

And Thomas does. Believe.

Jesus Is Still Jesus

Story A is the Provocation stories brought to fulfilment. Jesus is the new King who is building the new Temple, where God's presence dwells and sins are forgiven.

As in all the Provocation stories, Jesus starts the story. He made the whip. He sent the lame man off into the city carrying his mat. He rises in the midst of the Church. When he comes again a week later to rescue both Church and Thomas, he again starts the story.

As in all the Provocation stories, by building the Church as the new dwelling place for God on the earth, Jesus is saying stop to the corrupt system. But he is not saying stop to the idea. God will still dwell with his people. God will still bring true rest to his people. God's people have failed God. God has come to do it himself.

The disciples don't get it. They didn't get the Temple being brought to a halt. They didn't get why Jesus rode the donkey into Jerusalem. In this Resurrection story they are struggling, as with all the Provocation stories. We are no different. It takes time for all of us to really understand Jesus and get what he is doing.

A sign is demanded, in this case by Thomas. But the sign Jesus provides is not the one that was expected. The sign Jesus provides for the rest of time to come is not showing off his new-creation body. The sign he provides to show he is God's new King is the building of his Church with himself permanently present, with the gathered people of God filled and empowered by the Holy Spirit, sent into the world to proclaim and to recognise the forgiveness of sins. That's not what anyone had in mind at the time.

Seeing the sign does not mean that everyone will believe the sign. Plenty of people saw the whip in Jesus' hand. Many people saw the lame man walking and the blind man seeing. But they did not believe. They saw but they didn't see. In his resurrection, Jesus is bringing in the new rule of God. Jesus is building the new presence of God. But like all the Provocation stories, every person needs God's help to truly see what God is doing.

As with all the Provocation stories, we see Isaiah. A disturbingly large number of other scriptures are brought in underneath. This is Isaiah 2; God's new Temple is rising up. This is Isaiah 6; the presence of God is tangible but is not perceived by those who are blinded by their own certainties and their hardness of heart. This is Isaiah 11; the new King has come from the ancient roots and the Spirit of God is upon him. This is Isaiah 32; the new rule of God is both rock of safety and river of life. This is Isaiah 54; a new covenant of peace is spoken to an abandoned wife who has been rescued and brought back. The city of God is being rebuilt with precious materials. All the children of God will be taught by God and will know God. This is Isaiah 60; nations will come to God's light. This is Isaiah 61; the Spirit of God is on the people of God to speak good news to the poor. The ancient ruins will be rebuilt. This is Isaiah 66; God brings his children to birth and extends peace to them like a river. They are a sign among the nations until the new creation comes completely.

This is also 2 Chronicles 6:5–9, where the Son of David will build the Temple for God. It is Psalm 90:1; God is our dwelling place through all generations. It is Psalm 89:20–9, where the Davidic King will bring in the rule of God and establish the new covenant of God's love. It is Psalm 46; God is our refuge and strength, therefore we will not fear. And many others besides.

Story B is a Contention story. Part 1 is an unresolved argument between Thomas and the rest of the Church which Jesus resolves in Part 2. In Part 1, the Church do not speak of their identity as being the new people of God, the new dwelling place of God. They make no reference to the Exodus or the Exile. All they can talk about is what Thomas has missed.

To be fair to them, they do attempt to make a credibility statement. 'We have seen the Lord,' is in that territory. But in his Contention stories Jesus never starts there. He covers a lot of ground with Nicodemus before he says, 'I am speaking about what I have seen.'

Even in the fiercest of his arguments with the authorities, Jesus never shuts the door. He does speak strongly to people. But he is living in a culture that is very comfortable with strong, exaggerated speech. It shows that you care. But even then, Jesus never speaks with a closed hand. He keeps speaking about his identity, his relational authority and his biblically rooted authenticity. In this way, even his most robust critics always have the opportunity to step across to him.

Unfortunately, the Church do none of this. Instead, they shut the door on Thomas with him very much outside. Now, doubtless, Thomas' personality is in play. But I am not sure we should lay all the blame at his door.

In Part 2, Jesus invites Thomas to get hold of who he is. Putting your hands on the sacrifice provided by God is the Exodus story. Israel sacrifice their Passover lambs and then smear the blood on the doorframes of their houses. It is very hands on. And in doing so they are saved. The phrase that Jesus uses, 'Reach here', also means 'to bring', or 'to bring forth'. The priest takes the blood from the sin offering and with his finger 'brings' it to the corners of the altar (Lev. 4:28–30). The offering that Thomas is invited to get his hands on and to bring is Jesus himself.

Jesus then underlines the point he has already made to Thomas by asking him to see with his finger. Seeing is going to be without seeing: 'Because you have seen me, you have believed; blessed are those who have not seen and yet have believed' (20:29).

Blessing will come to all future disciples who will see without seeing. To see without seeing is what Ezekiel did. From the very beginning, his whole insight into what God was doing came from inner vision, not from the process of light waves entering his eyes and striking his retina: 'In my thirtieth year, in the fourth month on the fifth day, while I was among the exiles by the River Kebar, the heavens were opened and I saw visions of God' (Ezek. 1:1).

Everything we have looked at from Ezekiel in the other Contention stories requires inner vision to see, rather than the use of the eyes. Jesus as the bread from heaven. Jesus as the person from whose side the river of life flows. Jesus as the gate, the way to be saved and brought into a good place. No one 'sees' this by looking at the physical Jesus. Jesus is the means of revelation. But revelation does not come by simply looking at him. Seeing him is deeper than that.

This bringing into close relation of the Provocation and Contention stories is helpful. By doing this, John the author is showing us that Jesus, like all of us, doesn't fit into nice easy boxes. Jesus has aspects of his personhood where he is deeply consistent. The narrative panels are a way of showing that. However, he also integrates his personality. In this sequence of stories he brings different aspects of himself into close relationship. But he is still Jesus, the Jesus we have already met.

Who We Are and How to Live

What this means for us almost defies description. Jesus is God's new King, building the new dwelling of God on the earth. Jesus is permanently present in our midst. The gathered Church is the new people of God. Church is built with people. People are the precious building materials seen by Isaiah that God builds together to make his home.

This means that wherever and however believers are brought together and have community together, Jesus himself is in our midst. Not just in our organised meetings, large and small, although that is to be recognised and celebrated, but in our very relationships and being together.

We have been given a new-creation nature within our existing-creation bodies. The presence of the Holy Spirit has been breathed into us and we have been raised up as a new creation with resurrection life at work within us. A combination of Genesis 2 and Ezekiel 37 has happened to us. We were dead but have been made alive by the resurrection power of God at work within us. The power of the age to come has been manifested in us and through us.

The new covenant has begun: the knowing of God, obedience to God from our new nature within and the unconditional loving commitment of God to us.

The Church is the body of Jesus, sent to the world to represent him and to be him. As Jesus came to reveal the Father and make him known, we go to reveal Jesus and make him known. His identity is our identity. He is risen among us and we are in him. We have authority to forgive sins and welcome others into new creation life.

As we engage with others to make Jesus known, we are to do so with open hands. We are to speak, sometimes strongly, of our identity, our authority and, when challenged, our credibility. But we do not speak of these things in such a way that others are excluded and separated from us. The door to even our fiercest critics is to remain open.

All of this is happening in the time–space that we understand as realised eschatology. The new creation has begun but it has not fully come. We are new people. But who we are is not yet fully revealed. Our change into the likeness of Christ has begun because we have a new nature within. But it is not yet completed. All of us are a work in progress. But what this means is that to follow Jesus is to live out who we really are, not to try to attain to something that is beyond us. All New Testament calls to holiness are framed in this understanding. Throw off what is not you. Put down what does not belong to you. Take off what does not suit you. Do not indulge your existing-creation body which will soon pass. By the work of the Spirit, grow your new nature, which is like Christ.

33

Standing on the Shore

The Thomas story forms the backdrop to the author's purpose in writing the Gospel. If disciples are going to see without seeing, how will followers of Jesus become friends with Jesus? Answer: write the Gospel as a literary temple so that by the work of the Spirit of God within the Word of God the reader can meet with Jesus, form deep friendship and have life in his name.

But this is not the end of the Gospel.

Time passes. We are not sure how many days. John the author simply says, 'Afterwards'. You can read the next story in John 21:1–8. Peter decides to go fishing and invites his friends. Six go with him, of whom two remain unnamed. Is he going back to work? Are they running short of money? Or is it recreation? A chance for Peter to return to familiar territory and think things through more deeply? Or is it friendship? A chance to relax with people who have shared an incredible experience with him? Maybe it is all of these. Fishing with friends on a hot night is relaxing, especially if several of the party know what they are doing and have access to good-quality equipment. There is plenty of time to think and talk things through. And it also turns into a very lucrative night, from a business point of view.

The Start of the New Creation

We get a time check. It is early morning. The sun is about to rise. Jesus stands on the shore. We find out at the end of the story that the disciples are about 100m from the beach, looking for shoaling fish feeding in the shallower water. This is a subtle but important distinction from the previous stories. Jesus has risen near them, rather than in their midst. As we have seen, the new-creation Jesus is in the midst of the Church. But what we see in this story is that Jesus is also in every other part of life. He is alongside his friends at work. He is with them in their friendship.

They don't recognise him, until something else happens. The presence of Jesus comes quietly and unannounced. As far as the disciples are concerned, there is a man on the shore who wants to buy some of their fish. A perfectly ordinary practice. There isn't a Sainsbury's. People buy their fish from the fishermen who work the sea. The new creation enters the existing creation in fairly ordinary form. It is also a matter of the disciples' perception. If we are not looking for something, we tend not to see it.

Pastoring Through Change

In this story, Jesus is helping the disciples to become familiar with how the Holy Spirit is going to work in their lives. Jesus is going to be present in the Church, drawing close to his friends, filling them with resurrection power and sending them to reach the world. But Jesus is also going to come unannounced to their work and to their friendships. Jesus will come alongside and be with them at a time and in a manner of his choosing. You might even have to get dressed once you realise that he is there.

Jesus Is Still Jesus

This is the Demonstration story, almost identical in structure to The Feeding of the Five Thousand. Jesus starts the story with a request for help. He is holding a beach barbecue and needs some fresh fish. The disciples respond reluctantly. They don't have any fish. None at all. This is the Demonstration story going to another level. There aren't five loaves or even two small fish. Undeterred by that, Jesus gives instructions: 'Throw your net on the right side of the boat.' It is in the disciples' hands that the miracle occurs. This is the moment of recognition. They have seen this happening before. The outcome is an abundance: 153 large fish and no torn net.

All the other Demonstration stories are drawn in. Like The Wedding at Cana, does it really matter if they go back to Jerusalem with no fish? But Jesus is interested in everything about us. It would be shameful for Peter to return to Jerusalem with nothing. And some extra money will definitely come in handy as they stay longer than planned in the city to meet with Jesus. Like The Feeding of the Five Thousand, there is a tremendous abundance. They are taking fish home with them at the end of the story. Like all the Demonstration stories, Jesus is revealed to a small group who believe in him.

This is another Elisha story. You can read it in 2 Kings 6:1–7. There are no fish, but everything else connects well. A group of disciples decide to go off to the Jordan. They need wood, to help them build a bigger house for them to meet with Elisha. Elisha is with them. They go to a place that they know, where they can chop and collect wood that has been carried by the river close to the shore. But disaster strikes. The axe-head falls into the river. And it is borrowed gear. Not only is there no axe; there will be no wood. The disciple is standing in the water near where it is but can't see it or reach it. Elisha is standing near. He adds an ingredient: he throws in a piece of wood. The axe-head comes to the surface. He gives the disciple instructions to draw out the axe-head himself, which he does.

There are fifteen points of connection: (1) A group of disciples (2) decide to go to water (3) to get the resources they need to (4) build a place to meet with the prophet. (5) They are in the water close to shore (6) but lose the axe and therefore have no wood. (7) The disciple is standing in the water (8) very near to where what he is looking for is (9) but can't see it or reach it. (10) The prophet is standing nearby. (11) He adds an ingredient – a piece of wood. (12) The prophet gives instructions (13) which the disciple follows, and (14) what he needs comes to the surface and (15) he can now draw it out by himself.

Who We Are and How to Live

Jesus comes alongside us at work, with our friends and when we are recreating. We may not recognise his presence to start with, but he can and he will direct us to do things that will provide an abundance when we thought we would end up with nothing.

Adding the ingredient of Jesus and the cross can change any situation.

34

Do You Love Me?

We have reached the final story in the Gospel. There are so many beautiful symmetries in John. The last thing Jesus does is the same as the first thing he does: a meal with friends and time spent talking together. The final story of the resurrected Jesus is the same as the first story of the resurrected Jesus: meeting with a close friend and helping them to move forward well. This final story is an Invitation story. You can read it in 21:12–25.

The Start of the New Creation

In this story it would be easy to assume that it is the incarnate Jesus. Apart from the context of resurrection, there is nothing to show that the new-creation Jesus is anything other than he always has been throughout the whole Gospel. He is a wise, caring, insightful, challenging and ultimately helpful man. This helps us to see that new-creation life isn't going to be completely removed from what we already know and love. At the heart of new creation is close friendship.

Pastoring Through Change

Can you imagine reading the Gospels without this story? Every Gospel tells us of Peter's terrible failure with his repeated denial of Jesus at the trial. And then nothing. Can you imagine reading Acts and seeing Peter's incredible influence as apostle, Church leader and pastor without this story? Yet this story is only found in John.

Jesus knows that failure is not a problem. It is what happens next that matters. As we saw with The Woman at the Well, Jesus has an amazing way of helping people acknowledge the failings of their past and at the same moment enabling them to step into a future free of their past. That is quite a skill. Jesus puts on a beach barbecue with the specific intention of helping Peter. Flaky Simon will become rock-like Peter, the shepherd and leader of God's people. This story is another key milestone on that journey of change.

The breakfast barbecue comes complete with charcoal fire, echoing the one Peter stood by only a few days ago, saying three times, 'I am not a disciple of that man.' After the food, Jesus and Peter go for a walk to have a chat. The disciple whom Jesus loved tags along, listening in but staying back, so that Jesus' work as pastor can be done.

Jesus repeatedly questions Peter: do you love me? Much could be said about the important use of questions in pastoral situations, but now is not the moment. A lot has been made of how the author uses two different Greek words for 'love' in this story. In the first two questions, Jesus uses the word *agape*. In the third question, he uses the Greek word *philia*. Peter's three responses all use *philia* for, 'Yes, I love you.' However, in the Gospel, *philia* and *agape* are used interchangeably. For example, the disciple whom Jesus loved is described using the word *agape* in 13:23 and *philia* in 20:2. In the chat between Jesus and Peter, John the author uses other pairs of words, like lamb and sheep. He is using slightly different words to create a richness and depth of meaning rather than to suggest different meanings through the different words. It is the repeating of the question that is important.

Jesus repeats the question to get Peter to repeat the answer. It is a moment of healing. Peter is hurt when Jesus asks him for the third time, 'Do you love me?' He is having to face his failing while at the same time being invited to step free of his failing. Helping a person get free from past mistakes is often painful and so has to be done with great love and good skills, both of which Jesus possesses.

Jesus moves on to give Peter a heads up about his death by crucifixion. Why bring that up now? It may not seem like it, but it is a strong affirmation of Peter. Jesus is saying to him: 'You are like me. You will shepherd like me; you will die like me.' There is a deliberate reference back to how Jesus described himself: 'I am the good shepherd. The good shepherd lays down his life for the sheep' (10:11).

Jesus is moving Peter not just from failing as a disciple at a critical moment. He is moving him from fisherman to shepherd leader of the

Church. He is appointing him into a very significant responsibility while at the same time making clear to Peter what the qualifications are for that role. There are two: (1) love for Jesus; (2) caring for people. Do you want to be a senior leader in God's Church? That is the job description.

It is at this moment that Peter realises they are being followed. He turns and sees the disciple whom Jesus loved. Like all of us, there is some competitive anxiety in him. 'What about him?' is the first question on his lips. We don't know whether Peter is enquiring about the disciple's role in the Church or asking about how he will die. Jesus tells Peter to mind his own business and get on with his own life and do what Jesus calls him to do.

We have seen Jesus pastoring his friends individually in the stories of Mary and Peter. We have seen Jesus pastoring the Church, making clear to them their new identity and their purpose, and how their friendship with him will move forward now by the Spirit. We have seen Jesus coming alongside his friends in their work and in their friendships. We know there are many more stories that could be told. But we have seen enough to know that Jesus has succeeded in pastoring his friends through the momentous changes that have engulfed them.

Jesus Is Still Jesus

This is a classic Invitation story. Someone points out Jesus. The disciple whom Jesus loved takes the role of John who baptises. Like the meeting with the woman at the well, Jesus starts the conversation with a simple request. As in all the Invitation stories, people connect very closely with him. A meal happens. Conversation develops. Then, like with Nathanael and the woman at the well, Jesus uses his intuitive–prophetic insight to create a moment that is life-changing and healing for Peter. As with all the Invitation stories, those he invites close to him are profoundly changed and helped as people.

We are back in the Jacob story. Towards the end of his life, Jacob prophesies over his sons. He speaks of Joseph's fruitfulness and his resilience as a leader and attributes this to God, whom he describes like this:

because of the hand of the Mighty One of Jacob,
because of the Shepherd, the Rock of Israel,
because of your father's God, who helps you,
because of the Almighty, who blesses you.
(Gen. 49:24–5)

These are the two statements that Jesus makes to Peter in the Invitation stories. In the first one he gives him the new name and the new identity as Peter, the Rock. And in the final story of the Gospel he gives him the new role as Shepherd of his people.

Who We Are and How to Live

The ordinariness of this story helps us. New-creation Jesus is still doing the same things we have seen him do so well before. There is the lovely miracle of the 153 fish. But having got breakfast organised, the focus of Jesus' attention is on deepening friendships and enabling change. We can have great confidence that Jesus, by the Spirit, is right now doing the same things with us.

Maybe Jesus is calling you to lead in his Church. Well, you know the qualifications. And you know you will need Jesus' help to change. Suffering and death may well await you. But he will be with you. As you think about your own future there is no need to be concerned about others'. Jesus has their lives in hand, just as much as yours. There is no need to compare yourself to others. Following Jesus is all that matters.

Maybe you have slipped up badly. Jesus will come to you. He will talk it through with you. It might be a little bit painful. But it is ultimately good for us to face the reality of our own shortcomings. Jesus will not make you linger there. But you need to step through what has happened. You can't ignore it.

Making mistakes is part of leadership development in Jesus' world. Failure is not the problem. It is what you do next that counts.

If you are a leader already, try not to get too big-headed about it. You are only following Jesus, just the same as everyone else. There are two men in this final story. One is invited into a very high-profile leadership role. The other is invited to look after Jesus' mum. You can

make your own mind up about whether one is more significant than
the other.

*

The narrative structure of the Resurrection stories is very similar to
the timeless time:

| 20:11–18 | 20:19–23 | 20:24–5 | 20:26 | 20:27–9 | 21:1–8 | 21:12–25 |

Invitation Provocation Contention Demonstration Invitation
The Resurrection Unwrapped

Conclusion

Written That You May Believe

John's Gospel was written so that we can know Jesus.

The Jesus we encounter through the Invitation stories calls us to be friends. We come close to him. Spend time with him. Discover that he knows us. Hear him as he opens his heart extravagantly to us. And our lives change. Simons becomes Peters. Rejected people rejoice. Friends become followers. Followers become priests, as we find ourselves invited inside his Father's house.

The Jesus we see through the Demonstration stories does come, perhaps with a little delay, when we seek his help for others' needs. Sometimes in deliberately strange ways, and through all our struggles to believe, he helps us to trust in him. He sees our need. He feels our pain. And then he draws us into being part of his miracle. He turns our shame into praise, our sickness into life and our lack into abundance. He tells us to stop trying to control everything and to trust him.

The Jesus we find through the Provocation stories speaks to power without taking up arms. He is King by laying down his life. He brings into the light the things that have gone wrong. He speaks of God's justice to come. He opens our blind eyes. He is the Son who builds God's house and brings in God's reign where all things are just and beautiful and right and true.

The Jesus we discover through the Contention stories is strong and deeply secure, knowing who he is from Scripture. He is completely authentic and speaks truly of what he has seen and heard. He has powerful authority, which surprisingly comes solely from being Son to his Father. He is not frightened to let truth be challenging. And even in the most bitter conflicts he never closes his heart to those who oppose him.

The Jesus we know through the Declaration stories is nothing less than the embodiment of the entire history and theology of Israel. He is indeed the Word made flesh.

The Jesus we meet in the Admission story silences all the voices of condemnation, shame and guilt. And we enter in to be one with him. Adultery stops and true intimacy with him begins.

John the author has achieved his purpose. He has written. Written to reveal Jesus that we might know him and receive life. The story of Jesus has been woven inside the story of Israel, beautifully crafted into narrative panels so that we can see Jesus as he truly is, and we can enter into living friendship with him. Going through death to the Father, Jesus has risen in our midst. He is with us by the Spirit. We can know him through his Word.

Friends know each other. Friendship is mutual, a giving of self, one to the other. There is a never-ending richness to true friendship.

You will hear his call to follow him and your life will never be the same again. You will step into an open heaven and find a covenant-keeping God speaking promises to you (1). Shame will be turned to honour. Disaster to abundance. You will find fresh hope. Even the darkest of corrupt places can be demolished so that he can rebuild all that is good (2). You will stop being in control of your life. You will make a new start. The life of God will blow through you and take you forward in ways that you could never imagine possible on your own (3). You will find that your worst failings and deepest pain can be reframed. Your past will no longer determine your future (4). You will not lie paralysed, clinging grimly to false superstitious dreams. Neither will you be burdened by the empty accusations of legalistic religion trapped in its own self-important righteousness (5). You will feed on him. His death will bring life. As you join the new Exodus moving from Exile into new creation you will be nourished by all he has done for you by his death on the cross (6). You will come to him. Rivers of his life-giving Spirit will flow from within you for the healing of the nations (7). You will live without shame or condemnation and walk free into purity and intimacy with him (8). He will open your eyes. You will no longer be blind to your own blindness but will worship him (9). You will hear his voice. He will speak to you as your Shepherd protector. You will recognise that it is him and you will follow his lead (10). In your grief he will weep with you. In death he will speak life to you (11). You will know him. You will love him as a wife loves her husband. You will gladly pour out your riches to serve him. Your King will come. Your King – your friend (12). He will wash you and welcome into his Father's house (13–14).

We truly have found friendship with God.

We have also, by the by, discovered a way to read the Bible. There are other important ways to read the Scriptures, but this is a fruitful one and I hope you have enjoyed it. You can read the whole Bible like this, paying attention to the narrative, getting into the story – and finding Jesus, risen in your midst.

With grateful thanks

I am profoundly grateful for the influence of so many people who have all, in significant ways, enabled this book to be written. Rev Malcolm Hanson formerly of Jesmond United Reformed Church, my first pastor, who taught me to love the Bible and teach it faithfully. Dr Peter Forrest, who mentored me. Matthew Clifton-Brown, who first told me that I had a gift in teaching. Ray Lowe, who encouraged me to enter the mysterious world of academic theology. Rev Dr Richard Briggs, my tutor when I was a student at Cranmer Hall, whose wisdom opened up the Bible in ways I had never imagined. Arnold Bell, now among the great cloud of witnesses, who first asked me to teach John's Gospel to church leaders and started the journey that led to this book. All my students who have patiently participated in my ponderings. Terry Virgo, John Hosier, Mick Taylor and everyone in the Theology Forum of the Newfrontiers family of churches who continually encouraged me to think deeper about God's word. Rt Rev Prof Tom Wright who graciously came for a weekend of teaching at our church when Bishop of Durham, and whose teaching and friendship have profoundly helped us all to see Jesus in richer, clearer ways. Everyone at City Church, whom I loved to serve, who gave me the time to write the book. And Katherine Venn, my editor, who has given me so much encouragement and wise direction on the way.

Bibliography

Alter, Robert. *The Art of Biblical Narrative* (Basic Books, 1981)

Ashton, John. *Understanding the Fourth Gospel* (Oxford University Press, 2nd Edition, 2009)

Bailey, Kenneth E. *Jesus through Middle Eastern Eyes: Cultural Studies in the Gospels* (SPCK, 2008)

Bauckham, Richard. *Jesus and the Eyewitnesses: The Gospels as Eyewitness Testimony* (Eerdmans, 2nd edition, 2017)

Bauckham, Richard. *The Testimony of the Beloved Disciple: Narrative, History and Theology in the Gospel of John* (Baker Academic, 2007)

Beale, Gregory K. *The Temple and the Church's Mission* (Apollos, 2004)

Carson, D. A. *The Gospel According to John* (Apollos, 1991)

Davis, Ellen F., Hays, Richard B. (Eds). *The Art of Reading Scripture* (Eerdmans, Cambridge, 2003)

Fokkelman, J. P. *Reading Biblical Narrative* (Westminster John Knox Press, 1999)

Lincoln, Andrew. *The Gospel According to St John, Blacks New Testament Commentary* (Continuum, 2005)

McGrath, Alister E. *Christian Theology: An Introduction* (Blackwell Publishing, 2nd Edition, 1997)

Morison, Frank. *Who Moved the Stone?* (OM Publishing, 1999)

Schneiders, Sandra M. *Jesus Risen in our Midst* (Liturgical Press, 2013)

Schneiders, Sandra M. *Written That You May Believe: Encountering Jesus in the Fourth Gospel* (Independent Publishers Group, 2003)

Wright, Tom. *Simply Christian* (SPCK, 2011)

Notes

2. Knowing God

1. Greg Beale, *The Temple and the Church's Mission* (Apollos, 2004), pp. 29–80.
2. Alister E. McGrath, *Christian Theology: An Introduction* (Blackwell Publishers, 1997), pp. 299–300.

3. Temple Space

1. Tom Wright, *Simply Christian* (SPCK, 2006), p. 178.
2. Sandra Schneiders, *Jesus Risen in Our Midst* (Liturgical Press, 2013), pp. xii–xviii.
3. D. A. Carson, *The Gospel According to John* (Apollos, 1991), pp. 38–40, 68.

7. Come and See

1. Kenneth E. Bailey, *Jesus through Middle Eastern Eyes: Cultural Studies in the Gospels* (SPCK, 2008), pp. 202–5.

8. Going Deeper

1. Frank Morison, *Who Moved the Stone?* (OM Publishing, 1999), pp. 30–42.

10. Back to the Beginning

1. Beale, *The Temple and the Church's Mission*, pp. 100–4, 130–1.
2. Beale, *The Temple and the Church's Mission*, p. 102.

16. Death and Life

1. John Ashton, *Understanding the Fourth Gospel* (Oxford University Press, 2nd Edition, 2007), p. 95.

HODDER & STOUGHTON

Hodder & Stoughton is the UK's
leading Christian publisher,
with a wide range of books from
the bestselling authors in the UK
and around the world ranging from
Christian lifestyle and theology to
apologetics, testimony and fiction.
We also publish the world's
most popular Bible translation
in modern English, the New
International Version, renowned
for its accuracy and readability.

Hodderfaith.com   Hodderbibles.co.uk
 @HodderFaith    /HodderFaith